# Colonial America
## From Jamestown to Yorktown

## American History in Depth

General Editor: A. J. Badger
Advisory Editor: Howell Harris

# Colonial America
## From Jamestown to Yorktown

Mary K. Geiter and W. A. Speck

First published 2002 by
PALGRAVE MACMILLAN
Houndmills, Basingstoke, Hampshire RG21 6XS and
175 Fifth Avenue, New York, N.Y. 10010
Companies and representatives throughout the world

PALGRAVE MACMILLAN is the global academic imprint of the Palgrave
Macmillan division of St. Martin's Press, LLC and of Palgrave Macmillan Ltd.
Macmillan® is a registered trademark in the United States, United Kingdom
and other countries. Palgrave is a registered trademark in the European
Union and other countries.

ISBN 0–333–79055–3 hardcover
ISBN 0–333–79056–1 paperback

This book is printed on paper suitable for recycling and made from fully
managed and sustained forest sources.

A catalogue record for this book is available from the British Library.

A catalog record for this book is available from the Library of Congress.

10   9   8   7   6   5   4   3   2   1
11   10   09   08   07   06   05   04   03   02

Printed in China

# Contents

# Maps

# Preface

The events of 11 September 2001 became a defining moment for the American people in a variety of ways. But perhaps more than any previous event in American history, the murderous acts perpetrated against the Pentagon, Flight 93, and the World Trade Center clarified once and for all the problem of American identity.

This book investigates the historical roots of that problem. Historians of America have wrestled with how to define what is an American ever since Hector St John Crèvecoeur posed the problem when he asked: 'who is this American?' Hitherto, it has been suggested that Americans were given their appellation externally from the British. Yet within the British American colonies, people began to see themselves as separate from the mother country. The outcome of the American Revolution seemed to clear the problem somewhat when British subjects became American citizens.

These explanations are rooted in geography. Indeed, the term 'America' implies the United States and quite pointedly ignores Canada. In recent times, arguments over immigration laws again raised the question as to who was an American. The Cold War years, however, expanded the idea of citizenship beyond the shores of the United States. American foreign policy demanded long tours of duty overseas for American military service members and American contractors working for the American government, which resulted in a generation whose dependents were born and reared outside of US territory. This posed a psychological problem for citizens who had never seen the shores of North America. Were they really Americans or just citizens of the United States? While they were legally Americans, feeling like an American was another matter. Yet, in one horrifying morning, being an American transcended geographical boundaries. The tragedy on that day in September fused together what had been almost mystical ideals, lost in time and rhetoric, and bound them up in one word: 'freedom'. In that instant the definition moved from the external or material evidence of being a member of American society, to the internal. The ideals embedded in the language of the forefathers were no longer resting amongst the dusty pages of history books, but now were given life and force. Americans now could say: 'we are Americans not because we live in America, but because America lives in us.' That is the essence of being an American and, on that terrible day, the whole world, in this sense, became America.

The authors of this book, one an American citizen, the other a British subject, wrote it in the conviction that an exploration of American identity can best be undertaken by placing colonial history in an imperial context. For the colonists regarded themselves as English, or British, during the seventeenth and eighteenth centuries. That is, they identified themselves more with the mother country than with the continent of North America. It was only gradually that they drew distinctions between themselves and Europeans, and only suddenly, towards the end of the colonial period, that they dropped their identification with the British and called themselves Americans. Thus, this Anglo-American approach requires the reader to think beyond the normal constraints of the subject and to look to Britain for the roots of America's development.

We would like to thank Professor Tony Badger, the general editor of the series of which this book is a part, for his support throughout the writing of it. Tony and Betty Wood read the whole text and made many valuable suggestions for improving it. They are not responsible for any infelicities or errors that remain, for which we take full responsibility.

Carlisle<br>4 May 2002

# Introduction

The relationship of Great Britain to her American colonies in the century before the Declaration of Independence is too often treated in the shadow of that document. Until recently, most textbooks focused on the 13 mainland colonies which declared their independence of Great Britain and became the United States. To treat the period before 1776 as the first chapter in the history of the USA, however, is to misunderstand its significance. For one thing it overlooks the fact that the thirteenth British colony to be acquired on the eastern seaboard of North America was not Georgia but Nova Scotia, which the French ceded to Britain at the Treaty of Utrecht in 1713, 20 years before the launching of the southern settlement. More seriously, it ignores the West Indies. During the seventeenth century, the English acquired 11 islands in the Caribbean, of which the most significant were Barbados, Jamaica, Antigua, Montserrat, Nevis and St Kitts. These were regarded in many ways as more important than the continental colonies. Certainly Barbados was seen as the jewel in the crown, its sugar being more profitable to the royal revenues than the tobacco of the Chesapeake Bay or the rice of South Carolina.

The area which became the United States was therefore but a part of the British Empire until the outbreak of the War of American Independence. Divorcing its history from this imperial context inevitably distorts it. How far the colonies were influenced by Great Britain is a matter of considerable dispute. Some historians view them as separate entities from their establishment whose development can be treated almost without reference to the mother country. America was different from the start in their view, and grew ever-more away from Britain culturally, socially, economically and, finally, politically. Others insist that they were an integral part of British history and can only properly be appreciated in that respect. Thus, the cultures, societies, economies and political systems in the various colonies reflected those in Britain.

1

Paradoxically, the colonies were becoming more like England on the eve of their separation from it.

The idea that America was exceptional from the first settlements onwards was dominant in the 1950s. Perhaps its most committed advocate was Daniel Boorstin, whose prize-winning book *The Americans: The Colonial Experience* (1958) asserted the differences between the colonists and their English cousins in the very title. In the text effete Englishmen were contrasted with audacious Americans. The colonial experience was the boyhood of Crèvecoeur's 'new man'. The English were idealists and thinkers, while the colonists were pragmatists and doers. Philosophies formulated to interpret European realities were irrelevant to the facts of the wilderness, which had to be interpreted afresh in the light of new experiences. Common sense thus became a sound American virtue long before Thomas Paine appealed to it in his celebrated Revolutionary pamphlet of 1776.

Since the 1960s the pendulum has rather swung the other way, to stress the import of English norms into America during the colonial period. It received its most extreme expression in the influential, if controversial, book by David Hackett Fischer, *Albion's Seed: Four British Folkways in America* (1989). Again, the very title expressed the thesis that the seeds of American culture were to be found in Britain ('Albion'). The text investigated four British regions, and argued that they were the seedbeds of different parts of the colonies. Thus, East Anglian migrants to Massachusetts carried their cultural baggage with them, as did 'cavaliers' from southern England to Virginia, Quakers from the 'north midlands' to the Delaware, and migrants from the borderlands of England and Scotland to the back country. Such features of colonial life as architecture and marriage customs were traced to these four 'cultural hearths'.

In their more extreme manifestations the theories of American exceptionalism and of English transplantation can become too simplistic. Boorstin claimed, for instance, that the American colonists invented the degree-awarding college in Harvard, William and Mary and Yale. In Oxford and Cambridge the colleges were little more than halls of residence, which were federated into universities which regulated the award of degrees. This was to ignore the model of Trinity College, Dublin, founded by Elizabeth I, which performed the functions allegedly invented in America. Again, Fischer's four British regions, on investigation, have been shown to be artificial geographic areas which did not share common cultural features.

This book accepts, nevertheless, that, within reason, there is something in both theories. That is, the climate and terrain of the North American continent, and its native inhabitants, made the colonies markedly different from the mother country. The colonists did develop distinct societies during the colonial period, particularly in the south with the introduction of chattel slavery, which was unknown in Britain. Moreover, the colonies did develop a distinctly American culture by the mid-eighteenth century, while the colonists increasingly came to regard themselves as Americans by contrast with Europeans.

At the same time, when they compared their condition with that of the mother country, they identified themselves more and more as Englishmen as they defended what they called their English liberties against the threat to them which they perceived to be posed by the policies of the British government. It was not until they resolved to defeat that threat by declaring themselves independent that they adopted an American political identity. Before that, their participation in the 'great war for empire' helped to boost the colonists' consciousness of themselves as both British subjects and Americans. This sense of twin identities was not paradoxical, since they were not at this stage rival alternatives. People in the eighteenth century, as now, identified themselves with different cultural groupings without feeling confused. Thus, Britons could identify with their county or with their country, as well as with the new national concept of Great Britain brought into being by the Union between England and Scotland in 1707. For instance, they could consider themselves to be Yorkshiremen, Englishmen and Britons simultaneously. Similarly colonists could identify themselves with their colony, or their region, or their continent, as well as with the mother country. They could regard themselves as Rhode Islanders, New Englanders, Americans and British without thinking that it involved a choice. Benjamin Franklin thought of himself as a Pennsylvanian, an American and an Englishman. When he first visited England, he referred to it as going 'home'.

This involvement in the imperial context meant that the colonies interacted with the mother country continuously and increasingly throughout the colonial period. Their interaction is often conceived as that between, on the one hand, a Britain which scarcely changed from the early days of colonisation to the War of American Independence, and, on the other, a dynamic America which was transformed almost out of recognition between the foundation of Jamestown and the defeat of the British at Yorktown.

Certainly the colonies developed remarkably, their populations expanding until by the eighteenth century they were doubling every 25 years. Their composition was also changing, from being largely composed of English settlers to that of a melting pot of peoples of European and African ancestry. Yet, though this created a society very different from that of the mother country, its leaders continued to regard themselves as English. Above all, they spoke English, perpetuating a significant cultural distinction between them and the French to the north and the Spanish to the south. There are signs that American English was beginning to diverge from the language of the mother country as early as the 1740s. Nevertheless, the colonists and the British inhabited an Anglophone world which even today gives America and Britain a special relationship based on a common language and, even though they have since developed along divergent historical paths, a shared history for 170 years from which they still derive mutual values.

While the colonies were developing dramatically, the mother country was far from being static either. On the contrary, it too was transformed during the course of the colonial period. At the start, Stuart England was a minor power compared with the superpowers of Bourbon France and Habsburg Spain. By the end, Hanoverian Britain was itself a great power, replacing Spain as the principal rival to the French. This transformation was accelerated by the Glorious Revolution of 1688. As we shall see, it replaced the last Stuart King, James II, with the Dutch William of Orange. But the change was by no means just that of King Log for King Stork. Absolute monarchy became limited monarchy. William III was dependent upon Parliament for supplies to pursue the war with Louis XIV, which was his main objective in invading England in the first place. This was the first in a series of conflicts with France which has been seen as the second Hundred Years' War. The need for money triggered off a 'Financial Revolution', which enabled the state to anticipate Parliamentary revenues through a system of public credit which sustained an unprecedented national debt. This system brought into being what has been described as a fiscal-military state. England, and following the Union with Scotland in 1707, Great Britain tapped into the economy to sustain its war footing on a scale which no other power could match.

The fiscal-military state impacted on the empire. Among the economic resources which underpinned its war effort, and which it protected, was a growing Atlantic trade. One of its features was the traffic which took hundreds of thousands of enslaved Africans across the ocean to enforced labour in the mainland colonies, especially in the south, and the West Indies. Much as we deplore the slave trade now, it was considered by most contemporaries as essential for the development of the colonial economies. Though there were critical voices raised in the colonial period, which grew louder towards the end, the trade and its attendant slavery survived. Together with the primary produce, such as tobacco, rice and sugar, which they harvested and shipped out to exchange with British manufactures, they helped to generate a hugely profitable trans-Atlantic commerce.

Ensuring that this would benefit the British state led to the enactment of navigation laws, and a system for enforcing them, which tied the economies of the mother country and the colonies together. While this provoked some friction between them, it did not lead to serious resistance from the colonies as long as they felt that they were involved in the same 'glorious cause' with Britain. The resounding success of British and American arms in the war against France from 1754–63 brought the imperial connection to its culmination. It was when the fiscal-military state thereafter tried to tap colonial resources to help finance the policing of its expanded territories in North America that tensions developed which eventually reached breaking point.

The arrangement of the book is intended to convey the theme of the American colonies being a part of imperial history. The first part places it in an imperial context. First, it delineates the settlements of the colonies established in the Americas during the seventeenth and eighteenth centuries. It then describes the social structure of Britain in that era to provide a yardstick of how far British society was replicated in the colonies. Relations with the Indians, as Native North Americans are described throughout the book to avoid a rather cumbersome expression, following the example of leading ethnohistorians, are dealt with as an aspect of imperial policy. This provides a dimension often missing from treatments of Indians, either as inhabitants of individual colonies or 'in their own right'.

Part II describes the settlements made in the Americas and how they developed. The colonies are placed in five regions which have come to be generally accepted by historians. Thus, Virginia and Maryland are treated in the context of the Chesapeake Bay. New England groups together Plymouth, Massachusetts, Rhode

Island, Connecticut and New Hampshire. New York, New Jersey, Pennsylvania and the three lower counties on the Delaware River, which were to become the state of Delaware, are discussed as the middle colonies. North and South Carolina and Georgia constituted the lower south. The Caribbean islands are dealt with separately in the chapter on the West Indies.

Part III discusses the close interaction of colonial history with that of the mother country in the period following the Glorious Revolution. That pivotal event on both sides of the Atlantic involved British America with the wars fought between Great Britain and France between 1689 and 1763. These conflicts increasingly impacted on the colonies, integrating them ever more tightly into the British empire, despite the later view that they had been treated with 'salutary neglect'.

Part IV investigates the partial disintegration of that empire with the declaration of independence by the 13 colonies which formed the United States of America. Chapter 13 compares and contrasts the colonies with the mother country on the eve of independence, showing that, while there were many differences, there were also striking similarities. The period 1763–76 is divided into two chapters to stress that the friction between Britain and her American colonies did not lead inevitably to separation immediately after the end of the Seven Years' War. It is argued that, to the contrary, the disputes of the 1760s were due to the aftermath of that war, while those of the 1770s marked a new phase in their relationship.

# PART I
# The Imperial Context

# 1 The British Empire in America to 1750

As early as the reign of James I, Britain's American possessions were already being referred to as the British Empire. For, although the empire only became formally British when the Union of 1707 fused England and Scotland into the United Kingdom of Great Britain, the notion had earlier antecedents. However, while the English and Scottish Parliaments were not merged until then, the accession of James VI of Scotland to the English throne in 1603 had earlier united Great Britain in a composite monarchy. James promoted the idea of a British empire, particularly in the plantation of Ulster in Northern Ireland by subjects who were regarded not as Scots, nor as English, but as Britons. The Irish settlements under Elizabeth and James are generally seen as part of the colonising impulse in their reigns. The Scottish Presbyterians who went to Ulster, known to Americans as Scotch-Irish, were to become a significant element in the later establishment of the Middle Colonies. The Jacobean attempt to project plantations as a British endeavour was however thwarted by the English, who resisted Scottish aspirations to British imperial status. Thus, during the short-lived English Republic following the civil wars, when Parliament passed the Navigation Act in 1651 to protect colonial trade, it specifically excluded Scots. This was upheld when the Act was re-enacted after the Restoration of Charles II in 1660. North America and the West Indies were to constitute an English Empire until the Union of 1707 allowed Scots entry into its commercial system.

The idea of empire implies dominion, and, apart from the abortive attempts to settle a colony on Roanoke Island in the 1580s, the Crown was a party to colonisation from the start. Although the colony at Jamestown was planted in 1607 by the Virginia Company as a trading venture, its legal title was a royal charter. The original charter even gave James I a role in the company's affairs, though the second made it virtually autonomous. When the company failed, however, the King took over and Virginia became the first Crown colony in North America.

Yet initially, the Crown does not appear to have adopted any coherent policy towards the colonies. As Edmund Burke was to put it: 'the settlement of our colonies was never pursued upon any regular plan; but they were formed, grew and flourished as accidents, the nature of the climate, or the dispositions of private men happened to operate'.


## ROANOKE ISLAND

The Roanoke venture was a perfect example of Burke's dictum. A group of adventurers led by Sir Walter Raleigh sponsored the project. They hoped to interest Queen Elizabeth, flattering her by calling the projected colony Virginia, and pointing out its strategic value as a base against Spanish possessions in the Caribbean. But the Virgin Queen was not persuaded to make it a state enterprise. Instead, Raleigh and his associates undertook to settle the island of Roanoke in the Outer Banks of what became North Carolina a century later. The first settlement in 1585 had to be abandoned the following year. In 1587 John White, a survivor of the first expedition, was appointed governor by Raleigh and took a party of English men and women to the island. They suffered from his failure to provide firm leadership and persuaded him to return to England for fresh supplies. Unfortunately, the rapidly deteriorating relationship with Spain in the run up to the Armada led Elizabeth to forbid a return voyage until 1590. When White eventually reached Roanoke, there were no signs of the colonists. A few clues to their fate suggested that they had taken refuge with friendly natives on the island of Croatoan in the Outer Banks. Certainly, they would have been in need of Indian allies as their relations with most of the tribes in the region had been disastrous. At first, they had found the native inhabitants friendly, and even living in recognisable village communities. White himself had captured their primitive civilisation in a number of drawings. But then the settlers encountered other tribes who were not friendly, but downright hostile. The fate of the lost colonists remains an intriguing mystery. The most convincing explanation of what happened to them is that they survived for some years, and even cohabited with local natives, until the expanding confederacy of chief Powhatan conquered the area and exterminated the settlers.

## EARLY STUART SETTLEMENTS

Powhatan's empire was well established when the next band of English settlers arrived in his territory. This comprised 105 colonists sent out by the Virginia Company of London, established in 1606. They founded Jamestown in April of the following year. Though the colony recalled Elizabeth's patent to Raleigh, the town was named after her successor, James I. The settlers also demonstrated their allegiance in a curious ceremony in which Powhatan was crowned as a vassal of their King. James's interest in the colonial venture was at that stage limited to the granting of charters to the Virginia Company. When the company failed to make a profit, however, and was dissolved in 1624, James took over Virginia. Thus where the company had previously appointed a governor, now one was nominated by the King.

James granted several charters to the Virginia Company of London before it was wound up. The third, issued in 1612, included the grant of Bermuda, claimed in his name by Sir George Somers when he was shipwrecked on his way with provisions for the infant colony at Jamestown.

James had also granted a charter to the Virginia Company of Plymouth as well as that in London. In 1619 it issued a patent to a group of English colonists known to history as the Pilgrims. These were separatists from the Church of England who wished to preserve their own congregation from the taint of popery, which they claimed still survived in the established Church. In 1608 they had gone to Leiden in Holland seeking a more godly society, but had become disillusioned with the secular aspects of Dutch civilisation, especially when they seemed to be corrupting their teenage children. They therefore decided to remove them from temptation by taking them across the Atlantic in the *Mayflower*. There the Pilgrims, as they were known, founded Plymouth Colony in 1620. Religious motivations also led the Massachusetts Bay Company to establish a Puritan settlement in Boston in 1629. The propensity of Puritanism to spawn rival sects led to the secession of groups from Massachusetts to Connecticut and Rhode Island in the mid-1630s. Religion was a main consideration in the colonisation of Maryland and Providence Island. Catholicism found a haven in the Chesapeake when Maryland was granted to the Catholic Cecilius Calvert, second Lord Baltimore, who sent a number of co-religionists led by his brother to settle St Mary's in 1634. Puritanism provided the stimulus for 'the other Puritan colony' of Providence Island in the Caribbean off the coast of Nicaragua, which members of the opposition to Charles I played a prominent part in settling in 1630.

Commercial prospects had previously drawn English adventurers to South America and the Caribbean. Hopes of getting rich quick in the fabled El Dorado led to sporadic settlement on the Amazon river, though these were fairly quickly eliminated by the Spanish claimants. Attention was then focused on the West Indies. In 1622 Sir Thomas Warner, on his way back to England from one of the abortive settlements on the Amazon, landed at St Christopher in the Leeward Islands. By then, the success of tobacco cultivation in Virginia encouraged colonisers to hope for similar results elsewhere, and Warner saw opportunities for tobacco planting in St Kitts, as it became generally known. Backed by London merchants, he returned to the island with a number of settlers in 1624. From this base, Nevis was settled in 1628 and Antigua and Monserrat in 1632. In 1625 John Powell claimed Barbados for the King of England. Charles I granted the island to Sir William Courteen and the Earl of Pembroke in 1627, but confused the issue by also granting the 'Caribee Islands' to the Earl of Carlisle. Rival claim-ants for the two earls actually fought to establish their proprietor-ships over Barbados. One governor sent out by Carlisle subdued the Pembroke agents into submission, then turned against his patron and executed the governor sent out to replace him. He held out for another year before succumbing to another governor. Charles I intervened to resolve the dispute in favour of the Earl of Carlisle.

By 1650, therefore, there were scattered settlements along the coast of America and in the West Indian islands. These had come into existence more through private than state enterprise. Although Charles I proclaimed on taking over Virginia that he intended to provide 'one uniform course of government' for all the colonies, no such policy was in fact adopted.

## COLONISATION UNDER CROMWELL
## AND THE LATER STUARTS

From the middle of the seventeenth century, there was a second wave of colonisation which was positively promoted by the government. It began with the 'Western Design' of 1655, an expedition sent out to the West Indies by Cromwell with the intention of taking Hispaniola from the Spanish. Although it failed to 'wrest a horn from the head of the beast', as Puritans characteristically put it, the expedition did take Jamaica. This aggressive colonial policy was followed in the 1660s by the restored government of Charles II. In April 1663 a commission to investigate New England was set up, which drew up a proposal that was put to the Council for Foreign Plantations the following January. It recommended the grant to the King's brother James, Duke of York and Albany, of a vast proprietorship in North America, which stretched from Maine to the Delaware Bay, and included the whole of the Dutch colony of New Netherland. When this was seized from the Dutch in 1664, it was renamed New York. James ruled his own proprietorship of New York with the authority with which he was invested as proprietor by his brother's charter of 1664. This was reissued in 1674 after the colony's reconquest by the Dutch in the third Anglo–Dutch war, when New York again became New Amsterdam for over a year. They finally relinquished their claim to the colony to the English Crown at the Treaty of Westminster in 1674.

James not only became proprietor of New York, but also of adjacent New Jersey, or Albania as it was initially called, again after his ducal titles. He ceded the territories of East and West Jersey to his old comrades Lord Berkeley and Sir George Carteret, but kept the government or dominion for himself. Later, when he tried to grant the right of ruling to the proprietors, Charles II objected that it was his and not the Duke's to concede. A judicial decision in 1680 appeared to confer the right on James, but it remained in doubt throughout the 1680s. Similar dubiety arose over his concession of the territories on the west bank of the Delaware River to William Penn when Charles II granted him the proprietorship of Pennsylvania in 1681. The three lower counties which James added to the royal grant in 1682, and which ultimately became the state of Delaware, gave rise to much dispute as to whether the right of government had been conceded to Penn along with the proprietorship of the soil.

James only reluctantly yielded the lower counties, under pressure from his brother.

The expansion of the empire under Cromwell and Charles II thus aggressively challenged Spanish and Dutch claims in North America and the West Indies. This was true even of the Carolinas, for although they were granted by a charter of 1663 to eight proprietors, and were not Crown colonies, they nevertheless were regarded as a threat by Spain to its settlement in Florida to the south. This was especially the case when the King granted another charter to the proprietors in 1665, extending the southern border of the colony to 29 degrees north, which included the Spanish settlement of St Augustine. The establishment of Charles Town (later Charleston) in 1680 persuaded the Spanish to fortify St Augustine more securely. The wooden fort there, which had been burned down twice by English raiders, once in 1586 by Sir Francis Drake and again as recently as 1668, was replaced by a massive fortress, constructed out of 'coquina', a unique sedimentary rock.


IMPERIAL POLICY

The second phase of colonisation, from the conquest of Jamaica to the launching of Pennsylvania, not only saw more active involvement by the government in acquiring colonies, but also attempts by it to impose a coherent pattern on the relationship between England and the 'plantations'. This policy began in the Interregnum, when the Rump Parliament passed a Navigation Ordinance in 1651 which laid the basis of future legislation. It was in essence a bid to restrict the carrying trade of goods from and to America to English merchant ships or colonial vessels. It was primarily aimed at the Dutch, who had achieved hegemony in extra-European commerce largely because of their superior merchant marine, which could undercut any rival nation's shipping rates, including England's. But it was also aimed at Scottish interlopers. The first British Empire was very much an English concern. This was made clear at the Restoration, when the Navigation Ordinance was re-enacted. Foreigners, including Scots, were forbidden to trade directly with the colonies. Scottish goods, excepting servants and horses, were to be sent to America by way of England according to the Staple Act of 1663.

The Navigation Act of 1660 also enumerated certain colonial products which could only be shipped directly to England. These included sugar, tobacco, cotton, indigos, ginger, fustic and other dye woods, which all paid a duty upon arrival in English ports. By far the most lucrative of these was the impost on sugar, which since the 1640s had replaced tobacco as the main crop of Barbados. Most tobacco shipped to England came from the Chesapeake Bay colonies, though some was grown elsewhere, in the Delaware Bay for example.

What was not foreseen at the time was a loophole in this Act whereby the enumerated commodities could be sent from one colony to another and then exported to England without paying a duty. This was blocked in 1673 by the Plantation Duties Act, which provided for the duties to be collected in the colonies. It was not that the government was particularly interested in raising duties in America. As the Lord Treasurer observed at the time, the object of the Act was 'to turn the course of trade rather than to raise any considerable revenue to his Majesty'. The Act stipulated that 'for the better collection of the several rates and duties...this whole business shall be ordered and managed and the several duties hereby imposed shall be caused to be levied by the commissioners of the customs in England'. In November 1673 the first officials were appointed for the colonies, a collector and a surveyor being assigned to Barbados, Maryland, Virginia and the Carolinas. By 1677 they had been introduced into all the mainland colonies south of New England. In 1678 Edward Randolph was sent out as collector, surveyor and searcher of the customs in New England, thereby completing the system.

Randolph's was a controversial appointment, since he was an abrasive man who had already rubbed many backs up the wrong way in North America. He was in no doubt about the purpose of his mission, claiming that evasion of the Navigation Acts by Massachusetts alone cost the Crown over £100,000 a year in lost revenues. Randolph claimed that the only way to force Massachusetts to obey the Navigation laws was to make it a Crown colony. Although his proposal met with stiff resistance in New England, he stuck doggedly to it until eventually he obtained a writ of *quo warranto* against the Bay colony 'for usurping to be a body politick'. Such writs required those upon whom it was served to explain by what authority they exercised their jurisdiction. The Puritans were unable to satisfy the

Crown that their rule rested on the terms of the Massachusetts Bay charter, which was annulled in October 1684.

The attack on Massachusetts coincided with a review of several colonial charters, including Connecticut, Rhode Island, Pennsylvania and Maryland. It seemed as though the English government was engaged in a concerted policy of tightening its grip on the colonies.

In the view of Stephen Saunders Webb that policy was motivated more by strategic than by commercial considerations. He maintains that 'the structure of the imperial constitution was completed on January 27, 1682'. On that date Lord Culpeper's commission as Governor of Virginia gave him effective military as well as civil control of the colony. 'It was then imposed on colony after colony', Webb insists, 'as the organic law of the English empire.' He therefore concludes that the empire was not primarily 'a commercial system', but 'a military system'. His justification for this claim rests primarily on the Crown's reaction to Bacon's rebellion in Virginia and King Philip's war in New England. These events, coinciding in the mid-1670s, forced the English government to put security at the top of the imperial agenda. The result was the imposition of a system of 'garrison government', in which the colonial governors exercised military, even martial authority. In Webb's striking phrase, the year 1676 marked 'the end of American independence'.

While defence doubtless concerned the Crown, retrenchment was even more of a priority to Charles II. He wanted to make a profit from the colonies, not incur a loss. Virginia was worth about £100,000 a year in tobacco revenues. The King indicated his dependence on these when, in 1680, he got the governor to persuade the Assembly to impose a duty of two shillings per hogshead on exported tobacco, one of the few taxes raised in America before the reign of George III. Charles II did not intend to reduce his income from the Old Dominion by maintaining a large military establishment there. By 1681 the forces sent out to suppress Bacon's rebellion, who had arrived after it petered out, were in considerable arrears. The following year, they were disbanded. A crucial part of Webb's case for the imposition of 'garrison government' on the colonies is that the 'Governors General' were all military men. Yet the Governor of Virginia who succeeded Culpeper, Lord Howard of Effingham, was not an army officer.

The piece of the jigsaw which cannot be made to fit Webb's thesis, however, is the last colony to be settled in the seventeenth century:

Pennsylvania. The greatest proprietary grant ever made, stretching from Delaware Bay to the Great Lakes, was given not to a military man, but to a Quaker, William Penn, the leader of a pacifist sect.

Pennsylvania was the last colony to be granted to a proprietor. In 1682 the Privy Council refused a proprietary grant south of the Carolinas to Lord Dorchester on the grounds that it was not convenient for the King 'to consolidate any new proprietary in America nor to grant any further powers that might render the plantations less dependent on the Crown'. The desire to bring the colonies more firmly under control is to be seen in the issue of writs of *quo warranto*, asking by what warrant those which were not Crown colonies exercised their authority. Besides Massachusetts, writs were prepared against Connecticut, Rhode Island, New Jersey, Pennsylvania, Maryland and the Carolinas. James, as Duke of York until 1685 and then as King of England, was embarked on a policy of transforming the charter and proprietary colonies into Crown colonies to build up royal authority in America. It culminated, as we shall see, with the establishment of the Dominion and Territory of New England, which ultimately stretched from Maine to the Delaware. Although the Dominion was swept away in the Glorious Revolution, the revolutionary regime in England still showed a determination to retain as much control over the colonies as it could. Thus Sir William Phips, Governor of Massachusetts, also commanded the militias of Rhode Island, Connecticut and New Hampshire. In 1698 Lord Bellomont was made Governor of New York, Massachusetts and New Hampshire, and also commanded the militias of Connecticut, Rhode Island and New Jersey.

The drive to bring all the colonies more directly under control from London also continued. In 1696 another Navigation Act was passed which laid down further restrictions on colonial commerce. Thus, vessels engaged in the Atlantic trade had to be built, and not merely owned, in England or the colonies. Colonial governors had to take oaths to uphold the navigation system and to place £1000 bond as security against failing to comply with this requirement. Admiralty courts, which tried breaches of the navigation laws without juries, were introduced into England's American territories. In 1696 too the Board of Trade and Plantations was established. It was charged with supervising trade and 'inspecting and improving our plantations in America'. It was also 'to consider of proper persons to be Governors or Deputy Governors or to be of our Council or our Council at law or Secretaries on our respective plantations, in order to present their names to us in Council'; that is, the Board was to advise the Privy Council on the personnel of colonial government. The Board was also authorised to examine legislation passed by the colonial assemblies to ensure it was compatible with the interests of the Crown, 'to consider what matters may be recommended as fit to be passed in the Assemblies there, to hear complaints of oppressions and maladministrations in our plantations . . . and also to require an account of all monies given for public uses by the assemblies.'

The Board was particularly charged with ensuring that the navigation system was sustained by the colonies. After an investigation, it concluded that those colonies not directly under the Crown were flagrantly defying the laws, and reported in 1698 that 'if the proprieties and charter governments do not speedily comply with what is required of them, we see no means to prevent a continuance of this mischief without calling in the further assistance of Parliament.' The colonies in question did not satisfy the Board that they were putting their house in order, for in 1701 it concluded that their charters should be resumed and 'all of them put into the same state of dependency as those of your Majesty's other plantations'. A bill for their 'reunion with the Crown' was actually introduced into the House of Lords in 1701. One of the reasons given for introducing the measure was that the proprietary and charter colonies were depleting the royal revenues because of the encouragement they gave to illicit trade. Although the Lords dropped the bill, it was placed before them again early in 1702. It had to be dropped again when the death of William III put an end to the Parliamentary session. Nevertheless, in 1702 New Jersey was transformed from a proprietary into a Crown colony. Maryland had been taken from Lord Baltimore and resumed by the Crown in 1689 because of its support of James II, as had Pennsylvania in 1691 because of William Penn's Jacobite leanings. Although Pennsylvania had been restored to Penn in 1694, he nevertheless had his work cut out to avoid forfeiting his proprietorship of the colony again. He even entered into negotiations with the Crown to agree a price for its surrender, but these were never brought to a definite conclusion. Only the Carolinas remained in the possession of proprietors throughout the period 1689 to 1714.

Colonial policy under the Queen became the special concern of her favourite the Duke of Marlborough, a military man concerned about defence in America during the War of the Spanish Succession.

Marlborough's solution to the problems of imperial defence, however, was not to superimpose royal control, but to insist that only military men should be colonial governors. William Byrd of Virginia found this out the hard way when he tried to buy the governorship of that colony from the Earl of Orkney, only to be overruled by the Duke because he was not an army officer. Marlborough even foisted a military governor on Pennsylvania, persuading Penn, who was intimately acquainted with the Duke, to accept Charles Gookin, a comrade in arms, as his deputy in the colony. His most notable appointment was of Daniel Parke to govern the Leeward Islands. Parke had been his aide-de-camp at the Battle of Blenheim and took the news of the victory to London. When he got out to Antigua, he retook Nevis and St Kitts from the French. He even offered to take Martinique if the government could spare 10,000 Scottish soldiers 'with oatmeal enough to keep them for three or four months'. In 1710 Parke fell foul of settlers on Antigua after ordering troops to disperse the assembly at bayonet point. Those who opposed his arbitrary ways led an uprising against him. He defended himself gallantly, killing one of the insurgents with his own hands, but he was overpowered and brutally murdered. Parke was indeed the only governor of an English colony in the Americas to be assassinated.

Marlborough's insistence on nominating colonial governors usurped one of the powers granted to the Board of Trade. His influence over the colonies in time of war led to an erosion of the Board's authority. At the Treaty of Utrecht, which ended the war in 1713, the French recognised the English claims to Hudson's Bay and Newfoundland, and ceded Nova Scotia to them. These now became part of the British rather than the English empire, as Scots were allowed to trade directly with the colonies following the Anglo-Scottish Union of 1707. There was no question of Nova Scotia becoming a proprietary colony. Moreover, although Maryland was given back to the Calvert family in 1715 after its head converted from Catholicism to Anglicanism, North Carolina became a Crown colony in 1719, to be followed by South Carolina in 1729. When Georgia was launched under 20 trustees headed by General James Oglethorpe in 1732, it was with the specific condition that it would revert to the Crown after 21 years. In fact it did so in 1751, two years earlier than required.

At that time the British Empire in North America and the West Indies was still very much a commercial concern. The jewel in the crown was the sugar produced by Barbados and other West Indian islands. By 1750 sugar had become the most valuable commodity among British imports. They had doubled in the first half of the eighteenth century and were to quadruple in the second half as an expanding population increasingly demanded it, so that consumption rose from 4 to 20 pounds a head between 1700 and 1800. This helped to boost the West Indies' share of Britain's overseas trade from 10 per cent to 20 per cent. As the tonnage of sugar imports expanded from 20,000 tons to 160,000 over the century, so the revenues accruing to the Crown from customs duties increased. In 1750 the import duty on sugar was 4 shillings and 10 pence per hundredweight. The political clout of the West Indian lobby in Parliament was correspondingly considerable. It was largely responsible for the passage of the Molasses Act in 1733, which placed punitive duties on imports of sugar, molasses and rum from non-British sources, particularly the French West Indian islands of Guadeloupe and Martinique. Foreign sugar was charged with a duty of 5 shillings per hundredweight, molasses at 6 pence per gallon, and rum at 9 pence per gallon. This was much resented by New England merchants who relied on French molasses for much of their rum, but their protests were unavailing against the power of the Caribbean pressure group. Its influence also helps explain the British government's controversial decision at the Peace of Paris, which ended the Seven Years' War in 1763, to take Canada rather than their sugar islands from the French. The British sugar planters did not want to expand the imperial sources of production and thereby bring about a fall in prices and in their profits. It was a decision which profoundly affected the nature of the British settlements in America, transforming them from being primarily a commercial concern into a vast territorial empire.

# 2 British Society in the Era of Western Migration

## STUART ENGLAND

How English was colonial America? How far did the American colonies replicate the society that the settlers left? Did those settled under the Stuarts largely reproduce the social structure of seventeenth-century England? Or did they create different kinds of communities? These questions are integral to any investigation of the relationship between the mother country and the colonies. They have been variously answered in the past. Some historians have argued that only certain sections of English society provided the colonists who settled across the Atlantic Ocean in the first century of colonisation. These have been identified as the middle classes, the farmers and tradesmen of early modern England. The United States has thus been seen as a middle-class society from its origins, and thereby to have avoided the class struggles of the Old World. Moreover, these 'middling sort of people' have been regarded as morally superior, being ambitious, enterprising, hardworking, intrepid, sober individuals, the backbone of English society. Many, especially those who went to New England, were imbued not only with the Puritan work ethic but also with Puritanism itself. Above them was an idle, semi-pagan aristocracy; below them was the godless mass of the labouring poor.

Against this, others have maintained that the colonists did span a much wider spectrum of English society. While they admit that few members of the landed elite of aristocrats and country gentlemen migrated to America, they insist that emigrants from both the middle and lower orders were shipped across the ocean. As a consequence, the social tensions of Stuart England were imported into the colonies. Religion only motivated an untypical few, most migrants going for economic motives.

In order to resolve this debate a model of the social structure of Stuart England is here constructed. This is then compared with information about the emigrants to the colonies in the seventeenth century. This comparison enables some conclusions to be drawn about the extent to which the colonial settlements under the Stuarts emulated society in the mother country.

## The Aristocracy

Under the Stuarts, English society was dominated by the large land-owners, the nobility and gentry. Noblemen who were summoned to the House of Lords were a very elite group indeed, numbering fewer than 200 peers of the realm. But, though legally distinct from the other great landlords, they were socially and economically indistin-guishable. Contemporaries referred to both together as the aristoc-racy. They lived in country houses surrounded by estates divided up into farms and leased out to tenants who paid them rents. These houses and estates varied in size. At the top of the landed elite were noblemen whose palaces rivalled those of the King. The Marquis of Salisbury's palatial house at Audley End prompted James I to remark that it was too big for a king, but quite fitting for a Lord Treasurer, the post Salisbury held. During the reign of Queen Anne, the last of the Stuarts, Blenheim Palace was constructed on a massive scale to reflect the greatness of its occupant, the Duke of Marlborough. Below these magnates, lesser lords and country gentlemen lived in more modest mansions. Beningbrough, an exquisite baroque structure built a few miles from York for the Bourchier family, also in the reign of Queen Anne, afforded a comfortable country residence away from the bustle of the city. The social exclusiveness of their stately homes characterised the aristocracy, who considered themselves to be so far above the rest of the population as to constitute not so much a class as a caste.

Their lifestyles were distinguished from most others by conspicuous consumption and leisure. The country house was described by Sir Henry Wotton in 1622 as 'the theatre of hospitality'. It was the stage on which the nobility displayed their wealth and their paternalism. The building and maintenance of a stately home involved huge expenditure on architects, bricklayers, glaziers, masons and other tradesmen. It had to be furnished and decorated by a range of craftsmen from cabinet makers to upholsterers. It employed a retinue of servants both inside the house, such as butlers and chambermaids, and outside, such as coachmen and gardeners. It was a centre for lavish display and costly entertainment. This made it probably the biggest employer of labour in its immediate neighbourhood. Owners of such houses enjoyed enormous economic, social and ultimately political power.

**The Middle Classes**

Relatively few business or professional men acquired country estates. Most pursued their trades or callings in cities and towns. They were on the next rungs of the ladder below the aristocracy. Gregory King, in a contemporary table of the social structure in 1688, counted 26 rungs in all, from the lords down to 'vagrants: as gypsies, thieves, beggars etc.' On the 12 below the gentry, he placed freeholders, farmers, members of the professions and businessmen.

England remained a predominantly agricultural society throughout the period, and land was central to the economy. Aristocrats rarely farmed it directly themselves, its cultivation being undertaken by freeholders and tenant farmers. The greater landowners below the level of the country gentlemen were traditionally referred to as yeomen, although the actual term was gradually falling into disuse as the period progressed. Below them, the lesser farmers were known as husbandmen. To be called a yeoman was to aspire to social status of a sort, albeit one less exalted than that of gentleman. Some yeomen slipped over the border if they could. James Fretwell of Pontefract described himself as a yeoman in his will, but appeared as a gentleman on his tombstone. Some of the better off yeomen were indistinguishable economically from the landed gentry anyway. Probate inventories of the seventeenth and early eighteenth centuries record that in Essex and Gloucester some left effects worth several hundreds of pounds, while one had goods valued at £1873 14s. Husbandmen were less wealthy. An analysis of inventories for 14 counties between 1598 and 1700 revealed that yeomen left effects worth an average of £206 compared with £76 for husbandmen.

The professions included officers in the armed forces alongside clergymen, lawyers and doctors. At the beginning of the seventeenth century there was no permanent armed force in England. The Cromwellian period changed all that, and while there was demobilisation at the Restoration of the Stuarts in 1660, Charles II kept some soldiers on foot throughout his reign. James II expanded the army from 20,000 to 40,000 men. Under William III they were increased to fight the French to about 80,000. Following the peace of 1697, Parliament reduced the total on paper at least to 7000, though William kept more than that number, mainly in Ireland. The Royal Navy also grew under the Stuarts. Army and navy officers, numbering at least 10,000 even in peacetime, were added to the professions during the seventeenth century. There were about 11,000 clergy of the established Church of England, to whom should be added the Nonconformist ministers of the dissenting chapels after the Toleration Act of 1689 allowed them freedom of worship. Their wealth varied enormously, from the 26 Anglican bishops, who were regarded as spiritual peers and sat in the House of Lords, to the humblest curate or dissenting preacher struggling on a pittance. Some of the lesser clergy had to augment their incomes by farming or practising a trade. Yet by the end of the seventeenth century, the vast majority of the Anglican clergy had attended Oxford or Cambridge Universities and obtained degrees, which could be regarded as a professional qualification. Dissenters were barred from the Universities, but their congregations usually insisted on educated preachers, many of whom received their training in Nonconformist academies such as those at Stoke Newington and Warrington. Physicians too had to have degrees at Oxford, Cambridge or Trinity College Dublin if they wished to enrol as full members of the Royal College. Many Dissenters went into medicine, who again could not attend these Anglican institutions. Instead, they went to Edinburgh or Leiden, whose medical schools were superior to those in England. Below the physicians in status were the apothecaries and barber surgeons. Apothecaries were dispensers of drugs who set up dispensaries, where they also diagnosed and prescribed for poorer patients. The very name of barber surgeons indicates the even more lowly reputation of surgeons, who did not separate from the barbers until 1745, and did not get their own college until 1800. In the seventeenth and early eighteenth centuries, they kept shops where they would sell goods to customers or treat them as patients, for instance by bleeding them. In this respect, apothecaries and barber surgeons were scarcely distinguishable from other businessmen such as shopkeepers and tradesmen.

The business community was largely urban, spanning the social range from merchants trading overseas to master craftsmen who had served an apprenticeship in some trade, such as cabinet making or weaving, and employed journeymen and apprentices as day workers. A recent study of merchants in London, Liverpool and York who traded overseas looked at them in their natural urban habitat, pursuing their business activities, and also getting involved in municipal affairs and associating with others involved in similar pursuits. This built up a profile of a merchant community with its own lifestyles and values, espousing bourgeois rather than landed aspirations.

Even before England was industrialised, the multiplicity of trades was remarkable. Daniel Defoe's *The Compleat English Tradesman* dealt with a great variety, such as 'grocers, mercers, and woollen drapers ... tobacconists, haberdashers, glovers, hosiers, milliners, booksellers, stationers', etc. As for their numbers, he considered it impossible to calculate: 'we may as well count the stars'. Tradesmen who had served their time as apprentices and had enough capital to set up their own workshops were masters. These earned a livelihood from the profits made on the goods they manufactured and sold. They employed apprentices and craftsmen who had served their time, but had not sufficient resources to set themselves up independently. These were called journeymen, who were paid wages.

**The Labouring Classes**

Labourers and servants formed the great bulk of those who worked for a living in early modern England. Although most labourers had not been apprenticed to a trade, this did not mean that they were totally unskilled. Those who were employed on farms had to acquire a whole range of skills, caring for livestock or cultivating crops. Almost every urban trade employed labourers, many of whom were expected to assist craftsmen. In town and country there were heavy jobs for unskilled workers such as carters and porters. Women too found employment as milk sellers, hawkers and rag pickers, while even children were to be found in labouring jobs like chimney sweeping.

Women were more likely to find themselves employed in domestic service. This was far and away the biggest single employer of labour. In 1694 approximately 20 per cent of the population of 40 London parishes consisted of servants. The capital apparently had a higher proportion employed in domestic service than elsewhere, however, for in 100 villages the ratio was 13 per cent.

At the bottom of English society were the masses described simply as 'the poor'. There was a significant number of permanently poor people or paupers, as well as those who fell into the category temporarily because they were down on their luck. Sixteenth-century legislation had provided for their relief to be organised by their parishes. Parish officials oversaw the collection and distribution of the poor rate. The amounts raised nationally were of concern to contemporaries who were convinced that the poor were not only with them always, but were on the increase. Between 1685 and 1701, they rose from £665,000 to £900,000. The numbers of people sustained by these sums fluctuated according to the state of the economy. A poor harvest followed by an increase in the price of bread put intolerable pressure on the household budgets of the labouring poor, and increased the amounts handed out in relief. But even in good years, the proportion of the population dependent upon parochial relief or private charity was prodigious. Gregory King calculated that it could include half the total population. While this is a staggering figure it has by and large been confirmed by historians investigating the operation of the Poor Laws.

## MIGRATION FROM ENGLAND TO THE COLONIES UNDER THE STUARTS

The main evidence for English emigration to North America in the seventeenth century concerns some 3000 indentured servants who sailed from Bristol between 1654 and 1661, and a further 750 who went from London in 1683 and 1684, all bound for the Chesapeake Bay colonies, Maryland and Virginia. The data provided by the records has been variously interpreted. One analysis concluded that, apart from a tiny handful of gentlemen and members of the professions, amounting to about one per cent of the total, the bulk of the migrants could be identified as yeomen and husbandmen, with another substantial proportion comprising tradesmen and artisans. This seemed to confirm the view that the majority of those who crossed the Atlantic in the seventeenth century came from England's middle classes. Another investigation, however, challenged this interpretation of the lists. It concluded that the bulk of the migrants were divided almost equally into four groups: yeomen and husbandmen; tradesmen and craftsmen; apprentices or servants in husbandry; and unskilled labourers. Thus, they spanned the spectrum between the gentry and the paupers. Further analyses of the data rather confirm the latter than the former view. Thus, English emigrants to the Chesapeake under the Stuarts came overwhelmingly from the middle and labouring classes. This was not a cross-section of English society, since hardly any members of the aristocracy and gentry, or of the mass of the labouring poor who made up half the population of England, were represented. As we shall see, the indentured servants who went to the tobacco colonies under the Stuarts were largely young single men, producing an age and gender imbalance in the Chesapeake which did not replicate the social structure of the mother country in the early years of settlement.

Quantitative evidence for the settlers of the New England colonies is much sparser than that for the Chesapeake in the seventeenth century. From the few ships' lists which have survived, it seems that most of the adult males who migrated to the Massachusetts had been urban tradesmen in England. Moreover, while individuals went to Virginia whole families crossed to New England, including not only parents and children, but also domestic servants. They thus came closer to replicating the middle ranks of English society in age and gender ratios than did the tobacco colonies.

The main evidence for migration to the middle colonies concerns Pennsylvania. Although the proprietor of the colony, William Penn, cast his net wide and obtained colonists from Ireland and Scotland in the British Isles, and from France, Germany and the Netherlands in continental Europe, they mostly went from England and Wales. It has been claimed that they were drawn predominantly from the northern counties of England. Most of those who purchased property from the proprietor, however, came from counties scattered through-out England and Wales. Moreover, London accounted for nearly a fifth of all the first purchasers. Most of these were craftsmen and tradesmen such as carpenters, shoemakers and tailors. They thus came from the same sections of English society as the majority of settlers in New England. Where their Puritan counterparts had to adapt to a largely rural lifestyle, becoming farmers rather than con-tinuing to practise their trades, those in the Quaker colony had more opportunity to pursue their callings with the rapid rise of Philadelphia, which made early Pennsylvania the most urbanised of the colonies settled under the Stuarts.

Religious rather than economic motives have been ascribed to the majority of those who went to Puritan New England or Quaker Pennsylvania. Some account of religion in Stuart England is therefore necessary to assess the validity of this claim.


## RELIGION

At the beginning of the seventeenth century, on the eve of colonisation, England was nominally a country where the only recognised creed was that of the Church of England as by law established. This had been formally set out in the Thirty-Nine Articles of 1563. Although the Elizabethan Settlement is often referred to as a *via media*, or middle way between Roman Catholicism and Calvinist Protestantism, in fact the theology of the Articles was closer to Calvinism. Salvation came through grace alone, not through good works. Grace was the unmerited gift of God. Only three of them were criticised by Protestants under Elizabeth and her successor, James I. These upheld the authority of the Bishops and of the traditions of the Church. The more zealous Protestants, who were known as Puritans, objected to the episcopal hierarchy in the Anglican church and to the role of traditions going back beyond the Reformation. They claimed that neither bishops nor some of the traditional forms used in the Church of England were sanctioned by the Bible, the ultimate authority to which they appealed. Although their theological objections to the Elizabethan Settlement were few, they objected to many of the practices which had survived from the era of Catholicism, which they called 'relics of popery'. Such rituals as bowing at the name of Jesus, exchanging rings in marriage and crossing an infant's head in baptism smacked to them of superstition. They also criticised the clergy for wearing surplices and other vestments distinguishing them from the laity. Shortly after his accession, James I summoned a conference at Hampton Court to discuss these differences. Although little came of it beyond the decision to issue the Authorised version of the Bible, the debate was largely contained within the Church of England. Few seceded, though these included the Pilgrims who initially moved to the Dutch Republic and eventually sailed in the *Mayflower* to found Plymouth Colony. Most so-called 'Puritans' remained as Anglicans because they accepted that the Church of England was reformed, even though they wanted a more thorough godly reformation. They were prepared to 'tarry for the magistrate', to wait until the King, as Supreme Governor of the Church of England 'insofar as the law of Christ allows', was ready to move further away from Catholicism and towards Calvinism. Unfortunately for them, King Charles I seemed to move in the opposite direction. This was because he appeared to be supporting Arminianism in the Church of England. Arminius had been a Professor of Theology at Leiden University in the Netherlands and was seen as a threat to the Calvinism of the Dutch Reformed Church through his teaching that men could choose to accept or reject grace. Strict Calvinists preached that grace was irresistible. He seemed to be preaching free will against Calvinist predestination. Arminius was tried at the Synod of Dort in 1618, where his doctrines were condemned. Where James I approved of their condemnation, Charles I promoted bishops in the Church of England whom Puritans accused of being sympathetic to Arminianism. At the head of these was William Laud, whom Charles made Archbishop of Canterbury in 1633. While Laud claimed not to be an Arminian, he set in train changes in the Church of England which he maintained upheld the beauty of holiness, but which struck his Puritan critics as showing an inclination towards Catholicism. Thus, he insisted that the communion table should be moved back from the middle of the church to the east end and that it should be called an altar. His case that he was not a crypto-Catholic was not helped when the Pope offered him a cardinal's hat. Even though he rejected it, many Puritans were no longer prepared to 'tarry for the magistrate'. Some, while insisting that they remained members of the Church of England, removed themselves effectively from its jurisdiction by going to Massachusetts. Others waited for an opportunity to reverse the Arminian tendencies in the established Church. One came when Charles summoned Parliament in 1640 for the first time in 11 years. At the dissolution of the previous Parliament, resolutions had been passed protesting against 'Arminian' innovations in the Church of England. Now the innovators were to be brought to book. Charles thwarted those behind this move by dissolving the Parliament shortly after it met in 1640, for which it became known as the Short Parliament. But he was obliged to call another before the end of the year, which was to go down in history as the Long Parliament. By 1646 Laud had been executed, episcopacy had been abolished and the Anglican Church had been reformed along Presbyterian lines.

This had come about because Charles's religious policies had provoked civil war in his kingdoms of Scotland and England. The Scottish Church had been reformed in the sixteenth century, when Presbyterianism had been established. Like the Anglican Church it was Calvinist in theology, which was accepted by all but a small minority who accused it of not being completely on the model of Calvin's Church in Geneva. Unlike its English counterpart, it had no bishops, but practised a Presbyterian form of government, with control from below rather than from an episcopate above. Thus, parishes chose their ministers, and combined into local assemblies which sent delegates to a General Synod. James I of England was the sixth of that name in Scotland, and came to the Scottish throne before he ascended the English. He grafted a system of bishops on to the Church of Scotland. Although this provoked protests it was when his son Charles I tried to impose a version of the Anglican Book of Common Prayer on the Church of Scotland that there was national resistance. This took the form of the Covenant of 1638, whereby Presbyterians contracted to defend their Church against innovations from England. When resistance resulted in the so-called Bishops' War, Charles I found himself unable to subdue his Scottish subjects, who invaded England. It was to raise the resources to deal with them that the King had been obliged to summon the English Parliament in 1640. But a majority in the Long Parliament proved to be more sympathetic to the religious position of the Scots than to that of the King, and their intransigence resulted in a civil war in England too. In 1643 the Parliamentary majority accepted the Solemn League and Covenant which allied them with Charles's Scottish opponents. After the defeat of the King, however, the reformation of the Church of England to place it in conformity with that of the Scottish Church, an aim of the Solemn League and Covenant, proved impracticable. Instead, the Westminster Confession of 1646, and the Directory of Public Worship which replaced the Anglican Prayer Book, proved to be less than satisfactory to Scottish Presbyterians.

Meanwhile, under the pressure of civil war, English Puritanism split into many parts. The main sects to emerge from the process, besides the Presbyterians, were the Baptists, the Independents and the Quakers. Where the Presbyterians still stood for the reforms discussed in the Hampton Court Conference, the others had moved on. It was no longer a question of dropping three of the Thirty-Nine Articles and removing episcopacy. The Baptists insisted on adult baptism. The Independents were just that – they sought the independence of the parish churches from any kind of national organisation. While Baptists and Independents were within the Calvinist tradition, the Quakers preached a new doctrine of the inner light in all men, and dispensed with clergymen.

During the English Republic, established after the execution of Charles I in 1649, and the Protectorate of Oliver Cromwell which followed, England came close to religious anarchy as these and other sects such as the Fifth Monarchists and the Seekers jostled for supremacy in the localities. At the restoration of Charles II, an accommodation of them all in a monolithic Church of England was impossible. Even an attempt to comprehend moderate Presbyterians within the restored Episcopal Church, by limiting the power of the bishops and modifying some of the Thirty-Nine Articles, failed. Instead, an intransigent established Church insisted that its clergymen should subscribe to all of the articles. Some 400 could not bring themselves to do so and left the Church. They became the first Nonconformists, or Dissenters as they were known at the time. They were not allowed to leave in peace, but subjected to statutes passed by the Cavalier Parliament in the early 1660s which penalised any worship other than that of the established Church. Thus Catholics and Protestant Dissenters were persecuted under Charles II. The Catholic James II ended the persecution with his Declarations of Indulgence. But attempts to get the Anglicans to cooperate with this policy proved abortive. Instead, they took the lead in the resistance to the King, which culminated in the Revolution of 1688 when he departed the realm. In the Revolution Settlement of 1689 another attempt at comprehension of Presbyterians in the established Church failed. Instead, a Toleration Act was put on the statute book which allowed Protestant Dissenters who believed in the Trinity to worship separately from Anglicans.

**Religion and Migration to America**

The chequered religious history of Stuart England has been seen as the main motivation for emigration to the colonies, as first Puritans and then Quakers sought to escape persecution. It is notoriously difficult to disentangle spiritual from worldly motives. There were undoubtedly zealous aspirations behind John Winthrop's vision of a 'city upon a hill' and William Penn's 'Holy Experiment'. But how far they had the backing of a majority of colonists in New England and Pennsylvania is difficult to ascertain. In recent years, however, secular trends in England have been established which seem to have influenced migration to the colonies more powerfully than perhaps they have been given credit for in traditional accounts.

## POPULATION

One of the most important trends in the period was the growth of the population. At the turn of the sixteenth century there were about four million people in England and Wales. This was the result of an increase which was still occurring in the early seventeenth century, so that by 1650 there were a million more. Then the upward turn was reversed, and the population shrank back to 4,800,000 by 1680. Thereafter, there was a slow recovery, though it did not reach five millions again until 1720.

The rise in the population was natural and not the result of immigration. Indeed, more people left the country than arrived under the Stuarts, perhaps as many as 400,000 going across the Atlantic to the American colonies. This in itself probably accounts for the trough in the overall numbers between 1650 and 1680, especially since many of the emigrants were single young men.

The slowing down of the rate of increase of the English population in the early seventeenth century has been ascribed to the impact of famine and disease on the death rate. During the 1590s there was a series of bad harvests which caused food prices to rise to levels which the very poor could not afford, and some actually starved to death. Others had their resistance to disease lowered, and fell victim to typhus. The plague also took its toll, with a severe epidemic in 1604. The last visitation of the bubonic plague to England between 1665 and 1667 was the most deadly of the diseases which ravaged the population, killing between 70,000 and 100,000 in London alone. Even when the plague mysteriously stopped taking its toll, other diseases, including influenza, smallpox, and typhus, continued to reap a grim harvest. Famine, however, did not, for even when poor harvests recurred in the 1690s, nobody in England appears to have starved to death. They also seem to have been less prone to disease. Indeed, a decrease in the virulence of diseases in the late seventeenth and eighteenth centuries used to be cited as a main reason for the increase in the overall numbers of the population of England and Wales in those years. Thus, inoculation against smallpox, introduced in the 1720s and widespread by the 1750s, was held to be almost solely responsible for the surge in the overall figures for the second half of the eighteenth century.

Of late, however, an increase in the birth rate rather than a lowering of the death rate has become established as the primary cause of the growth of population in early modern England. This is due to the conclusions reached by the Cambridge Group for the History of Population and Social Structure after an intensive investigation of parish registers. The results of their analysis were published in 1981 in *The Population History of England 1571–1871* by E. A. Wrigley and R. S. Schofield. They indicated that a rise in the proportion of the population which married, together with a fall in the mean age at marriage of brides, made nuptiality the main reason for increasing numbers. Economic considerations were primarily responsible for the deferment of marriage until the mid- to late twenties in this period, since couples were expected to be able to maintain themselves and set up their own independent households. The notion that the extended family was the norm in pre-industrial England has been shown to be a myth. The nuclear family of husband, wife and children was far and away the most common. To sustain this family unit required marriage to be deferred until it was economically viable. There are signs that better economic opportunities encouraged earlier marriages and thus a rise in the birth rate in the second half of the sixteenth century. By 1600 the population was increasing at the rate of one per cent per year. Then, although overall numbers continued to rise, the rate of increase steadily fell, until it reached 0.2 per cent by the 1650s. Thereafter, for three decades, it stagnated and even became a minus figure. Recovery was slow until 1720, but thereafter accelerated until by the time of the 1801 census, the population of England and Wales stood at just under nine millions.

The principal agent of the seventeenth-century decline in the rate of increase seems to have been an increase in the proportion of the population which, although nubile, did not marry or have children outside wedlock. In the sixteenth century between 5 per cent and 10 per cent of the population never married. In the seventeenth century the ratio increased to between 20 per cent and 25 per cent. This has been explained as a response to the increasing pressure of population on resources, causing the price of food and other essential commodities to rise to the point where real wages declined. The result was that people could not afford a family. As the pressure on resources slackened at the same time as steps were taken to increase them, for example through more efficient farming, the rate of inflation dropped, causing real wages to rise in the later seventeenth century. This was especially the case in manufacturing districts, creating a migration to London and other towns. These began to experience a rise in the proportion of the population which married, and even an increase in illegitimate births. There are also signs that couples married at an earlier age, which had an impact on the birth rate, causing the population to grow again in the eighteenth century. The mean age at marriage of brides dropped from over 25 to under that. Where this occurred, it could have the effect of reducing the period in which the population would double from 200 years to 40.

Thus, where the early seventeenth century was an era of austerity, the later years saw unprecedented prosperity. The push factors behind migration significantly slackened. Under the early Stuarts, young men not only deferred marriage because they could not afford it, but went in large numbers to the colonies. Under the later Stuarts, they were no longer subjected to such pressures. As economic conditions improved at home, so the attractions of indentured servitude in the colonies lessened, and the supply of servants dwindled.

These trends largely affected the southern colonies. But economic circumstances in the mother country perhaps go far to explain migration to the northern and middle colonies too. The 'great migration' to New England in the 1630s occurred not only in years of religious persecution, but also in a decade of economic dislocation. The fact that Penn had difficulty recruiting colonists for Pennsylvania despite the fact that persecution, especially of Quakers, was resumed shortly after he obtained the grant of Pennsylvania, suggest that economic motivation was stronger than religious motivation in the seventeenth century.

## EARLY MODERN BRITAIN

In the eighteenth century a significant number of emigrants from other parts of the British Isles than England went to the colonies, especially from Scotland and Northern Ireland. When the English Empire became officially the British Empire with the Act of Union between England and Scotland, opportunities for trading with the colonies were opened up to Scots, who took full advantage of them. The empire as a consequence became British in reality as well as in theory. The people who went from the British Isles to North America in the early modern period used to be regarded as having peculiar qualities which distinguished them from their neighbours. It was thought that village communities, in which most Britons lived, were stable. Children were born into extended families which had lived in the same parish for generations. They were brought up by parents, grandparents, aunts and uncles who lived in the same dwelling or in close proximity. After a rudimentary education, boys were employed on the family farm or in their father's trade, while girls went into domestic service with a local family. They chose their marriage partners from among their contemporaries whom they had known since childhood. After raising families themselves, they died surrounded by familiar faces and were buried alongside their ancestors in the parish churchyard. Those who left these sheltered communities to venture across a wild ocean to a primitive colony threatened by hostile natives must have had some extraordinary psychological characteristics. They were hardy, intrepid souls daring to carve out their fortunes in the unknown. Early Americans therefore bequeathed such characteristics to the New World, and created a new kind of man or woman there. This view has, however, been demolished as a myth by social historians who have investigated the realities of life in early modern Britain. One of their key findings is that village communities were very far from being stable.

## SOCIAL MOBILITY

The death rate in London and in other large towns remained so high that their populations were not even reproducing themselves. The growth in the number of London's inhabitants, therefore, from 200,000 in 1600, to 490,000 by 1700 and to 675,000 by 1750 was due to internal migration. In 1757 George Burrington thought it 'very probable that two-thirds of the grown persons at any time in London come from distant parts'. According to a modern estimate, as many as one in six of the population of England and Wales spent part of their lives in the capital in the seventeenth and eighteenth centuries.

This rate of geographical mobility seems remarkable in a country whose inhabitants mainly lived in scattered village communities. For London was a giant, no other town in Britain and few in Europe approaching it in size. In the early seventeenth century only Bristol and Norwich could number their inhabitants in five figures, and then barely, with about 12,000 or 13,000. By 1700, when Bristol had some 20,000 and Norwich 30,000, they had been joined by Colchester, Exeter, Newcastle upon Tyne, Yarmouth and York. By the middle of the eighteenth century, a further seven towns had passed the 10,000 mark – Coventry, Leeds, Liverpool, Manchester, Nottingham and Sheffield. Liverpool prospered from the growth of trade with North America and the West Indies, which also boosted Bristol and helped Whitehaven to increase from 4000 in 1710 to 9000 in 1760. By then, Whitehaven was the largest port on the west coast of England measured by the tonnage of its merchant shipping, though Liverpool was to eclipse it by 1800. Glasgow too grew under the stimulus of the North American trade, to leap from fifth to second place in the league of Scottish towns, of which Edinburgh remained the head, with 85,000 inhabitants in 1800.

Nevertheless, though the proportion of the population living in towns had increased, the majority of English men and women still lived in villages with a few hundred inhabitants. However, the view of pre-industrial villages as stable communities in which the same families lived and died generation after generation has been shown to be a myth. Every investigation of village communities in the early modern period has revealed a remarkable turnover in their populations. In Cogenhoe, of 180 inhabitants in 1628, 94 had arrived since 1618. In Cardington there were 109 families in 1782, of which only seven had parents who had been born there, while both parents had been born elsewhere in the case of 51. It has been estimated that, of the families living in a particular parish in 1600, the descendants of only 16 per cent would still be there in 1700. However, most internal migrants moved within their counties. A study of five eastern counties in the seventeenth century showed that few people moved more than ten miles from their birthplace. Although 64 per cent of the boys and 57 per cent of the girls in Cardington in 1782 left the village before they were 15, for most of them this meant only a move into a nearby parish for employment or marriage. Geographical mobility appears to have been more marked in Scotland. In the North East, around Aberdeen, where most of the land was held by a few great landowners, the turnover of tenants on some farms bewilders social historians. Their tenure was much less secure than those of tenants in England, since leases were rare and, where they existed, were for short periods, sometimes only a year. Even in the South West, around Glasgow, where there were more landowners below the stratum of the aristocracy and tenure was less precarious, tenancies still changed more frequently than in England. Scottish landlords had much more control over their lands than those in England. The different legal system north of the border gave greater protection to property rights, which they used to evict tenants at will. Those who moved did not migrate to other villages, for they were rare in early modern Scotland. Most Scots lived in smaller more scattered communities, or 'farmtouns', than their English counterparts. As in England most seem to have moved relatively short distances.

Nevertheless, this geographical mobility has been taken by some historians as evidence that the decision to migrate to the American colonies was not the great emotional trauma that it appeared to earlier scholars, who assumed that English society in the seventeenth and eighteenth centuries was static. Thus, the statistical data on emigration from Britain to the American colonies gathered by the British government on the eve of the War of Independence has been placed in this context as just another move for economic betterment. This might have been true of the single young men who again are seen shipping themselves across the Atlantic from southern England, especially the Home Counties around London, to find work in the ports of New York and Philadelphia. But it scarcely explains the decision of families in the north of England and in Scotland to uproot themselves from their farms to the Carolina backcountry. On the contrary, to decide to travel 3000 miles across an ocean, never to see one's family again, suggests that those who went to America were at least psychologically different from those who remained in Britain.

# 3  Anglo–Indian Relations

Some Americans in the eighteenth century described North America as having been an uninhabited wilderness when their forefathers first arrived there from England. Until recently, even historians treated the colonies as though they had been settled from Europe with hardly any contact with native peoples. When they did encounter them, as often as not they were dealt with as problems to be eliminated. In the past 30 years or so, however, scholars have stressed that the eastern seaboard was inhabited by native North Americans, or Indians as the colonists called them, long before any white people arrived there. Indeed, one account graphically describes the arrival of the English as 'the invasion of America'. The numbers of Indians living in the areas which the invaders occupied has been calculated at about half a million in 1600. Contact with Europeans, and with the diseases which they brought with them, precipitated a demographic catastrophe in the seventeenth century which wiped out perhaps half of them, reducing their numbers to a quarter of a million by 1700.

Relations between the two peoples were more complicated than a simple clash between 'civilised' whites and 'savage' natives. The English were not unprepared for encounters with natives in North America, since Europeans had become acquainted with the aborigines of the New World ever since Columbus 'discovered' it. Two stereotypes of the Indians had formed in the intervening years, corresponding to rival models of what human nature was like. Indeed, the aboriginal Americans were to be invoked by both Thomas Hobbes and John Locke as exemplars of their theories about how men behaved in a state of nature. Hobbes developed the notion that viewed them as savages, warring on their neighbours, making life poor, solitary, nasty, brutish and short. Locke preferred the alternative view of them as 'noble savages'. They lived a life of primitive virtue, respecting the lives and property of others. Recent studies of the Indians in their own right have tended to side with the latter view. Indeed, some environmental historians have argued that the Indians lived in harmony with nature, respecting the ecology of their habitat, until it was invaded by the English. Then, they were corrupted by their invaders, for instance by selling them furs in exchange for alcohol and firearms until the peltry was exhausted on the eastern seaboard and had to be hunted further and further inland. England's invasion of North America thus had a devastating effect on its environment. It was even claimed that Europeans introduced scalping to the Indians, though archaeological evidence has established that it was practised long before contact between the two peoples. The Indians gained as well as lost from encounters with the English. For although alcohol, to whose toxic effects they appear to have been singularly prone, was detrimental to their wellbeing, they benefited from the textiles, tools and utensils which they purchased from the settlers.

Generalisations about Indian culture are now at a discount following studies of Indian communities, which have shown that there was considerable cultural diversity among those who inhabited the areas of North America which were settled by the English. Those whom they first encountered inside the Outer Banks of what later became North Carolina, and then in the Chesapeake Bay, lived in villages which were initially at least more attractive than the pallisaded forts of the settlers. John White's drawings of the former depict an idyllic society engaged in fishing and harvesting. The draconian laws introduced into Virginia in 1609 to make the settlement viable pronounced the death penalty for those who went to live with the Indians. Presumably, many were doing so in preference to trying to survive in the bleak conditions of Jamestown.

Relations between the Indians and the colonists were not just cultural but diplomatic. It was part of English imperial policy to get the natives in America to recognise the sovereignty of the Crown over them. It is the interaction of polities as well as of peoples that must be considered when dealing with the relationship between English settlers and the Indians. The diplomatic relationship can be reduced to a balancing act, one where ultimately the scales tip in favour of the British. There was already a dynamic culture operating in North America when the first settlers arrived. Tribes competed with one another for territory through a show of force as well as through alignments with one another. The advent of settlers meant, for the Indian societies, yet another element in the competition.

## THE CHESAPEAKE

One of the earliest examples of this interaction can be seen with the Powhatan Empire which stretched along the tidewater region of Virginia and the Potomac River in the north to the Great Dismal Swamp in the south. Powhatan's main competitors were the Iroquois to the north and the Sioux to the west. By 1608 Powhatan had established an extensive monarchy which included about 30 tribes. This was powerful enough to exact tribute from tribes from outer lying areas across the Chesapeake Bay. Powhatan, himself, was an impressive figure who, as John Smith described him, was every bit as regal as European monarchs. He was able to instil fear and respect among his people through swift justice and largesse. His brutal punishment of offenders sent a strong message to anyone who contemplated even a minor offence. But he was also astute enough to provide sustenance to his subjects in order to gain their loyalty and support. Powhatan's rule may not have been on as grand a scale as that of his European counterparts, nevertheless, it was every bit as powerful. Thus, when the settlers arrived in 1607, their fate was in his hands.

English traders had been involved in the North American continent since the middle of the sixteenth century, while the settlers in the lost colony at Roanoke clearly interacted with the Indians there. But it was not until the establishment of Jamestown that there was any substantial interaction between the two peoples. The Jamestown occupants were there as part of a contract by the Virginia Company to set up a commercial venture. There was awareness on the part of the English company of the importance of establishing a working relationship with the 'naturals'. Following instructions, settlers traded with the Indians for food so that their meager supplies could be supplemented. Powhatan was quick to realise the significance of the white people and their guns. Possibly for that reason, he warned an expedition, led by Captain Christopher Newport, not to go any further inland than the area near what is today Richmond where they would come into contact with his enemy, the Monacan tribe. The settlers already claimed an alliance with the Paspehegh, who granted them the area of Jamestown. Powhatan saw this incursion as the first step in the erosion of his power. From the settlers' point of view, they were competing not so much for Indian territory, but within the imperial nexus of competition. The dynamics of the two worlds overlapped at this point and caused two peoples to put into play a fatal game of alliance making. Powhatan's relationship with the colonists was strategic and although there were violent outbreaks between his people and the settlers, he kept them dependent upon his good will by intermittently supplying them with food. The capture of John Smith and his release being equipped with guides and food was part of the cat and mouse game where Powhatan was showing his power and his good will at the same time. He sent his symbolic 'son' to England to establish an alliance with the English king. Later, he used his favourite daughter, Pocahontas to keep the alliance he had with the English.

The English policy toward Indian relations was based on survival and trade. They were aware of the necessity to keep on even terms with the local inhabitants so that they could secure food supplies in order to survive. To that end they traded hatchets, copper items, knives, etc. for corn and fish. This was all predicated upon firm leadership. After Smith's departure in 1609, Powhatan reverted to ambushes and withholding supplies to the settlement. Together with the severe winter which followed in what became known as the 'starving time', this added to the troubles of the settlement. Powhatan's aim to eliminate the threat of the outsiders seemed to be about to be realised. Only when reinforcements showed up, literally as the survivors were removing themselves to Indian camps, were his objectives thwarted. After Powhatan's death, his nephew Opechancanough renewed his attempt to eliminate the settlers in the 'massacre of 1622' in which 347 were slain, and more might have been killed if a converted Indian had not warned them. He tried again in 1644, when perhaps even more were massacred.

The ambivalent relationship which emerged between the two groups set the pattern for future relationships with Indians in other colonies. The European and Native American policies on alliances were similar in that they were based upon survival and power. Their differences were only that the customs involved varied. How these would be played out can be seen by examining other crucial periods in Anglo–Indian contact.

## THE PEQUOT WAR

Although imperial policy toward Indians had not changed since the establishment of Jamestown, the aim of the New England immigrants was primarily religious. They wanted to establish the city upon a hill as a beacon for all the world. This motive included the conversion of the heathen Indians. Sometimes this took the form of coercion. 'Praying towns' were populated by enforcing the natives at gunpoint to submit to the will of the Lord. But the people at the other end of the gun were often 'friendly' natives. The missionary efforts to Christianise the Indians can be seen within the imperial context and the acceptance by some native people can be seen as a response to the pressures of expansion. It can also be seen as another avenue for American Indians to effect a balance between the growing numbers of Europeans and themselves. To this end and in this upper region of North America, there was the opportunity for the Indians to play the French off against the English in their competition for land. Divide and conquer seemed to be the plan. But that is to accept that Indian nations were acting in unison. The Indian peoples were still in competition with one another. Thus, the chance to align themselves with one or the other European cultures was considered in relation to their own competition for territory and power. The colonists's alliance with the Narragansetts illustrates the continued division between the Indians. It enabled the settlers in Saybrook at the mouth of the Connecticut River to isolate the Pequots when sporadic hostilities developed into open warfare in 1637. In June a force consisting of colonists and Narrangansetts went from Saybrook to the Pequot base at Mystic. They set the fort on fire, burning to death 400 inhabitants; men, women and children. As William Bradford, the governor of Plymouth colony, observed: 'it was a fearful sight to see them thus frying in the fire and the streams of blood quenching the same, and horrible was the stink and scent thereof, but the victory seemed a sweet sacrifice, and they gave the praise thereof to God.' 'Savagery' was not a monopoly of one side in the Pequot War.

## THE COVENANT CHAIN AND CHAIN OF FRIENDSHIP

The virtually simultaneous outbreaks of Bacon's rebellion, sparked off by clashes with Indians on Virginia's frontier, and 'King Philip's War' in New England, created a crisis in Anglo–Indian affairs (see below pp. 80–2). It seemed as though the natives were uniting to resist the continued encroachment of the colonists on their lands.

Imperial policy remained that of negotiation rather than confrontation. However, it was not keeping up with the rapidity of population movement. The friction between settler and Indian was enhanced by the refusal on the part of the metropolis, in the case of Virginia, Jamestown, under Governor Berkeley, to offend the Indians. The trading relationship between the two groups determined the timidity with which the policy toward the Indians was enforced. From the Indian viewpoint, both in the incident involving Nathaniel Bacon and the expansion problems in the Massachusetts area, the natives resented the increasing numbers of settlers encroaching into the areas inhabited by the ever-receding Indians. The attack by Metacom, or King Philip, upon the New England settlements was a response to this sinister flow of people. On a deeper level, the alliances which the Indians were making with one another can be seen as a significant turning point in Indian relationships. Instead of competing with one another, they tried to drop differences in face of a common threat, that of foreign invasion. An alliance amongst the Algonquian-speaking peoples was made under the leadership of Metacom. These peoples occupied the eastern seaboard from New England down to the Chesapeake. Hence, Indian attacks in the areas of Virginia and New England at this time could be seen as a concerted effort. It became essential to find Indian allies to offset the threat.

Governor Andros of New York went to Tinontougen in August 1675 to negotiate with the five nations of the Iroquois League: the Cayugas, Mohawks, Oneidas, Onondagas and Senecas. Their sphere of influence extended from the Mohawk River in upper New York westward to the Great Lakes and the Ohio River valley. They entered into an alliance with Andros in which the Mohawks agreed to help the English in New Haven in their war with Metacom. The following June, they met together again at Albany to begin to forge the Covenant Chain. When the process was completed a year later the chain bound the Iroquois, the Governor of New York and 'the great King Charles who liveth over the Great Lake'. There was recognition of the French threat which bordered the western and northern boundaries of the English colonies and of the French interest in supporting Metacom. Thus, the balancing act took on the French and Algonquian peoples on one side with the English and Iroquois nations on the other.

The negotiations over the Covenant Chain had involved the Indians living along the Delaware and Susquehanna Rivers. Relations with them were not the least of the considerations which led Charles II to grant the whole area to the Quaker William Penn. As with other colonies, settler and Indian relations were controlled from the imperial standpoint. Penn has been credited with being the most liberal and far-sighted statesman in terms of Indian policy. When Penn took over the Pennsylvania territory, he created a separate peace treaty with the very Indians that Andros had established within his Covenant Chain: the Lenni Lenape of the Delaware valley and the Susquehannocks along the river from which they derived their name. Unfortunately, Penn's Chain of Friendship encroached and came into conflict with the Covenant Chain.

Penn was instructed in the Charter for Pennsylvania 'to reduce the savage natives by gentle and just manners to the love of civil society and Christian Religion'. As far as it was possible to do so he succeeded. Penn established a reputation for fair dealing with the Indians of Pennsylvania, who called him 'Brother Miquon'. On his second visit to his colony in 1701, he signed a peace with the Susquehannocks in which they agreed not to assist any other Indians who were not friendly to the English.

As a result, Pennsylvania was immune from Indian attack in King William's War and Queen Anne's War. The Iroquois supported the English in the first, but were neutral in the second until 1711. They were partly persuaded to break their neutrality and assist the British against the French by Governor Nicholson of New York. Nicholson was so anxious to get the mother country to back an invasion of Canada that he sent four Mohawk chieftains to London in 1710 as goodwill ambassadors. Their visit aroused considerable interest in the imperial capital, but did not produce the desired effect. Nevertheless, the colonial war effort was assisted not only by the Mohawks, but also by their allies in the Iroquois Nations, which increased from five to six with the addition of the Tuscaroras.

## THE MIDDLE GROUND

During the period between Queen Anne's War and King George's War an equilibrium was maintained between the British and the French in North America, with the Iroquois occupying the middle ground. The outbreak of King George's War found most of them again attempting to remain neutral. At the outset of the French and

Indian War the Covenant Chain was snapped. The Conference at Albany in 1754, best known for its abortive attempt at colonial union, was convened to try to renew it. The six nations, however, were divided between neutrality and support for either the English or the French, most of them initially siding with the latter, hence the name by which the war is known in America. When Braddock marched towards Fort Duquesne, he had only eight Indians with his army, while the French had hundreds drawn from nine tribes including some Senecas. The failure of Braddock's expedition left the Pennsylvania frontier exposed to attack, and this time the Indians did not spare that colony. The change in their attitude was partly due to the notorious 'walking purchase' of 1737. William Penn had negotiated a deed with the Lenape in 1686, which conveyed to him all the lands west of Neshaminy creek in the Delaware valley 'as far as a man can go in a day and a half'. Penn himself had never invoked this deed, but in 1737 his sons insisted that it be implemented. Their agents, determined to maximise the amount of land which could be obtained, procured athletes to walk over it and cleared the ground for them before they set out. The fastest of these covered 64 miles in a day and a half, thereby acquiring 1200 square miles of the Lenape's land. The embittered Indians were obliged to vacate it and remove themselves to the upper reaches of the Susquehanna. The goodwill between the proprietors of Pennsylvania and the Indians which had been built up in Penn's lifetime was squandered by his sons. Indians, including Delawares, invaded the western frontier of Pennsylvania in 1755. Over 3000 settlers were killed or captured that year, and another thousand in 1756. Many more fled east across the Susquehanna.

These setbacks seemed to bespeak the failure of British imperial policy in the opening stages of the French and Indian War. The need for Indian allies to assist the war effort against France was made starkly obvious. As Lord Halifax expressed it in the House of Lords in December 1755: 'it is evident that an alliance with any one of the wild nations in North America would be of more service to us than an alliance with the powerful empire of Russia.' In desperation they sought an alliance with the Cherokees, but found that the French too were bidding for their support. A series of disastrous diplomatic blunders led the Cherokee to attack the British, a full-scale war breaking out between them in 1759 which lasted until 1761. By then, however, the tables elsewhere were turned. The taking of

Anglo–Indian relations out of the hands of the colonists and in 1756 placing them in those of superintendents for Indian affairs, one for the northern district and another for the southern, paid off, in the north at least. At the siege of Quebec, and in other victories in that 'wonderful year', the British had most of the Iroquois fighting for them, while the French were almost deprived of Indian allies.

## PONTIAC'S WAR

Helping the British to drive the French from North America, however, proved to be the undoing of the Indians. They were no longer needed to maintain the balance between the two European powers. This was made quite clear in the Peace of Paris when their lands were allocated to the British without any thoughts of negotiating with them. Those who had sided with the French, led by Pontiac, a chief of the Ottawas, realised this and made a last-ditch effort to assert their independence. In 1763 they attacked British forts in the Great Lakes region, capturing them all except Niagara and Detroit, to which they laid siege. Pontiac's allies also besieged Fort Pitt. Amherst sent Captain James Dayell to the relief of Detroit and Colonel Henry Bouquet to that of Fort Pitt. Dayell attempted to surprise Pontiac in a night sortie, but his men were driven back into Detroit, while he himself was captured and burnt, his heart serving for his captors' supper. Bouquet managed to relieve the garrison at Fort Pitt after defeating Indians at Bushy Run in August. A force sent to the relief of Niagara in September, however, was massacred. It took until 1765 for the British first under General Amherst, then after 1763 General Bouquet, to retake the forts lost to the Indians and to crush Pontiac's allies. In their determination to defeat them they did not scruple to supply the unsuspecting Indians with blankets infected by smallpox, the first known case of germ warfare in North America.

Alongside this contempt for the Indians went a concern for the problems they faced from the uncontrolled influx of white settlers into their territory. This concern was not inspired by altruism so much as by awareness of the threat posed to the expanded British Empire in North America by disgruntled natives. Colonel Henry Bouquet, whose private views on colonists and Indians alike held them in disdain, published a proclamation in October 1761 which prohibited settlement west of the crest of the Appalachians. Amherst, despite infecting Indians with smallpox, gave his approval to this policy. In 1763 George III issued a Royal Proclamation similarly restricting westward expansion of the colonies. Future settlements in the new territories would be regulated from Whitehall and not by the colonies. This, the last major diplomatic gesture towards the Indians before the War of American Independence, is often seen as a step towards that imperial crisis. Certainly, it antagonised those who had moved into the Ohio region, and continued to do so notwithstanding the Proclamation. In 1768 the boundary line was adjusted to accommodate some of these settlers. Pressure for further concessions was resisted by the American Secretary Lord Hillsborough, but it became irresistible and forced his resignation in 1772. His replacement, Lord Dartmouth, was much more willing to approve further breaches of the Proclamation line, even as far west as the Illinois country. To all intents and purposes, the British government's policy of controlling the settlement of the interior was abandoned before the imperial crisis erupted. In 1774, however, they handed over the administration of the Ohio region to Quebec, and thereby transferred responsibility for Indian policy and white settlement in the area from the colonies to Canada. This, as much as its provisions for Roman Catholics, made the Quebec Act one of the 'intolerable measures' of that year as far as the Americans were concerned.

# PART II
# The American Context

# 4 The Chesapeake

The land which became Maryland and Virginia is located within the Chesapeake Bay, the great expanse of water extending from Cape Henry in the south nearly 200 miles north to the mouth of the Susquehanna River. The Eastern Shore is mostly flat and sandy, offering few enticements to the first settlers. But the Western Shore, between 10 and 20 miles across the Bay, is the outlet for several great rivers which attracted the English to settle along them. The most southern is the James, some three miles wide at its mouth, and navigable in colonial times to the falls at present-day Richmond. Further north is the York, more an extensive inlet than a river. Then the Rappahannock and Potomac Rivers, with the Northern Neck between them, enabled the colonists to expand along their banks with easy access to ocean-going ships for many miles. The Potomac marked the boundary between the two colonies named after two Queens of England, Elizabeth the Virgin Queen and Henrietta Maria, wife of Charles I.

## JAMESTOWN

There had been earlier attempts by the English to settle in the region, but it was not until 1607 that a permanent foothold was established in the area which was to become Jamestown, named after the King of England. The fort of Jamestown was intended as nothing more than a base of operations from which the English Crown could establish a presence in the New World. In doing so, James I's aim to propagate the Christian religion and increase trade went hand in hand with his ultimate goal of enlarging his empire. Therefore, the peninsula upon which the fort was erected was never intended solely as an agricultural settlement. The Virginia Company, organised to develop that part of the eastern seaboard of North

America, directed the captain of the expedition to secure a site which would be safe from Spanish attacks, yet open to the sea. The imperial intentions of the company were clearly stated in its charter, which stressed Crown claims on any valuable resources found in the new land. One-fifth of precious metals such as gold and silver were to be given over to the King. Trade was only to be conducted within the English Empire and independent foreign trade was prohibited. Another stipulation in the charter was concerned with the actual colonisation. Settlers were given all the rights of Englishmen held in the motherland. This last privilege was to have long-term consequences.

In order to attract people to migrate to this new territory, promotional literature was published which, typically, exaggerated its attractions. Thus, descriptions of the soil, climate and general environment were painted with an idealistic hue. Unfortunately, the picture was at variance with the reality. To begin with, the actual settlement was located on a peninsula which was connected to the mainland by a thin strip of land. The peninsula was little more than a mosquito-infested swamp. In addition to the bug problem, the water was contaminated by the incoming sea water during the summer months. Dysentery and typhoid quickly followed and salt-water poisoning made for lethargy and even death.

Furthermore, there was nobody equipped to plant and harvest so that by autumn, there was very little to live on. This was because the initial venturers were not equipped with the essential skills to make a success of the colony. The demographic makeup of the population added to the problems of survival. Of the 105 settlers, there were 35 gentlemen, one Anglican minister, one doctor, 40 soldiers, and a smattering of artisans and labourers who ventured from the shores of England. Hardly anyone had the ability to deal with the climate and soil and as the population dwindled, the gentlemen of the group had no desire to perform any menial, yet crucial tasks in order to survive. There was weak leadership from the governor of the settlement, Edward Wingfield and, as a result, arguments increased to the point where one member of the group was executed for mutiny. By the end of the first year of settlement, only 35 people had survived.

Clearly, something had to be done about the lack of leadership exhibited by Wingfield. The advent of Captain John Smith resulted in a strong, but dictatorial style of management. Though extremely unpopular, Smith was able to command the group and get it to plant, build and defend itself. By 1609, however, Smith left the colony after more arguments and challenges to his authority. By this time, the Virginia Company realised that reorganisation was necessary and so applied for a new charter which reduced the role of the Crown, allowing the company and the colony to operate with a little more autonomy. The company was converted into a joint stock corporation with stockholders. The council, which was hitherto appointed by the Crown, was replaced with one annually elected by the stockholders. There was now more scope for the corporation to make its own laws and regulations so far as they did not conflict with English law. The new charter also provided for the expansion of land some 200 miles north and south of the original boundaries, and westward clear across to the Pacific Ocean. While the far west expansion was somewhat unrealistic, the boundaries stretching immediately west, north and south would have a more direct impact.

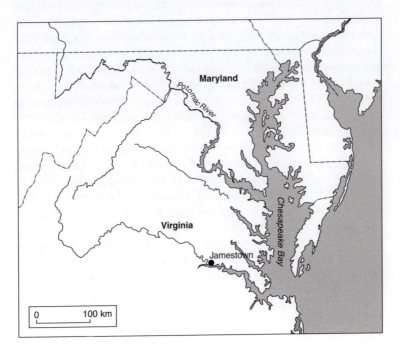

*Map 1*   The Chesapeake Bay

## RELATIONS WITH THE INDIANS

The best lands were on the Western Shore, where Powhatan, the Indian chief, was consolidating some 30,000 natives between the James and the Potomac into a confederation. At the time of the initial settlement of Jamestown in 1607, Powhatan was not concerned with the encroachment of the white settlers. In fact, he saw them as possible allies against those Indians who did not submit to him. This fact no doubt accounted for his initial friendliness and generosity in supplying sustenance to the struggling settlers. On the English side; the Crown directed that negotiations should supersede any hostilities with the native population. By 1609, however, the initial amicable relationship between settler and native began to deteriorate. This was partly due to the fact that Powhatan's expansionist aims and those of the settlers came into conflict. Accusations of theft and lying flew between the two groups with the result that violence broke out. Powhatan, who once supplied the settlers with food, now destroyed their means of survival. Livestock was killed and crops were burned. By the winter of 1609, the English settlers were facing starvation. That winter, known as the starving time, was the worst that the settlement knew. They had little choice between staying within the fortifications and starving to death or going out foraging for food and running the risk of attack. The situation became so bad that people were driven to eat the flesh of those who had died. There was one account of murder in order to consume fresh meat! It was impossible for any relief ships to make it across the Atlantic during the winter months. As summer neared, the settlers decided to abandon the New World. Then, in June, the first convoy from the motherland approached. On board was the new governor, Lord De La Warr, carrying supplies and a copy of the new charter. Although De La Warr fell ill and returned to England, his successors, Sir Thomas Gates and Sir Thomas Dale, were able to implement the provisions of the 1609 charter to its fullest intent. Also, because of their military experience, they were able to bring Powhatan to heel by way of a truce. Later, peace was ensured through the nuptial liaison between John Rolfe and Powhatan's daughter, Pocahontas.

## SURVIVAL

Once peace was established, the settlement was able to be repositioned 50 miles inland in a healthier location. Under Gates, a code of law was drafted, entitled, 'Divine, Morall and Martiall', which allowed for the prosecution of the law with the stiffest penalties. Among the strict codes was the requirement to attend the services of the Anglican Church outside of work hours. Disobedience incurred heavy fines and possible imprisonment. The moral laws also included penalties for blasphemy. Because martial law was part of the code, desertion and mutiny meant the death penalty. Consequently, within a few years, the colony was able to survive and grow.

Another innovation enabled the colony to flourish. The introduction of a new strain of tobacco plant, nicotiana tobaccum, was an immense improvement over the original but bitter tasting nicotiana rustica. As a result, exports to England increased and made the colony prosperous. Although the colony's fortunes were turning for the better, the financial turn around was not fast enough to satisfy the company's needs. A new charter was therefore issued in 1613 which allowed for a lottery, a means by which the company could raise cash through speculators' investments into the colony.

There was the ongoing problem of limited growth in population and an unbalanced gender ratio. Along with the depletion of numbers of settlers through the troubled early years, there were more men than women. Initially, men outnumbered women by three to one. This was hardly conducive to a permanent settlement. Although the ratio had improved over the next seven years, the investors found it difficult to convince families to risk leaving the security of their homelands for an uncertain future. By 1616, the population had declined from 450 in 1611 to 324. The combination of initially poor geographical location, bad management, the wrong type of immigrants, and now the imminent release of servants from their contracts threatened to reduce the workforce further. One last attempt was made by Sir Edwin Sandys when he granted subpatents to investors who, in return, would get administrative and judicial privileges. Although the company did not totally divest itself of land holdings, the end result was a transition from a company-based investment to one of private property. The way the grant worked was through a headright system whereby everyone who had paid their own way across the Atlantic would receive 100 acres plus 50 acres for each dependent. Land was also set aside for colleges, churches and schools, including one for Indians. Furthermore, areas or boroughs were carved out. In total, four boroughs emerged which included Charles City, Jamestown, Henrico, and Kiccowtan with the company maintaining a few thousand acres in each.

With a new charter, a more viable form of government was devised. Because land investors travelled to claim their properties in person, they also wanted similar rights as they had in England. These rights included the right to be represented in the House of Commons. The company responded to their expectations by granting an Assembly. The government of the colony was composed of a governor, council and two elected burgesses from every parish. Together, these three elements made up the Assembly. The Assembly was required to meet once a year in order to pass laws which they saw fit for the colony. There was a distinction between rights and privileges. Rights were reserved to the adventurers who were eligible to attend company meetings. This left the bulk of the population without the rights of Englishmen. However, Sandys did grant the vote to every adult male. This, in effect, went a long way to assuage the colonists by giving them some participation in government. Thus, on 24 July 1619, the first Assembly in North America met in Jamestown. It passed laws one of which stated no harm was to be done to the native population. However, though trade was permitted with the Indians, through the governor only, no liquor was to be sold to them. Although Dale's code of laws had earlier been made void, a new set of laws, albeit less harsh, was put in place against drunkenness, idleness, gaming and the wearing of ostentatious clothing.

At last, there was a feeling of optimism that the colony would survive. But there were still a lot of fatal illnesses which diminished the population. Approximately 4000 people were sent over in a four-year period between 1618 and 1622. Of those, only a quarter survived. The reason for this was largely due to the company's insistence on shipping settlers over during the spring instead of the autumn, when they could have had the winter to 'season' or acclimatise themselves to the new environment. In addition, James I had revoked the company's use of the lottery system. This severely cut into its revenue and had the effect of increasing tobacco production. Since the Crown banned the growing of tobacco in England from 1619, the price of the commodity soared. The Crown, in turn, capitalised on the soaring prices with a levy of one shilling per pound. The collection of the duty was farmed out, which added to the cost of production. Although Sandys tried to regain control of the distribution within England, shareholders were outraged at the proposed cost of the new scheme. In the end, the Privy Council suspended the arrangement.

Although the relations between settlers and the natives were generally amicable, they were also very fragile. The generous land policy instituted by Sandys meant expansion of the tidal waterways and encroachment into Indian territory. Disputes had broken out in the past, especially in the years 1609–14 which some see as England's first Indian War. But with the demise of Powhatan and Pocahontas, the links between native and colonist completely broke down. The misunderstandings and mistrust came to a head on a Friday, 22 March 1622, after breakfast when the Confederacy, now led by Chief Opechancanough, attacked the settlers, resulting in a blood bath. Approximately 350 men, women and children were wiped out. The most notable attacks occurred at Martin's Hundred and Charles City. Reprisals were made upon the Indian population. This continued into the next decade when a truce was reached by creating a boundary between the Indians and the settlers at the Jamestown peninsula. The only contacts that were allowed were through trade. Another major war occurred from 1644–46, in which Opechancanough attacked the settlement. Eventually, he was captured and murdered. The Powhatan Confederacy was no longer the force it once was because the growing numbers of immigrants and weaponry overwhelmed them. There was decreasing need to negotiate with the Indians and the growing recognition that the two cultures could not coexist.

## CROWN TAKEOVER

More immediately, however, such a devastating breakdown in relations was the final blow to the Virginia Company. In 1623 a *quo warranto* was issued through the Privy Council which questioned the company's legal right over the colony. Consequently, Virginia ceased to be a company-based operation and became a Crown colony, first under James I and then under his son, Charles I. After 1624 the King appointed the governor and his council. The Council was a more powerful body than the Assembly, comprising the great tobacco planters of the colony. Although nominated by the Crown, largely on the recommendation of the governors, they were not servile dependents. On the contrary, they showed their mettle in 1635 when Governor Sir John Harvey antagonised them by trying to restrict the expansion of the colony. They forced Harvey out of office, obliging him to sail for England. The Assembly survived the transition from company to Crown mainly because Charles I perceived it as essential to solving the problem of developing the colony's economy. Although he now appointed the governor and his council, after 1639 he was prepared to have them govern in conjunction with an annual Assembly, even though he himself experienced difficulties with Parliament and dispensed with it altogether in the 1630s. The Assembly's concern to protect its privileges from royal infringement resulted in a 'Brief Declaration', which it hoped would thwart any attempts at martial law being imposed. They also passed an ordinance whereby the governor was circumscribed from imposing any taxes without the authority of the Assembly.

Where under the company Virginia had nearly collapsed, as a Crown colony it began to flourish. The early years had been a disaster brought about by dispatching unsuitable settlers, the difficulties of acclimatisation to a strange environment with diseases to which Europeans had acquired no immunity, and deteriorating relations with the Indians. Only the cultivation of tobacco offered a way out of these difficulties, too late for the company but not for the Crown. Virginia continued to operate along the previous lines of government. The Assembly continued to function and membership grew as counties were carved out of newly settled lands. The county courts dispensed justice and the parishes performed tasks such as poor relief like the quarter sessions and vestries familiar to seventeenth-century Englishmen. Indeed, Virginia developed more and more into a recognisable copy of rural England by 1676. The early days of economic disaster and social dysfunction came to an end. Between 1629 and 1642 the white population grew from about 3000 to around 8500. By 1660 it had reached 25,000. Initially, much of this was due to immigrants from England, most of them indentured servants. Yet increasingly there was natural growth too. The economy continued to develop despite a steep drop in tobacco prices in the 1630s as exports increased. Society began to stabilise as life expectancy improved and the gender balance was redressed until the family could become the basic social unit. A hierarchy began to emerge by the 1670s as the heads of gentry families who had survived the upheavals of the opening decades became the leaders of provincial society in the Council or the Assembly, and of local communities in the counties and parishes.

As the development of the colony became more secure and the area under cultivation expanded, there arose a need for more labour. Although indentured servants supplied that need for much of the seventeenth century, the numbers depended upon the standard of living at home in England compared to the risk of emigration. In the 1680s the English economy enjoyed a boom which made economic emigration less attractive than it had been, and the supply of indentured servants began to dwindle. The demand for labour, on the other hand, continued to increase, and it had to be sought elsewhere. The first African labour force came in 1619, but their numbers remained small until the later seventeenth century. Prior to 1640, blacks made up less than one per cent of the population in the Chesapeake compared to 28 per cent by the beginning of the eighteenth century. Although there is evidence of racism, the low numbers of blacks and the need for work explains their similar status to that of the indentured servant. Both were essentially slaves with the possibility of freedom. Up until the 1670s in the Chesapeake area, there were free Africans who themselves owned servants. Most notable was the case of Anthony Johnson, a free black farmer who lived on the Eastern Shore and who employed servants. In the early years, though the numbers were small, it was not unusual for free blacks to have indentured male and female servants. The idea of slavery in perpetuity gradually came about through a number of factors which could have arguably been the result of prejudice. Africans, seen as non-Christians, were considered outside the laws which were, for the most part, the products of Christian morality. So not only did their colour set them apart, their belief systems were anathema to the monotheistic religion of the Western world. Once outside the laws of society, it would be easy to consider them as inferior. Also, blacks were thought to be descendants of the biblical Ham. His descendants, in turn, were condemned to permanent servitude. This last argument was seen increasingly as a justification for perpetual slavery. For the moment, however, such ideas were in a state of flux. Only after the African population began to increase dramatically, coinciding with a decline in the numbers of immigrant servants from Europe in the second half of the seventeenth century, were legal restrictions increasingly put on the status of black slaves. Bacon's rebellion also helped to condemn blacks to a life of repression.

## BACON'S REBELLION

When Nathaniel Bacon arrived in Virginia in 1674, it was governed by Sir William Berkeley who had first gone there as governor as long ago as 1641. Although his governorship had been interrupted by the Interregnum following the English Civil Wars, he had been restored to it after the Restoration of Charles II in 1660. By the time Bacon encountered him he was 70 years old.

Berkeley's influence on Virginia had been profound. 'He bent the young sapling of its social system', claims a leading historian, 'and made it grow in the direction that he wished.' Although this claim exaggerates the degree to which Berkeley personally recruited the colony's elite from royalist elements in England, he did recruit a clique loyal to himself, known from the name of his mansion as the Green Spring faction. Berkeley's cronies dominated the political life of Virginia, controlling the Assembly elected in 1662 which was so loyal to the governor that he kept it until 1676. It was the colonial equivalent of Charles II's Cavalier Parliament, which lasted from 1661 to 1679. This oligarchy kept tight control of Virginia at a time when its population was expanding and settling further and further west, towards the fall lines of the great rivers which emptied into the Chesapeake Bay.

The Green Spring faction grew increasingly out of touch, however, not only with the settlers on the frontier, but also with the people of the tidewater. They demonstrated their detachment in 1670 when an Act was passed in the Assembly depriving freemen of their right to vote, and restricting the franchise to freeholders. As one of them said of recent English immigrants, at whom the Act was partly aimed, Virginia served 'but as a sink to drain England of her filth and venom'.

Bacon might have felt that he himself was included in such remarks by the way he was treated by Berkeley and his henchmen. Expecting to play a role in Virginia commensurate with his rank in England, he felt himself to be cold-shouldered by the Green Spring faction. He in turn looked down on them as men of 'vile' extraction and education, and left Jamestown to seek his fortune on the frontier. The gap between Green Spring and the frontier widened when Indian attacks involving the Doeg and Susquehannocks were countered by the militia. Berkeley was endeavouring to maintain friendly relations with the Indians, and called off the colonial forces. This decision left the frontiersmen exposed to further Indian attacks. Encouraged by Bacon, they decided to take control of the situation into their own hands. Defying the governor, they launched a fresh attack on the Susquehannocks. Indeed Bacon indiscriminately fought any Indians he encountered, threatening to provoke a full-scale war which Berkeley was anxious to avoid. The governor was outraged at this defiance of his orders, and declared Bacon a traitor. The rebellion had begun.

At this stage it could be seen as a dispute between the tidewater settlers and the frontiersmen. But while the tensions between them had sparked off the uprising, there were also sources of conflict between the Green Spring faction and the rest of the population in the east. Economic difficulties created by a slump in tobacco prices caused acute problems throughout the colony. Berkeley had sought to resolve them by trying to diversify the Virginian economy. He had even introduced silk worms and mulberry bushes from France in an attempt to make it less dependent upon tobacco. As elsewhere in the colonies, such efforts were unavailing. There were also complaints about a poll tax, which bore more heavily on the poor than on the rich.

Berkeley has been accused of arrogance, browbeating, overweening ambition for power and even tyranny. While he was undoubtedly a proud man, he was not over-ambitious, let alone tyrannical. He asked the King to replace him as governor with a younger man. And he even agreed to dissolve the Assembly and hold fresh elections.

The new Assembly was dominated by Bacon, who was returned to it from the frontier constituency of Henrico. It dealt with the Indian threat by commissioning him to lead a force against it. Then it tackled the grievances of the tidewater inhabitants against the Green Spring faction. Thus, the grip of the elite on the county courts and even the parish vestries was relaxed, while an Act gave the vote back to the freemen.

The apparent reconciliation between Bacon and Berkeley, who gave his assent to the legislation passed by the Assembly, was, however, only skin deep. The governor delayed issuing a commission for the force to deal with the Indians. Bacon reacted by going to the Assembly with a body of armed men, forcing Berkeley to flee to the Eastern Shore of the Chesapeake. Bacon then published a Declaration 'in the name of the people of Virginia'. This indicted Berkeley:

> For having, upon specious pretenses of public works, raised great unjust taxes upon the commonalty for the advancement of

private favorites and other sinister ends, but no visible effects in any measure adequate; for not having, during this long time of his government, in any measure advanced this hopeful colony either by fortifications, towns, or trade...

For having abused and rendered contemptible the magistrates of justice by advancing to places of judicature scandalous and ignorant favorites...

For having protected, favored, and emboldened the Indians against his Majesty's loyal subjects, never contriving, requiring, or appointing any due or proper means of satisfaction for their many invasions, robberies, and murders committed upon us...

Some historians have read this Declaration as an anticipation of the Declaration of Independence. Yet its ostensible target at least was not the King of England but Governor Berkeley. It accused him of 'having wronged his Majesty's prerogative' and of betraying his loyal subjects. Bacon's intention was not to declare independence, but 'to represent our sad and heavy grievances to his most sacred Majesty'.

So, far from being an early example of a colony seeking independence, Bacon's confrontation with Berkeley should be viewed as an extension of the faction fighting at the Court of Charles II. Sir William Berkeley had been a client of the Earl of Clarendon, principal architect of the Restoration of 1660. When Clarendon fell in 1667, the governor lost his power base at Court. He wrongfooted himself there too by protesting against the Navigation Acts and by opposing the grant from the King of quitrents and other royal dues in Virginia to the courtiers Lords Arlington and Culpeper. Part of the tax burden he placed on the colony, against which Bacon's Declaration protested, was to raise funds to contest this grant. Arlington was at the time one of the most powerful courtiers in the kingdom. When the government of which he was a leading member collapsed in 1673, the incoming chief minister, the Earl of Danby, was no better disposed towards him. On the contrary, as Lord Treasurer he objected to a colonial governor who had criticised the navigation laws. The Plantations Duties Act, which Danby sponsored, took responsibility for administering the system, taking it out of the hands of colonial governors and placing it in those of the customs service. Giles Bland, one of Bacon's staunchest supporters, was a customs officer. He hoped to benefit not from any visionary scheme of independence, but from the victory of the anti-Berkeley interest in the English court. Chief among them was Lord Culpeper whose grant Berkeley had opposed. Ominously for Berkeley, Culpeper was declared governor-designate of Virginia in 1675. This was the English political background to Bacon's rebellion. He hoped to benefit not from severing the imperial link with the Crown, but from making it stronger. He threw in his lot with the forces ranged against the Green Spring faction because he knew that it was out of favour with Charles II.

When Bacon returned to the frontier to deal with the Indians, Berkeley returned to Jamestown. Bacon then turned back and besieged the capital, forcing the governor to flee once again. The rebel leader than issued a Proclamation freeing any servant or slave belonging to Berkeley or his supporters. This led to a breakdown of order in which indentured servants joined with slaves to attack planters, one of the plantations which they plundered being Berkeley's own at Green Spring. This rebellious alliance of servants and slaves has been seen as a major reason behind the shift from indentured servitude to slavery in late seventeenth-century Virginia. It is argued that planters expressed a preference for slaves over indentured servants since the latter had proved to be a threat to their ascendancy in Bacon's rebellion. Intriguing though this theory is, it seems that the supply of indentured servants from England was dwindling anyway, necessitating a switch to an alternative labour supply.

Bacon's rebellion ended with his death from dysentry in October 1676. But the aftermath lasted much longer. Berkeley had 23 rebels hanged. As Charles II wryly pointed out, this was more than he had executed for the death of his father. The King was indeed more lenient than the governor. Charles was inclined to lay much of the blame for the breakdown of order in Virginia on Berkeley. He sent 14 ships carrying 1300 troops to the colony to suppress the rebellion, together with a royal commission to investigate its causes. The commissioners confirmed the view that the Green Spring faction's unpopularity was the main source of discontent. Berkeley was persuaded to return to England, where he died in 1677. He was eventually replaced as governor by Lord Culpeper.

Unlike Maryland, Virginia did not become actively involved in the Glorious Revolution, though the Assembly did petition James II to recall his governor, Lord Howard of Effingham, whose arbitrary manner had offended them. The King was considering this when

William of Orange invaded England. After the Revolution, as William III, he conceded the Assembly's request, keeping Lord Howard in England and getting him to appoint a deputy governor, Francis Nicholson, who was to become one of the more effective governors of colonial Virginia. During his governorship the capital of the colony was moved from Jamestown to Williamsburg, named after William III. The new monarchs, William and Mary, gave their names to the College established there in 1693. The handsome buildings for the college, the governor's mansion and the Assembly, together with the wide streets and impressive town houses, made Williamsburg the finest colonial capital in British America.

## MARYLAND

Further up the Chesapeake Bay, Maryland was founded out of the failure of another settlement. George Calvert, the first Lord Baltimore, like many of his peers, invested in the Virginia Company. However, his first venture at Avalone in Newfoundland turned out to be less conducive to a permanent settlement than Jamestown. After visiting Avalone in 1627 and finding the climate and general environment inhospitable and hardly profitable, Calvert abandoned the plan for an area further south. By 1629, the Virginia venture had proved successful, but the Anglicans there would not allow for Roman Catholics to become full citizens. However, there was still enough land in the Chesapeake region which could be claimed. The fact that Calvert was a Catholic created problems at home and enemies who would try to limit his financial activities as such. Because he was a peer of the realm and closely connected to the King, however, he was able to get a grant of land which he named after the Queen. Although he died before the charter was granted in 1632, the terms of the grant were similar to that of his previous one for Avalone and substantially different from that of Virginia and Massachusetts. Whereas they were considered company charters, his was a sole proprietorship which gave him extensive powers over his new colony; over land rights, natural resources, trade, customs and other revenues. Moreover, his powers were such as those of the Bishop of Durham, who controlled the northeast of England up to the Scottish border as a palatinate. It was little less than a feudal fiefdom. As the Bishop had the power to collect duties and hold courts, so did Baltimore who had the power to incorporate towns, hold courts, and very importantly, allow for a variety of faiths to worship. This meant he could issue licences for Churches. Fealty to the Crown was nominal. In Baltimore's case, it amounted to 20 per cent of precious metals and a symbolic two arrows yearly.

The first Maryland settlement was made at St Mary's in the southern part of the colony. Investors who purchased 1000 acres or more were given manorial rights. These rights involved the right to hold courts, dispense justice and collect duties. A total of 60 manors were created. Initially, there was no representative body or Assembly, but one was called in 1638. The probable motive behind this can be located in English rather than in colonial politics. In 1631, one of the inhabitants, William Claiborne tried to set up a rival trading operation on nearby Kent island. Baltimore claimed that Claiborne needed a trading licence from the proprietor. A conflict broke out with Baltimore eventually taking over the island. However, a challenge to Baltimore's authority was raised by Claiborne's supporters in England. Events there during this time had a direct effect upon Baltimore's influence as proprietor. Charles I had married a French Catholic which created suspicion from the start of his reign. But this increased in the 1630s when he ruled without Parliament. Initially, he had the sympathy of the moderate section of the population. This included those merchants who backed the King, and subsequently Baltimore's claim over Kent Island's trade. So he was able to deal with Claiborne's to his own advantage. One of the ways in which the King financed his personal rule was through such uses of his prerogative as the granting of the charter for Maryland. Baltimore, however, aware of the appearance of subjugation of the rights of Englishmen which events in England were giving, combined with the problem over trading rights in Maryland, called for an Assembly of freemen to meet in 1638. One of its first Acts passed, an oath of loyalty to the King, was clearly an attempt to safeguard all non-Roman Catholic faiths in the colony. The other was to create a legislature, meeting on a yearly basis and based on the model of Parliament. The make up consisted of a governor, council, lords of the manor and one or two freemen who were elected from every hundred. Although initially opposed to the legislation, Baltimore eventually allowed the Acts setting out the system to pass.

The colony's situation was improving in some respects while deteriorating in other ways as the political situation in England crumbled. The proprietor had learned from Virginia's mistakes by requiring settlers to become self-sufficient while promoting the main crop of tobacco as an export item. But the events in England were spilling over into the political life of the colony. The outbreak of the English Civil Wars, which lasted from 1642–49, raised suspicion about the Catholic Baltimore. While his brother, the governor, returned to England, Claiborne and another conspirator, Richard Ingle attempted the take over of the colony in the name of protecting Protestantism. When the governor returned, he had to flee to Virginia for protection. Ultimately, he was able to enlist the aid of Virginia's Governor Berkeley and in 1644 he was able to retake the colony. Taking further advantage of the political crisis in England, Ingle returned there to accuse the proprietor of harbouring traitors to the Crown. Baltimore still was in a position of influence with the Court and London merchants to defeat Ingle's attempts. Nevertheless, in 1649, Baltimore appointed a Protestant governor, William Stone, and introduced a bill for religious toleration. This was in answer to the growing Protestant population, but it was also a last ditch effort to save his position as proprietor because the King had been beheaded and the rump Parliament with a radical Puritan bloc had taken over. By the end of 1650, a commission appointed by Parliament and including none other than Claiborne, took control of the English colonies of Bermuda, Antigua, Barbados, Virginia and Maryland. Baltimore was ousted as proprietor until events in England took another twist. In 1656, Oliver Cromwell took the reins of government as Lord Protector. Recognising the danger of an unstable colony with the radical element in charge, in 1657 Baltimore was reinstated. An Act Concerning Religion was passed which put religious toleration on the books.

After the Restoration, Baltimore consolidated his hold on the colony. He remained in England, where the ultimate power lay, sending first his brother and then his son to Maryland as his governor. The proprietor's friends, most of them Catholics, controlled the council. Meanwhile, the elections to the Assembly were returning more and more Protestants. This eventually provoked a clash between the Assemblymen and the proprietary faction. Faced by some opposition in the Assembly in 1669, Baltimore increased the property qualification for voting the following year, thereby reducing the electorate. He also decreased the number of representatives. In 1676, coinciding with Bacon's rebellion, protests were raised against the proprietor's high-handed actions in counties near the border with Virginia. These protests foreshadowed the Glorious Revolution in Maryland, which was to transform it from a proprietary to a Crown colony (see below pp. 128–9).

Over the next century, Maryland's growing population and limited territory gave impetus to modifications in its social and political structure. Like Virginia, Maryland went through a process of initial instability to become a stable colonial society. Indeed, the two Chesapeake colonies, however much they might have differed in their political and religious experiences, socially and economically were inevitably very similar.

Before 1640, the population of Maryland was less than 400. During the English Civil Wars, the numbers increased to about 500 due to Puritan immigrants from Virginia and a more liberal land policy in Maryland. Unlike Virginia, male servants received 50 acres, three barrels of corn, tools and one set of new clothes as a headright. Still, there was a high mortality rate which left the gender balance uneven. Males outnumbered females six to one which was socially significant. Of the children who survived into adulthood, most lost at least one parent. While there were many disadvantages to these two phenomena, one positive aspect they shared was more control over their young adult lives. For women, it meant having more choice in marriage partners. For the children, particularly the males, their inheritance came at an earlier stage thus freeing them from parental constraint over choices. Another significant aspect concerned the limited amount of land to be had. Because land in the territory was finite, the manorial system suffered.

By 1660 Maryland's white population had increased to 8400. As in Virginia, this increase was underpinned by a cash crop economy. In Maryland too the gender imbalance had been corrected and the family had become the norm. Also, the Hundreds were forming into counties and being governed as such until county courts superseded manorial or Hundred courts of justice after 1692, when the Anglican Church became established. As the supply of indentured servants to the Chesapeake began to fall off, so Maryland, like its sister colony, sought to supply its labour shortage with slaves. By 1700 the total population had increased to 29,600, over 3000 of whom were slaves. In 1740 the inhabitants of Maryland numbered 1,160,000; 23,000 of whom were black.

# 5 New England

After Captain John Smith left Virginia, albeit under a cloud, he explored the northeastern coast of North America looking for a location for a fishing and trading venture. He found such a place on the rocky coast of New England and returned to England to persuade the investors in the Plymouth Company that a business venture there was possible. Having been stung once before in the failure of the Sagadahoc investment, the company proposed to limit the enterprise to 40 eminent persons. Of those, Cecil Calvert, Lord Baltimore was one and Sir Ferdinando Gorges was another. While Baltimore eventually interested himself in the Chesapeake, Gorges took the lead in the organisation of the Plymouth venture. The venture was to be set up along the lines of Virginia under Sir Edwin Sandys in 1618. Once the area was under patent, the company would grant patents to groups who would in turn settle the area. The profits would then come to the company through quitrents and payments on the development of the colony's natural resources.

## PLYMOUTH

One of the first groups to apply was an English dissenting sect who resided in Holland. They had left their homeland after believing that the established Church was beyond redemption and themselves ostracised from society for their separatist activities. They left their homes in Yorkshire to live in Leiden, but the worldliness of the place was affecting their young. Also, the 12-year truce between Holland and Spain was due to expire and it was feared that the Spanish would once again threaten the people with the Inquisition. Their disillusionment and concern for their own safety led them to look across the Atlantic. The Dutch had already sent an expedition to the Hudson Bay area, but the Separatists wanted to create their own society.

Previously, they were contracted with the Virginia Company, but the problems of settling in the Virginia area where the Anglican Church was established was exactly what they wanted to avoid. Between 1618 and 1620, negotiations began with a group of London merchants lead by Thomas Weston which resulted in setting up a joint stock company. The agreement was that the Pilgrims would settle the area of the patent for seven years, at the end of which the profits would be shared between the two groups. The administration of the fledgeling colony was left to emigrants to decide, which they did on route across the Atlantic. Forty-one of the male passengers drew up an agreement, what was to become the Mayflower Compact, in which laws were to be established for the 'general good of the colony.' The intent of the document was to preserve the Godliness of the separatists by setting up a church based upon the principle that God made a covenant with man to provide a way to salvation. From this precept stemmed the political structure of the colony. They were determined to avoid any of the corruptions that had entered their lives in England and Leiden. Although two ships had started out on the voyage, the *Mayflower* and the *Speedwell*, the latter experienced problems in its first port of call, at Plymouth, England, leaving the *Mayflower* to sail across alone with 101 passengers.

In November 1620 they arrived in the New World and set up the Plymouth colony. They were lucky in that European diseases had decimated the local Indian population. In their view it was not luck, but God who had 'thinned the land' for them. Unfortunately, in their zeal to become self-sufficient by farming the land, they quickly realised that the land was rocky and lacking the depth of soil for extensive planting. After the first year, the investors in England became disillusioned and began to sell their shares. Although the colonists were allowed to extend their shareholding in the venture, their poor financial standing inhibited it. Only when a new settlement established itself up the coast in the 1630s was the Pilgrims' situation improved by the increased sales of livestock and grain.


## MASSACHUSETTS

The Plymouth colony was soon eclipsed and ultimately absorbed by the more dynamic one based in the Massachusetts Bay area. Where Plymouth's population reached at most 7500, some 13,000

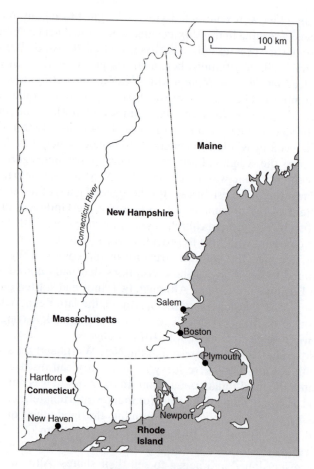

*Map 2*    New England

settlers moved to the Bay in the 'great migration' of the 1630s. The
Massachusetts Bay Company was dominated by Puritans within the
Anglican Church who found little satisfaction to their demands for a
purer church. Trends in Europe did not look promising for Protestants in general, whose faith seemed to be threatened by the Catholic
Counter-Reformation, while in England the rise of Arminianism
posed a local threat to them. These Puritans, rather than cutting
themselves off from the Church of England as did the Separatists
at Plymouth, decided to make their new society an example for the

world to follow, and hoped that the established Church would reform itself. In their view, toleration was not the answer, but conformity to one way, their way. The colony's origins stemmed from earlier attempts by a group of merchants who were also interested in the fishing grounds of the north. Their initial project, however, failed. One of the settlers, Reverend John White, moved to the area of Salem, known at the time as Naumkeag, where he was able to interest others in England with similar religious leanings. Ultimately, a patent was secured from the Crown in 1629 establishing the Massachusetts Bay Company. Most of the adventurers came from the vicinity of London and East Anglia.

One individual who was acutely aware of the climate in England was John Winthrop. A Justice of the Peace and member of a gentry family, Winthrop shared the view of many of his class that the established Church was headed in the wrong direction. He objected to the increasingly ornate rituals associated with its services. His views were proving detrimental to his own career when he was deprived of an attorneyship in the Court of Wards and Liveries. The combination of financial necessity and spiritual zeal probably decided Winthrop to take his family across to America. For him, the Massachusetts Bay Company was not just a trading venture. For the likes of White and Winthrop, keeping the corruption of the Church from their doors was paramount. The Puritan element which invested in the venture was able to buy out any who were not of the same religious leaning.

Luckily, the charter did not specify any requirement for keeping the company headquarters at home in England. Winthrop was instrumental in the decision to set it up in Massachusetts Bay and use the charter as the constitution of the new colony. The governor and general court of the company were transformed into the governor and legislature of Massachusetts, and the freemen who voted for them as investors became the voters for the lower house.

In March 1630, seven ships with some 700 passengers set off with Winthrop, elected as the colony's first governor, on board the *Arabella*. The Puritans had taken note of problems of previous settlements and had prepared themselves well by making sure they had enough supplies and foodstuff to make a successful start. In June, the group first set down in the area of Salem where there had been an earlier settlement, but the majority of the passengers decided to continue further down the coast. They eventually chose an area set on a peninsula situated near the Charles River. The settlement was named Boston after the home in Lincolnshire of some of the emigrants. Settlements spread out organised in congregations. Land was distributed through the council set up in Boston. Winthrop had made it clear in a celebrated lay sermon he gave to the passengers on the *Arabella* that there was to be no levelling of social distinctions in the Bay colony. A hierarchy was established where divisions of land were parcelled out according to rank. Gentlemen were given 200 acres while others were granted anywhere from 30 to 100 acres. Within the next decade, the number of towns expanded to over 20. The colonists' practical approach toward trade made their settlement self-sufficient and financially viable. Concentrating on lumber and fish and grain, they exported to the West Indies and southern Europe. Winthrop's sermon had held out the vision of Boston becoming a 'city upon a hill', a Puritan beacon to the world. But its burgeoning prosperity was soon to pose a challenge to that ideal.

The Puritans were determined that their city on a hill was to exemplify the work of God. They believed that God had made a covenant with men through which they could be saved. The first such covenant or contract had been with Adam, whereby in return for obedience to God's will he was to have eternal life. But this covenant of works had been broken by Adam and Eve. This was because of man's nature. Following the Fall, and the expulsion from the Garden of Eden, nothing men did in their lives could merit salvation. Left to their own devices they were literally beyond redemption. Only the unmerited gift of grace could save. God had therefore made another contract with them, the covenant of faith. Justification could only be based on faith, not on works. Faith that His grace alone could ensure salvation was what He demanded of men now. Those who were recipients of His grace would experience 'saving faith'. Since good works were a concomitant of grace, those who experienced its gift would become 'visible saints'.

From this flowed the notion of a church covenant. The will of God was extended to the Puritan form of government. Only those persons who had received grace were fit to govern. The church tested its members for evidence of saving faith. Those 'visible saints' who demonstrated that they had received grace were alone admitted to communion, thereby becoming full members of the church who could vote in elections to the general court. Winthrop's sermon the 'Model of Christian Charity' made explicit that society was to be ruled by those marked out or selected by God to be their guides.

These 'high and eminent in power and dignitie' were to be the 'visible saints' who would lead Massachusetts colony down the path of righteousness. Although the clergy did not hold secular office, their influence, especially in tests for church membership, was so great that political decisions, for the most part, were made after consultation with the divines. Church and state were intertwined. Laws were passed which required meeting houses to be built, preachers' salaries to be paid through taxation, and regular church attendance to be enforced. Blasphemers and divergent religious views were punished. There was no room for Quakers, Baptists, not to mention Roman Catholics. Consequently, many were banished and some were hanged.

The prime illustration of such intolerance occurred in the mid-1630s when Anne Hutchinson, the wife of a Boston merchant, questioned the authority of the church on the issue of salvation. She holds a central place in what has become known as the Antinomian controversy. Antinomianism is the belief that, since the covenant of works had been replaced by the covenant of faith, then the law is not binding on believers. The elect, those who have received God's grace and are thereby saved, can break all ten commandments with impunity. Anne was to be accused of this heresy when she herself attacked the ministers of the Bay colony for preaching that good works were not just a sign of salvation, but could contribute to it. This came about because the stark Calvinist doctrine that there was nothing the individual could do to be saved, since men are predestined to salvation or damnation before they are born, created doubts and anxiety in the laity. To alleviate these the preachers developed the notion that the heart could be prepared to receive grace. Though there was nothing men could do to merit it, if God extended it to them, it was like a seed which would germinate and thrive provided the ground were well tilled and fertilised. Hutchinson insisted that those who preached this, who in her view included all the clergy in the colony except one, John Cotton, were bringing in good works by the back door.

The ensuing controversy had political and social implications. Anne's belief that only the individual could tell whether or not he or she was saved was directly opposed to the ideas of the ministers, who played a key role in examinations of those who claimed to have saving faith. When she was asked how she knew this, her reply that it was due to direct personal revelation was included among the many errors of which she was found guilty. As a woman, she was also

accused of acting outside of her station in life. Anne had held meetings
after church services to discuss the sermons, and this was viewed
with suspicion by the authorities. Moreover, her ideas challenged
the structure of beliefs and hence the authority invested to maintain
that structure. Recent scholarship contends that Hutchinson was
only the catalyst to a larger debate involving a political power struggle
and a spiritual one. John Cotton, for instance, was a Puritan minister
whose differences with the other ministers arose over the question
of salvation. Did God reveal directly to the person his state of grace
or could it be determined only through those that were already in
a state of grace? In order to determine who was in a state a grace
an examination took place, where the candidate had to declare that
only God could save humanity. This was followed by convincing the
examiners of true repentance, a desire to be saved, then justification.
This last step was the most difficult because the candidate had to
prove that the Holy Spirit had entered them making them ready for
God's grace. If the candidate was successful, sanctification would
follow which meant that they were one of the visible saints or elect.

The controversy became a major political issue when Anne's
cause was taken up by Henry Vane, son of a leading politician in
England, who arrived in Massachusetts at this time. Vane challenged
the authority of John Winthrop. Winthrop, who also fancied himself
as a theologian, had the flaws of one who is convinced that he knows
what is best for the community. Any decisions taken to that end were
justified. Winthrop tried to ensure that his decisions and those who
supported him would prevail by getting a mandate to do so. At the
second general meeting in October 1630, it was decided that, though
the charter stipulated that freemen had the right to elect the assistants,
only the assistants would elect the governor and deputy governor.
Also, laws would be promulgated by the governor and assistants, and
key officers were to be chosen only by them. Subsequently, Winthrop
and his magistrates controlled the government in an arbitrary manner
for they did not call a meeting of the general court for a year and
a half. The mandate stood on shaky ground because not all communities had equal representation, and the wording of the charter was
at odds with Winthrop's claim that the passing of laws was within his
remit. After some argument, Winthrop agreed to two representatives
from every congregation, while the freemen's right to elect the
governor and deputy governor was re-established. The greatest
embarrassment for Winthrop, however, came at the annual meeting

of the general court in the spring of 1634 when some members of the council, Thomas Dudley, Israel Stoughton, and Roger Ludlow, demanded to see the charter, which revealed the right of the general court to make laws. Winthrop's credibility was so tarnished that he was defeated by John Haynes at the next election in 1635. The following year, he tried to get re-elected but was again defeated, this time by the newcomer from England, Henry Vane.

Hutchinson therefore had the powerful support of the new governor as well as that of John Cotton, one of the leading minsters in the colony. Unfortunately for her, Vane left for England and Winthrop was re-elected. With his new election, Hutchinson lost support. Even Cotton deserted her. Winthrop was able to bring the full force of the law on her and banished her from the colony. Anne and her family went to Rhode Island where she was killed by Indians in the growing conflicts between them and the settlers. Winthrop ascribed her fate to a punishment by divine providence.

From the beginning of the settlement, the relationship between the New England settlers and the Indians was guarded. They knew from the Virginia experience that circumstances are often not what they appear. Negotiations with Massasoit, chief of the Wampanoag nation resulted in a treaty in 1621. This proved to be beneficial for both sides. Massasoit obtained an ally in his nation's contest with the rival tribes of the Narragansett and Massachusetts peoples. For the settlers, the treaty meant some security and an outlet for trade. Because of the cordial and at times helpful relationship with the natives, the Pilgrims learned to plant native food, such as squash and corn, thereby enabling them to lay up enough store for the winter. About half of them had survived the first winter by the discovery of stores of food abandoned by Indians. In the spring a friendly native, Sancho, showed them how to cultivate land which his fellow natives had cleared beforehand. The harvesting of this crop in 1621, which they shared with local Indians, was the basis for the celebration of Thanksgiving Day. Nevertheless, because they had allied themselves with one group of Indians, they became involved in the conflict with others and they never felt at ease with the Wampanoags. By the time the Puritans arrived, there was a fragile coexistence between the various natives and settlers. The murders of two white traders in the years between 1634 and 1636 and subsequent vicious attack on the Pequots significantly brought the other Indians into line under the English. The tables were now turned. No longer did the Indian nations control the terms of the relationship, now the English dictated the conditions upon which the natives could go to war with others. The reason for this turn about was the fact that the numbers of settlers, along with their defensive measures, outnumbered the Indians. The Pequot War, as it became known, served the purpose of uniting the colonies from Massachusetts, Plymouth and Connecticut into a Confederation of the United Colonies of New England. Although these colonies had religious differences, they shared the common necessity of survival.

As Massachusetts became more secure in its establishment, there were attempts to educate the native population. This pressure emanated from England, where advocates of colonisation always promoted the effort to 'civilise' the savages through educating them. After all, the seal of the Massachusetts Bay Company depicted an Indian and bore the legend, 'come over and help us'. The Puritans were somewhat lax in this mission, partly due to their tenuous beginnings. By 1646, however, the Indians had been subdued and thoughts turned toward their education. The Reverend John Eliot established a mission where the Pequots and Massachusetts peoples were organised into 14 'praying towns'. The mission was somewhat of a success because by 1660, the main congregation of Natick was admitted to the main church at Roxbury.

The decade of the 1640s proved dangerous for the colony, not just internally with the Indian problems, but with an external threat from attempts to revoke the Massachusetts charter. An earlier attempt had not unduly alarmed the colonists. In 1634 the Privy Council had created a committee to look into the colony's affairs. Because the charter was not being held in England, the Council of New England, which was responsible for the charter, was disbanded. Forthwith, the King ordered a *quo warranto*, questioning by what authority the Massachusetts Bay Company claimed jurisdiction over the colony. He appointed Gorges as governor, but Gorges declined on account of age. Therefore, the *quo warranto* was never taken over to the colony. Also, the King's attention was on the troubles at home, so the colony's charter remained safe for the moment.

A more serious attack upon the charter came from a Presbyterian minister in 1646. Dr Robert Child visited Massachusetts in 1641 and discovered that the colony's laws did not conform to England's laws. He also charged that his rights as an Englishman were infringed there. Child noted that the Puritan Church, which after all claimed to be part of the established Church, did not conform to church regulations. Most of the colonists could not share in the sacrament and children were not allowed to be baptised. It was true that the colony had yet to devise a code of law and this accounted for the arbitrary behaviour of Governor Winthrop. The only thing they had was a quasi-legal code based upon religious tenets written in 1636 by John Cotton. It was later revised in 1639 and finally issued as the 'Body of Liberties' in 1641. With the new and more substantial attack on Massachusetts, a second edition was published based upon legal precedents set out in volumes imported from England. For the first time, Massachusetts law defined the political framework and the liberties of the individual. The result was that the new constitutional polity, as laid out in the *Book of General Lawes and Libertyes* of the colony was making inroads into its theocratic stronghold. Recognising the significance of this new direction, the ministers drew up the Cambridge Platform in 1648, which essentially warned the secular authorities, and Presbyterians in particular, not to meddle in the religious welfare of the colony. Although the secular and spiritual lines were now clearly drawn, the Cambridge Platform made no concessions with regard to church membership. However, with the growing population and not enough freemen, the 1648 code did provide for lesser offices such as constables, jurors and highway surveyors to be filled without the requirement of church membership.

The decline in the number of church members alarmed the ministers, who convened a synod in 1662 to consider it. Previously only full church members could have their children baptised. The second generation of settlers, however, were marrying and having families, but could not get their offspring christened without becoming communicants in their parish churches, even if they were themselves the sons and daughters of visible saints. That they were not seeking full membership has been attributed to a declension in mid-century Massachusetts. Certainly ministers castigated them for not living up to the high standards of their parents. But it could be that despair at not being worthy rather than indifference accounted for their attitude. Whatever the reason, the synod decided that there was a real problem, which it solved by proposing what became known as the 'half-way covenant'. The adult children of full members were to be allowed to have their offspring baptised without becoming visible saints. They could not, however, take communion or vote. This proposal was not endorsed immediately by most of the churches to whom it was conveyed by the synod for approval. Gradually, however, it was generally adopted.

Following the restoration of the monarchy in England in 1660, many Dissenters left for New England. Massachusetts experienced an influx of Baptists, Presbyterians and Quakers. The initial reaction of the Puritans was hostile. Four Quakers were hanged in Boston between 1659 and 1661. Pressure from England, not least from the King, was brought to bear upon the Bay colony to relax its intolerant laws. Although the colony's laws prohibited the establishing of public worship for these divergent groups without express approval, they were allowed to hold private meetings.


RHODE ISLAND

Dissenters, especially Quakers, were more welcome in Rhode Island. The colony had been established as a result of the banishment of Roger Williams, one time Plymouth colony separatist, from the Massachusetts colony. In 1633 he had objected to the extent to which the general court exercised its powers in spiritual matters. His advocation for the separation of church and state and disavowing any connection with the established Church of England, was tantamount to challenging the authority of the colony's government. His radicalism extended to physical acts such as tearing the English flag because it smacked of popish idolatry with the cross of St George emblazoned upon it. In 1635 the Puritan authorities' response to this challenge was to banish him. Williams and his supporters left Boston and travelled south of Plymouth to negotiate a purchase of land. They settled in an area on the Blackstone River, named it Providence, and set up a government whereby the separation of the secular from the spiritual was put into affect. Other settlements were established within striking distance of Williams's colony. Anne Hutchinson, who was also banished, along with a friend of Williams's, William Coddington, established Portsmouth. Coddington went on to establish yet another town, Newport. The central premise of the governments was freedom of conscience. While they believed in the freedom of individual beliefs, they were not advocating salvation for all. They believed in predestination and that nothing could be done for those who were damned anyway. They also believed that in order to survive, 'a democracy or popular government' in which freemen had the right to make laws and enact true religious toleration had to be put in place. One other town, Warwick, was established at this time by Samuel Gorton.

Williams recognised the necessity of getting a patent for his colony and went to England, where his friend the Earl of Warwick, influential in colonial affairs, supported his claim. Williams's view of toleration found favour in the current political climate. His pamphlet, 'The Bloudy Tenent of Persecution', was an attack on orthodoxy such as the one exhibited by the Massachusetts Puritans. The idea that civil authority should be vested in the people and not from some divine authority was in keeping with the views of Parliament. In March 1644, he received his patent from Parliament which gave the colony corporate status. In 1663 the Crown reissued this as a royal charter.


CONNECTICUT

Connecticut was also established in this period. Although the area was explored both by the Dutch and English for exploitation of the fur trade, the migration by Thomas Hooker in 1636 began the permanent settlement of the colony. Hooker and his congregation moved there from Newton in reaction to the Antinomian controversy. Hooker objected to the arbitrary actions of the general court, though he was not in sympathy with either Hutchinson or Williams. He particularly disliked John Cotton, clashing with his view that only the regenerate could be admitted to communion. Hooker argued that it was not for the church to decide who was and was not elect, and that the sacraments should be available to all. He settled in Hartford. Later, Windsor and Wethersfield were established and a frame of government was drawn up with the Fundamental Orders accepted in 1639. Laws similar to those operating in Massachusetts were introduced. Connections with Massachusetts were continued when John Winthrop junior was elected as the colony's first governor.

New Haven, which was absorbed into Connecticut in 1665, started out as an independent colony. John Davenport, a Puritan minister, and Theophilus Eaton, a London merchant, went to Boston from England, arriving there when the Antinomian controversy was at its height. They were not impressed at the Bay colony's attempt to set up a city on a hill, and moved to Quinnipiac, an Indian inlet off Long Island Sound. Finding it unsuitable to use as a port, they moved a few miles west to a better location they called New Haven. Unfortunately, they failed to get along with or to attract many settlers before becoming part of Connecticut.


## NEW HAMPSHIRE

Another New England colony which initially failed to develop was New Hampshire. After acquiring land along the Merrimack and Piscataqua Rivers in 1622, Sir Ferdinando Gorges and John Mason sent out settlers to establish settlements there. These did not really take off until colonists from Massachusetts moved to them in the 1630s. Massachusetts then disputed the claim to the area, a dispute which was not finally resolved until 1679, when Charles II took it over as a Crown colony This rounded off the establishment of colonies in New England, for Maine remained part of Massachusetts during the colonial period.


## KING PHILIP'S WAR

By the 1670s, New England had acquired a distinct identity. Puritanism was only one aspect of it, albeit one which stamped its mark on the character of Connecticut and Massachusetts. A story told by Cotton Mather early in the eighteenth century recounted how a preacher went from Boston to Cape Cod, where he met with indifference to his preaching from people who told him they had gone there 'to catch fish'. Fishing, indeed, became a leading industry in a region where thin rocky soil and impenetrable forests made farming difficult. Although settlements spread quickly after the arrival of colonists from England, they expanded principally along the seacoast and up rivers rather than overland. Fish were consumed not just locally, but exchanged for goods from a surprisingly wide market, which included the Azores, the Canaries and Madeira. Above all, New England became closely tied to the West Indies once sugar began to be produced in Barbados and Jamaica. Fish, meat and wood were sold and molasses and sugar bought for use in the distillation of rum. Lucrative though the maritime economy was, however, most people in New England were employed in agriculture. Family farms dotted the coastal strip and the fertile lands of the river valleys.

Families, indeed, were the nuclei of society from the start. Unlike the Chesapeake, where young single men were initially attracted as indentured labourers, typical migrants to early Massachusetts were middle-aged married couples and their children. Again, where life expectancy in the early days of Virginia was low and people died like flies, in seventeenth-century New England the environment was so healthy that the settlers lived longer than those they left behind in Old England. This, coupled with the tendency to marry younger than the English did, made the average family bigger. Consequently the population grew rapidly not just from immigration, but naturally. Between 1640 and 1700 it expanded from 14,000 to 90,000. Between 1675 and 1676, however, the physical expansion of New England was halted in devastating attacks on over half its towns, 12 of which were destroyed, in what became known as King Philip's War.

Relations between the Wampanoag Indians and the English settlers had changed since their joint celebration of the harvest in 1621. When Massasoit, the Wampanoag chief who had joined in the first thanksgiving with the Pilgrims, died in 1662, he was succeeded by his eldest son Wamsutta. Wamsutta, known to the English as Alexander, distrusted the English who seemed intent on driving the Indians from New England. When he succeeded his father, there were about 40,000 whites and perhaps half that number of natives in the region, and the imbalance was becoming greater every year. Wamsutta's suspicions of the colonists brought him to the attention of the authorities at Plymouth, who summoned him there for questioning. While being interrogated, he fell ill and was allowed to go home, on condition he left two of his sons as hostages. Shortly after leaving Plymouth he died, which his people took to be sinister, some believing he had been poisoned by the English despite their denials.

Wamsutta was succeeded as leader of the Wampanoags by his younger brother Metacom, whom the colonists called King Philip. Metacom was even more hostile to the settlers than his brother. He objected not only to their geographical, but also to their cultural imperialism. For Puritans were so intent on imposing Christianity upon the natives that they tried to stop them hunting or fishing on the Sabbath and tried to get them to marry in church. Such attempts to impose Massachusetts laws upon the Indians eventually led to the incident that determined Metacom to resist. In 1675 three of his followers were hanged for the murder of an Indian who had been converted to Christianity. This was the last straw, as Metacom protested against what he saw as an unwarranted extension of the jurisdiction of the colony over natives. For some years he had been constructing a coalition between the Wampanoags and other Indians, involving almost all the Algonquian-speaking peoples. They were now persuaded to strike to drive the English from the continent.

Hostilities commenced in June 1675 with raids on Dartmouth, Middleborough, Rehoboth, Swansea and Taunton, which were destroyed by fire. Over the summer some 52 towns, over half those in New England, were attacked. Panic swept through the colonies. Even Indians converted to Christianity were suspected of supporting Metacom. Those at Natick were removed to an island in Boston harbour where they spent two years in appalling conditions. Neutral Indians like the Narrangansetts of Rhode Island were attacked and in Cotton Mather's words 'terribly barbikew'd'. The killing of 600 Narrangansetts, including women and children as well as men, forced them into alliance with the Wampanoags with whom they had previously been hostile. As winter set in, Metacom's drive against the English was contained and then reversed. The settlers found allies in other Indians, notably the Mohawks of New York. The retribution was severe. Some 3000 Narrangansett, Nipmuck and Wampanoag Indians were killed, while hundreds were shipped as slaves to the West Indies, including Metacom's wife and son who were captured in a raid on his camp in August 1676. He himself managed to escape, only to be shot a few days later by an Indian paid as a mercenary by the colonists. His head was severed from his body and put on public display in Plymouth for the next 20 years.

King Philip's War was over. It has been seen as the most devastating ever fought on American soil, including the Civil War, in terms of the numbers who died in proportion to the population. Some 600 colonists were killed, while 1200 of their houses were destroyed. Although Metacom did not succeed in his aim of driving them into the sea, it was not for another 30 years that they reoccupied all the areas of New England that they had settled before 1675.

WITCHCRAFT

The devastation was seen by Puritans as but one of many judgements of God on their endeavours. They had been weighed in the balance and found wanting, having declined from the fervour and piety of their parents in the first generation of settlement. Their preachers harangued them constantly with jeremiads on this subject in these years. The impact of the Glorious Revolution on Massachusetts, when church members lost their privileged place in the colony's polity, seemed to fulfil their worst predictions (see below pp. 130–1). These crises affecting the rule of the saints formed the backdrop to the drama of the Salem witchcraft trials of 1692. Massachusetts had been invaded by the Indians in King Philip's War, by agents of popery and arbitrary power during the Dominion of New England, and now by the Devil.

Early in 1692, some girls in Salem Village amused themselves by playing a game in which they looked in a glass, serving as a crystal ball, to see if they could discern the likenesses of their future husbands. The game passed harmlessly enough until one thought she saw a coffin. This apparition induced hysteria which came to be diagnosed as diabolic possession. They accused the slave who had suggested the game, a West Indian called Tituba, of bewitching them. Eventually, Tituba confessed, the first of 43 accused of being witches who were brought to confess to being in league with Satan in the trials provoked by the outbreak, which were held between February and August. While there had been previous proceedings against alleged witches in New England, only four had confessed to being possessed by the Devil before this. All manner of bewitchments were divulged, including the making of a poppet to represent an adversary, who would suffer when pins were stuck into it. Those who claimed to be victims of the witches alleged that they had visited them in the guise of spectres. While their corporeal bodies were in one place, their spectral bodies could be in another. This was taken by the court to be evidence of diabolical possession, on the grounds that the Devil could only assume somebody's shape with that person's permission. It was only when doubts arose on this score, and that Satan could appear as spectres of human beings without their permission, that this kind of testimony was ruled out, and the cases then collapsed. Before that, however, some 19 of the accused had been executed, while five had died during the proceedings, one from the tortures inflicted when under interrogation, and four in prison.

Much scholarly ingenuity has been expended on trying to interpret this episode as historians have endeavoured to distinguish between the accusers and the accused. One very sophisticated analysis identified the 'victims' with Salem Village and the 'witches' with Salem Town, attributing their antagonism to economic tensions between the two communities. The village was mainly agricultural and associated with traditional Puritan values, whereas the Town was becoming increasingly commercialised and secular. More recently, it has been argued that the Devil appeared mainly in the shape of a woman. Most, though not all, of the alleged witches were women, while those who claimed to be their victims were mainly young girls. The women tended to be middle-aged or elderly, often widows, who violated gender norms by living independently rather than having a male head of the household. At first, they tended to be on the margins of society, but increasingly ladies from the colonial elite were drawn into the accusations. It has been claimed that as the charges began to involve the establishment, pressure to drop them grew. The girl victims were teenagers or even younger. Brought up in a repressive Puritan society, which quashed rather than encouraged individual expression, let alone rebellion, they suddenly found themselves encouraged by their parents and other adults to indulge their wildest fantasies against people they disliked. Psychologically, the temptation proved irresistible. In the final analysis, however, the phenomenon can only be explained in its own terms. People in seventeenth-century New England believed in witchcraft and practised magic. The collapse of the cases did not mark the triumph of secular ideas over beliefs in the supernatural. All those involved accepted that Satan had visited Massachusetts. They only disagreed about whether the witches were his agents or his victims.

The episode was finally brought to an end by the intervention of Sir William Phips, the first Governor of Massachusetts to be appointed by the King under the new charter of 1691. Phips arrived in Boston in May 1692 while the hearings were being held. Although he was a local man and a friend of Cotton Mather, who took a leading part in the proceedings, he was sceptical about the accusations of witchcraft and when Mather expressed doubts about the spectral evidence, he decided to bring the trials to a close.

# 6   The Middle Colonies

New York, New Jersey, Pennsylvania and Delaware were such a diverse group of colonies compared with those in New England and the Chesapeake that some historians have denied that they form an entity. To them, the term 'middle colonies' is a mere geographical expression. Certainly, there were great political and social differences between them. Although they all started as proprietary colonies, New York became a Crown colony on the accession of James II in 1685, to be followed by New Jersey in 1702. In this respect Pennsylvania and the three lower counties which became Delaware had more in common with Maryland, which like them had a single proprietor for most of the colonial period. In religion too they were distinct. Delaware was mainly Anglican, Pennsylvania, at least among its elite, largely Quaker, as was West Jersey, while East Jersey became predominantly Presbyterian. New York had a polyglot mixture of faiths, the Dutch Reformed Church appealing to the original settlers and their descendants who continued to speak Dutch until well into the next century. But by then, Pennsylvania too had a significant German-speaking population which attended Mennonite and Moravian churches. Unlike New England and the Chesapeake regions, there was no established Church in the middle colonies. Perhaps their diversity was what in the end distinguished them as a group from the northern and southern colonies.

## NEW YORK

Between the Chesapeake Bay and New England was an area which had not only been claimed by Europeans, but was actually settled by them before the English laid claim to them. It was indeed the only region of North America which had to be conquered by them from another European power in the seventeenth century. Swedes had settled in the Delaware valley and even called it New Sweden until it was taken from them by the Dutch in 1655. Before that, citizens of the United Provinces of the Netherlands had been active in the settlement of the Hudson River valley ever since the Dutch East India Company had contracted Henry Hudson to find a northwest passage through that northern part of the New World. The explorer got as far as present-day Albany and in 1613 set up a trading post. The Dutch were more interested in exploiting trade in fur than permanent settlements, and therefore viewed the New World merely as another outpost to their global trading network.

Although this venture only lasted a couple of years, another company, the Dutch West India Company, took over the interest. They had been dealing in the Caribbean and Brazil, but in 1624 the company sent some adventurers up to the old trading fort to re-establish connections with the native people. This time, the site became a permanent one, though still only a fort. The company also expanded its operations down as far as the Delaware valley and established another fort near what was to become Philadelphia. They named this Fort Nassau. Still another fort was begun a couple of years later when Willem Verhulst and Peter Minuit negotiated a purchase of land from the Manhattan Indians. They built a fort and named the new settlement, New Amersterdam. The whole of the territory was known as New Netherland after the homeland. Because the set up was primarily for trade, settlements were not given the financial incentive to become self-sufficient. Consequently, growth was slow. By 1628, the Dutch West India Company stopped investing. Interest in trade, however, remained and to that extent, incentive was given to settlement. Patroonships, or manorial rights were given to anyone willing to bring 50 or more people to work the area. Patroonships encompassed four-mile tracts of land along the Hudson River. Minuit was also responsible for promoting the Delaware region of Wilmington under a company chartered by the Swedish King Augustus Adolphus. In 1637, the company sent its first emigrants from Sweden under the guidance of Minuit. They established Fort Christiana.

Although they were well aware of native ownership of the land, the Dutch claimed the area in general. From that conception, potential settlers were required to first purchase the land from the Indians. The general outline of the venture followed the one set up in Virginia. Unlike Virginia, which grew fairly rapidly after discovering the viability of tobacco, New Netherland's economy was slower off the mark for a couple of reasons. As in Virginia, the expansion of land by the settlers brought them into conflict with the Indians. At first, the purchase of land seemed to avoid problems over ownership but because the two cultures had different ideas on what ownership entailed, the Indians not thinking in permanent terms, misunderstandings occurred. Also, the Dutch company and its settlers were seen as part of the contention between the Mahicans and the Mohawks over territory. Just like other colonists elsewhere in the New World, the Dutch became part of the Indians' strategy against one another. The company tried to avoid involvement by being neutral, but when the Mohawks defeated the Mahicans, company policy swung in behind the victors. The Dutch thought they had kept the situation fairly stable, but by signing a treaty with the Mohawks, they became part of the conflict. In 1643, after some attacks on the settlers by other Indians, the Dutch, along with the Mohawks, struck back and wiped out the Indian village of Pavonia. Further reprisals by the natives on the settlers followed. This time, it spread to the eastern part of Long Island where Anne Hutchinson had finally settled with her family. She, along with other settlers, was killed. Although peace was re-established in 1645, settlers were inextricably linked to the contests between native American groups.

Another factor which prohibited growth was the political setup of the settlements. Since a company owned and operated the endeavour, it followed along company lines. This meant that there was little or no room for representation. Decision making came from the director general and company officials. As far as there was representation, it came from the few wealthy patroons. The troubles with the Indians did lead to some concessions by the company in which a council was created to administer the colony. In order to avoid future problems, the company allowed, in vague terms, for a couple of representatives to report yearly on the state of the colony. Other concessions such as allowing more freedom of trade helped to sustain the colony's growth.

Significant change began to occur under the directorship of Peter Stuvyesant. Though short-lived, a body of representatives to the council was created. Also, New Amsterdam was given a sheriff and burghermaster. Although Stuvyesant recognised the need for public involvement in the affairs of what could be considered a fledgling colony, he still had the mind of a military and company man.

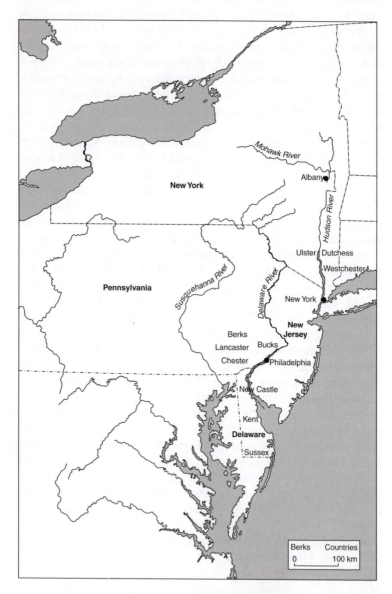

*Map 3*   The middle colonies

The experiment with representation was ended. During the 1650s, when war between the English and Dutch was on the horizon, the director tried to resurrect a representative body in order to get cooperation in funding the war coffers, but the colonists refused. Stuyvesant fell back to dictating tax impositions.

Another feature of New Netherland was its toleration of religious sects. By the 1650s, various groups had migrated down and over to the area. Jews, as well as Calvinists from other areas such as England and New England, not only settled there, but held official posts in government. This would have been seen as an incentive to migration, but the lack of representation and general poor governmental style kept people from coming. Lack of control over the Sabbath, which resulted in rowdy behaviour, and poor sanitary conditions were not inducements.

By 1674 there had been three wars between the English and the Dutch. One of the consequences of the Anglo–Dutch wars was the English acquisition of New Netherland. Stuyvesant had accurately gauged the imperial impact of the conflicts when he directed the forts in the colony to be reinforced. However, the forts were not completed by the time the second of the conflicts with England spilled over to North America.

Following the grant of New Netherland by Charles II to his brother James, Duke of York and Albany, in March 1664, Richard Nicholls was despatched from England with a fleet to capture it for him. On his arrival off New Amsterdam, Nicholls demanded that Stuyvesant surrender the colony to him. Although the governor was ready to resist the English, the Dutch colonists persuaded him to yield to them. Nicholls then renamed New Netherland as New York in honour of the Duke. New Amsterdam was similarly renamed New York City, while Orange, a Dutch fort up the Hudson River, became Albany. The Duke's claim was not confirmed, however, until after the third and final Anglo–Dutch war, 1672–74. The Treaty of Westminster concluded the peace with the handing over of the colony.

New York was a proprietary colony under the Duke and James ruled his proprietorship as an absolute monarch. William Penn thought his government of New York was a model of what he planned for England 'if the Crown should ever devolve upon his head'. Richard Nicholls, who acted as James's deputy governor following the conquest of the colony, introduced into it the so-called 'Duke's Laws'. The Dutch patroonships remained and limited representation continued. However, there was some integration of English law with Dutch customs. For instance, the justice system was bound along English lines with the court sessions and yearly assize meetings. However, the laws made no mention of elections to an Assembly or even to town meetings. Nicholls himself admitted that 'our new laws are not contrived so democratically as the rest'. There was a strong military presence in the colony, with New York City becoming the base for the first regular garrison of soldiers in British America. Following the final surrender of New York to the English in 1674, James appointed an army officer, Sir Edmund Andros, as his deputy. Andros re-established the Duke's proprietorship and reinstated the Duke's Laws. His arbitrary government provoked complaints about military rule and demands in some quarters for a representative Assembly. On being informed of these, James refused to give in to them, being convinced that to do so would be 'of dangerous consequence, nothing being more known than the aptness of such bodies to assume to themselves many privileges which prove destructive to, or very oft disturb, the peace of the government wherein they are allowed'. Andros, however, found it increasingly difficult to raise taxes without an Assembly to consent to them. Since James had invested his own money in the acquisition of New York, spending as much as £2000 to regain it from the Dutch in 1674, he wished not only to recoup his outlay, but to make a profit from the colony. The reluctance of the colonists to pay taxes to which they had not consented meant that he was losing rather than making money from his proprietorship of New York.

Consequently, when Andros went to England in 1681, he was able to persuade the Duke that the only way to turn his financial situation round from loss to gain was to summon an Assembly. 'We believe his Royal Highness will condescend to the desires of that colony in granting them equal privileges in choosing an assembly', the Duke's secretary Sir John Werden observed, adding significantly 'as the other English plantations in America have'. He was right, for when Colonel Thomas Dongan replaced Andros as governor of New York, he was instructed by the Duke to convene an Assembly there. The first was elected in October 1683 and sat for three weeks, this short session resulting in some important laws for the rights of the colonists. The right to trial by jury and punishments to fit the crime were instituted at this meeting of the Assembly. Taxes could only be imposed through the consent of the governor and council. Lands were protected from arbitrary seizure. This Bill of Rights also included the right of religious freedom so long as those who practised divergent faiths did not disturb the peace of the government. The assembly met again in 1684. The following year James became King, upon which New York was transformed from a proprietary into a Crown colony. Following James II's accession, his deputy governor there, Thomas Dongan, dissolved the Assembly and called fresh elections for another, which met in October 1685. After a brief session, however, further meetings were called only to be cancelled until in January 1687, the Assembly was dissolved. It never met again under James.

The reluctance of James to concede representative government to his proprietary colony of New York, and his apparent preference for arbitrary and even military rule, ensured that the Glorious Revolution would have more of an impact on New York than on any other colony. Moreover, the effects of his rule there and the reaction to it were to have more long lasting effects than elsewhere in British America (see below pp. 131–5).

## NEW JERSEY

When the Duke of York acquired the New York area in the first instance in 1664, he had its outer territories between the Hudson and Delaware divided and sold to two adventurers as rewards for their part in the Anglo–Dutch war. John, Lord Berkeley, and Sir George Carteret thus acquired the area which was to become New Jersey. Berkeley and Carteret were members of a group of London investors, albeit in the upper echelon of society, who were linked to companies which had global investments. The New World was seen as another market. Berkeley, in particular, had links with the Levant Company whose main interest was in the southern part of Europe. Companies like the Levant were looking to expand their trade without the restrictive practices that were operating in Europe. North America seemed not to have such limitations. Additionally, dissenting religious groups found the colonies to be places free of prohibition on their participation in investing. The Quakers, particularly, found the area of New Jersey a possible venue for investment. By 1674 Berkeley had sold his share, which became West Jersey, to two Quakers, John Fenwick and Edward Bylling. But within a few years of the sale, Fenwick and Bylling fell into financial dispute with one another and, as Quakers, resorted to mediation within the Quaker community. Three prominent men were appointed as trustees to oversee their investment: Gawrin Lawrie, merchant; Nicholas Lucas, maltster; and William Penn, from the landed gentry. Carteret's share, East Jersey, was sold to the Quakers shortly after his death in 1680. Among the proprietors for that section was William Penn.

At the outset of the new colony, Berkeley and Carteret issued a document, 'The Concessions and Agreements of the Lords Proprietors', to attract settlers primarily from within the colonies. It was not until after the proprietors had divided the colony into East and West Jersey in 1676 that settlers came from the British Isles in any numbers; West Jersey became virtually a Quaker colony. About a hundred settled there in 1675, to be followed by over 1000 more by 1680.

East Jersey, by contrast, became Scotland's first colony in North America. Scottish proprietors became dominant in its governing body. Although prominent among them was the Quaker Robert Barclay, the Scots who went to East Jersey were not on the whole from the Society of Friends. Even more prominent were the brothers James and John Drummond, respectively Earls of Perth and Melfort, two of the most powerful ministers at the Court of James VII and II. While both converted to Catholicism, the main body of settlers they attracted tended to be Episcopalians from the northeast coastal strip between St Andrews and Fife. Alongside these were Presbyterians who eventually became the most salient sect in East Jersey.


## PENNSYLVANIA

By far the largest grant of land made by the Crown was in the area of Pennsylvania. By 1681, the only stretch of land between the English colonies which was not settled by England was located between New York and Maryland. Strategically, the land was open to encroachment by other powers. The French Empire had expanded down the west side of the mountain range from the Adirondacks to the Alleghenies. The territory was in essence a weak spot. Although the land was under the auspices of the Duke of York, and up to the fortieth parallel claimed by Lord Baltimore, it needed investment and settlers in order to complete a contiguous boundary of England's territorial claims. There were investors always interested in new ventures, but it was a matter of organisation and timing. The combination of the two came in the person of one of the New Jersey proprietors, William Penn, and the political crisis in England.

Why Charles II granted the largest of the colonies to Penn has been a puzzle ever since. The only hard evidence is that he did it to settle an outstanding debt to Sir William Penn, the proprietor's father. Certainly, the Crown seems to have owed Admiral Penn some £16,000. But few accept this as a sufficient explanation of the King's grant. One difficulty in accepting it as such is that the collateral was colossal. Charles gave the Earl of Arlington and Lord Culpeper the quitrents of Virginia below the northern neck for a period of 31 years ostensibly to settle a debt of £12,000. Governor Berkeley protested that the gift was out of all proportion to the amount owed. The granting of the territory and government of Pennsylvania in perpetuity was therefore extravagant beyond belief for a mere £16,000.

Historians traditionally ascribed religious motives to the grant. The King sympathised with the plight of Quakers who were suffering persecution. He therefore granted Pennsylvania as a refuge for the Friends. Penn consequently undertook to settle the colony as a 'holy experiment'. Certainly, Friends flocked there in the 1680s and stamped their mark on the Quaker colony. This seems to confirm the conventional view that it was established as a refuge for a persecuted sect.

However, it is a historical fallacy to deduce intentions from results. If we discount the advantage of hindsight, there are some problems with the prevalent interpretation. For one thing, the Quakers did not lack refuges in North America. They were tolerated in Rhode Island, Maryland and New Jersey. Puritan Rhode Island and Catholic Maryland were celebrated for their religious toleration. How far Quakers had flourished in Lord Baltimore's colony can be gauged from the fact that almost all the Assemblymen for Anne Arundel county in 1680 were members of the Society of Friends. More to the point, West Jersey had been acquired by Quakers, including Penn himself, from the proprietor. It was scarcely overstocked with Friends when Penn petitioned for his charter. Moreover, he insisted on the three lower counties which became Delaware being part of his jurisdiction. These had to be separately ceded to him by the Duke of York. The lower counties became an Anglican rather than a Quaker settlement, which goes far to explain why they seceded from Pennsylvania in 1701.

Another problem with seeing Pennsylvania as a refuge for persecuted Quakers is that they were not suffering from persecution at the time when Penn applied for his charter. On the contrary, the year 1680 was the high point of a move to relax the penal laws against Dissenters. Nonconformists had certainly been prosecuted for breach of the penal laws in the first decade of Charles II's reign, and Quakers had been most severely affected by the Conventicle Act of 1670. But the King's Declaration of Indulgence of 1672 had granted relief, and this continued even after the Declaration was revoked in 1673. The outbreak of the Popish Plot in 1678 and the onset of the Exclusion Crisis had shifted attention away from Dissenters towards Catholics. The consequent rise of the Whigs led to calls for Protestant reconciliation. In the second Exclusion Parliament a bill to tolerate Protestant Nonconformists had been introduced by the Whigs, which among other provisions would have allowed Quakers to affirm, thereby relieving them from the imposition of oaths. Only the King's prorogation and ultimate dissolution of the Parliament had led to the dropping of the measure.

If, then, religious reasons do not give a sufficient explanation for the launching of Pennsylvania, how can it be explained? The answer has to be sought in the convoluted politics of the Exclusion crisis. The Whigs, who sought to exclude the Catholic Duke of York from succeeding his brother as king, triumphed at the polls during the two general elections held in 1679. Following the second Whig victory Charles II prorogued Parliament for the best part of a year, during which he sought to drive a wedge between his opponents, to separate the die-hard Exclusionist Whigs from the more moderate elements in the opposition. Among the latter was William Penn, who, though a radical critic of the government, had never sought to exclude James from the throne. They also included an influential group of London merchants, many of whom were in the Levant Company. The company was experiencing difficulties in its Mediterranean trade, partly because of heavy duties levied by the Ottoman Turks. Some of its members sought new outlets across the Atlantic. When Penn obtained his charter, he established a Free Society of Traders, among whose members were several prominent Levant merchants. Later a so-called New Mediterranean Sea Company was set up to profit from the expansion of Pennsylvania; again its membership overlapped with that of the Levant Company which traded in the Old Mediterranean. By granting to Penn a colony with promising economic potential, Charles II succeeded in drawing away from the hard-core Whigs a number of influential City merchants who backed the new colonial venture. It was therefore one of the many ploys adopted by the King to win over support to his and his brother's cause during the Exclusion crisis.

Penn, though a Quaker, was in a larger sense, a Dissenter. Thus, his political and mercantile connections extended beyond the Society of Friends. He also had personal experience in colonial investments. The political climate in England between 1679 and 1681 was one of paranoia over plots by Catholics to overthrow the monarch and suspicion of the King's religious leanings toward popery. The King's need for money exacerbated the tensions between Parliament and Crown to the extent that three Parliaments were called and dismissed and talk of another civil war was heard. The mercantile section of society feared popery and arbitrary power, but they also feared a war that would disrupt their business. The Duke of York was looked upon as a threat to the Protestant religion and as the crisis escalated, investors looked to his colonial holdings. While they wanted to expand their investments in the New World, they also wanted to make sure the investments were secured within a non-Catholic organisation. Penn's reputation for honour and the fact that he was a Dissenter, but not aligned with the radical elements of the opposition which threatened the crown, put him in the right place at the right time.

The charter for Pennsylvania was granted in 1681, but not without many revisions. The changes reflected the concerns of the English government over the potential power of a proprietor. One clause in the charter, the Bishop of Durham clause, would have given Penn semi-regal powers in his colony, such as Baltimore had in Maryland whose charter contained a similar clause. The King's Privy Council disallowed the clause, but did not impose the necessity for the establishment of an Anglican church unless 20 or more parishioners requested one. However, the charter left enough scope for Penn, as sole proprietor, to fashion the colony's constitution in any manner he decided as long as it did not circumvent the laws of England. When Penn was granted the charter for his colony, he seized upon the political moment to force terms for acquiring Delaware. This colony was also in the remit of the Duke of York, but Penn needed the territory for its commercial potential and for the securing of the Delaware River. In the end, the Duke was forced to hand over the territory, but he never acknowledged releasing the dominion. When James became King, he made moves toward regaining his lost territories including New Jersey, Delaware and Pennsylvania.

Penn set about organising a company, The Society of Free Traders, which represented investors from diverse religious background, thus fulfilling the desires of traders for entrepreneurship without religious restrictions. Advertisements for the kind of emigrants needed for the venture reflect the lessons learned from the problems of the other colonies. Penn warned prospective migrants to consider carefully their decision to go: 'I desire all my dear country folks, who may be inclin'd to go into those parts, to consider seriously the premisses, as well the present inconveniencies.' He also stressed the type of immigrant who would be suitable. 'Industrious husbandmen and day labourers', and 'carpenters, masons, smiths, weavers, taylors, tanners, shoemakers, shipwrights', attest to Penn's practical and methodical plan for his colony.

The colony's governmental structure was derived from Penn's Fundamental Constitutions of Pennsylvania, in which government was exercised by a governor, a council and an Assembly made up of an upper and lower house. The governor, appointed by the proprietor, together with the council acted as the executive power. The Assembly, both of whose houses were elected by the freemen of the colony, held the legislative power. Penn wanted the council to propose legislation and the lower house merely to assent to or reject it. Though Penn believed in passing on English liberties to his colonists, he was no democrat. He was aware of the 'ambitions of the populace' who could threaten the colony's stability and acted against these inclinations by controlling prime offices. If the proprietor thought that he had arrived at an equitable settlement, it was short-lived. Those who had objected to the frame of government formed factions between representatives supporting the proprietor and those who did not. Consequently, proprietary and anti-proprietary groups emerged. The latter are often referred to as 'the Quaker party', though this is a bit misleading as the great majority of Assemblymen, including the proprietor's supporters, were Quakers. David Lloyd emerged as the leader of the anti-proprietary group in the 1690s. He upheld the rights of the Assembly when Pennsylvania became a Crown colony between 1692 and 1694. The royal governor, Benjamin Fletcher, allowed the Lower House of Assembly to debate as well as to vote on legislation, as in other Crown colonies. After Penn resumed the proprietorship, the Assemblymen wished to retain this right. In the final version of the Frame of Government which Penn agreed in 1701, he conceded it. Indeed, the Council, now to be nominated by the proprietor and governor, ceased to be the upper house of the Assembly, which became unicameral, a unique situation among the colonies. The Assembly continued to be chosen by the freemen of the colony, though the definition of a freeman changed. To be a freemen required ownership of at least 50 acres of land in the counties, and of property worth £50 in the city of Philadelphia. This represented a gain for the counties over the city since previously the property qualification to vote for county representatives had been at least 100 acres, while in Philadelphia all inhabitants paying taxes had been allowed to vote. Elections to the Assembly were to be held annually, with voting by secret ballot.

The settlement of Pennsylvania grew rapidly so that within ten years, some 10,000 emigrants arriving from England, Holland and Germany, as well as from within the colonies, had the effect of establishing a multi-religious society. The majority of settlers, though, came from England and Wales. Slaves from Africa were also shipped to the colony and constituted a significant portion of its population. It has been estimated that one in ten of the families inhabiting Philadelphia in 1700 owned slaves. The plurality of the colony was noted by one settler who said, 'we are a mixt people'. Except for Jews and Catholics, people from different faiths could participate in the political process.

In so far as Penn set up his colony as a 'holy experiment', it was this general religious toleration, then unknown in England or in Europe outside the Dutch Republic, which he had in mind. Could religious pluriformity coexist with a 'peaceable kingdom'? The verdict of historians generally has been that the experiment was a failure. By the 1690s, conflict emerged even within the Quaker community when George Keith sought to impose a more rigorous orthodoxy on the Friends. His 'Confession of Faith' caused a split known as the Keithian schism. In 1692 Keith and some of his followers left the Society of Friends and called themselves Christian Quakers. The following year saw violent confrontations between the rival sects. The dispute eventually petered out when many Christian Quakers, Keith included, became Anglicans.

Conflict also occurred over land claims. Daniel Pastorius, a German pietist, purchased a 25,000-acre tract of land northwest of

Philadelphia and in 1686 he, along with pietists from Frankfurt and Quakers from Kreveld, arrived to claim their land. They settled in Germantown, at the time an 'urban village' outside Philadelphia, though so close to it that in the nineteenth century it became a suburb. Penn also granted territory to the southwest of Philadelphia in the Delaware region to some settlers from Wales, partly to strategically create a boundary between him and Lord Baltimore. This area, straddling Chester and Philadelphia counties, became known as the Welsh Tract. The area in the lower Delaware, including the three counties of Kent, Newcastle and Sussex, became a battleground between the rival proprietors in which houses were burnt and people killed.

In addition to the contest between Maryland and Pennsylvania over the Delaware area, there was conflict in the Pennsylvania Assembly between the Anglican dominated lower three counties and the Quaker dominated upper counties in Pennsylvania. Often times, it centred over defence and swearing oaths. Threats from rival colonies and countries were felt much more keenly by the Delaware inhabitants because of their proximity to the Bay, while the Philadelphia inhabitants were further up river and more inland. These strategic differences between the upper and lower counties were exacerbated by the pacifism of the Quakers in Pennsylvania, who refused to raise forces for their defence, and the anxieties of the Anglicans in Delaware who wanted to maintain a militia. These disagreements lay behind the secession of the lower counties in 1701. They also resented the way that the growth of Philadelphia had eclipsed the prosperity of New Castle. This was illustrated forcefully when the Assembly for the lower counties passed an Act in 1705 requiring the payment of duties by ships passing by New Castle on their way up or down the Delaware River. Penn's deputy, Governor Evans, who as an Anglican himself sympathised with them, actually fired upon a New York ship in the river which refused to pay duties to the colony. The resulting outburst of anger from the Pennsylvania Assembly was instrumental in persuading the absentee proprietor Penn to dismiss his deputy.

Within the first year of its founding, Pennsylvania was producing a surplus. This was because of good planning and the geographic location of the colony. Most of the emigrants who arrived in the colony came in family groups. This was conducive to a high birth rate. The position of the colony was such that it did not experience the effects of disease-ridden Virginia, nor the freezing long winters of New England. Penn's promotional literature boasted that Pennsylvania was along the same latitude as that of Naples and some '600 miles nearer the sun than England'. The summers were long enough for the farmers to have two, and sometimes three, harvests. Penn's careful planning extended to the design of the colony's first city, Philadelphia. Having travelled in Europe in his youth, Penn was struck by the designs of new towns such as Turin, Italy. Turin was laid out in a grid pattern with large grassy areas called piazzas. The design helped to impede any potential chaos in building and its consequences of overcrowding and related unhygienic conditions. Philadelphia became the pattern for future cities in the United States.

After Penn's death in 1718, his descendants inherited his problems. During Anne's reign he had negotiated to sell the proprietorship of Pennsylvania to the Crown, and a deal had actually been struck but was never ratified. This raised some doubts as to whether the colony was under proprietary or royal control. To further complicate the situation, his estate was disputed between his children by his first marriage to Guilielma Springet and those by his second to Hannah Callowhill. It took a decade to resolve the dispute in favour of Hannah's children John, Thomas and Richard.

The last Governor of Pennsylvania to be appointed by Penn, Sir William Keith, exploited the situation created by the proprietor's death for his own advantage. One of the ways in which he did so was by distinguishing between his appointment to the governorship of Pennsylvania and that of the lower counties. The first was without limitation, but the second was during the King's pleasure. Keith interpreted this to indicate that Delaware was now regarded as a Crown colony, and proceeded to act as if he were the King's rather than the proprietor's deputy. Thus, he called himself Excellency, and issued a charter to New Castle with no reference to the proprietor. When Penn died, Keith even began to assert his own authority in Pennsylvania, until in 1726, the Penns thwarted his ambitions, dismissing him as governor.

The long lasting saga of the border dispute between Maryland and Pennsylvania was another colonial issue which was fought out more in the corridors of power in London than in North America. Thus, the moves and countermoves of the Calverts and Penns were often reactions to developments at Court rather than in the colonies. The eventual resolution of the boundary problem by the running of the Mason-Dixon line in the 1760s was a victory for the Penns over the Calverts, for the survey established the southern border of Pennsylvania significantly below the fortieth parallel, which the proprietors of Maryland claimed to be the northern boundary of their colony according to the charter granted to their family by Charles I. Although they spent considerable time and money in the law courts at Westminster fighting to make good their claim, in the end it was the superior influence of the Penns with successive ministries which prevailed.

The influence of the Penn family with the ministers was put to its severest test when Benjamin Franklin was sent by the Pennsylvania Assembly to England to protest against alleged abuse of the proprietary powers in 1757 and 1764. On the first occasion, Franklin attempted to curtail the proprietors' prerogatives. On the second, he tried to persuade the Crown to take over the colony from the Penns. In both cases the interest of the Penns at the Courts of George II and George III was too entrenched for Franklin to prevail.


## THE SIGNIFICANCE OF THE MIDDLE COLONIES

However amorphous the concept of the middle colonies might appear historically, by the end of the colonial period contemporaries did see the 'middle settlements' or 'middle provinces' as forming an entity. Historians seeking the colonial origins of modern American culture have also begun to take notice of them. Traditionally Puritan New England was held to be the seedbed of what is typical about America. Certainly, Puritanism informs a distinctive American attitude. But the connection between Calvinism and the capitalism which became the economic dynamic of the United States is now harder to establish than seemed to be the case in earlier accounts. New England economically became something of a backwater in the colonial period. Boston stagnated relative to the vigorous growth of New York City and, above all, of Philadelphia. The spirit of enterprise in these major eastern seaboard ports was noticed by contemporaries. They also commented, sometimes less favourably, on the motley ethnic mix of the middle colonies. The Dutch of New York, the Scots of New Jersey, the Germans and Scotch-Irish of Pennsylvania, to name but the most prominent alongside the English, provided colonial America with a melting-pot society, anticipating that of the nineteenth and twentieth centuries far more than did New England or the southern colonies, whose white inhabitants continued to be predominantly English in origin.

# 7 The Lower South

The colonies of the lower south were carved out of the original Virginia grant and were established after the restoration of Charles II. These colonies included the Carolinas and Georgia. Geographically, the Carolinas and Georgia are located in the same region, but Georgia was settled some 70 years after the Carolinas.

## THE CAROLINAS

Although the charter for the Carolinas was granted in 1663, there is evidence of settlements in them as early as 1655. The first initiatives in exploring the area began around 1654 when Francis Yeardley extended his search for a better climate to grow silk, olives and wines where they would be free of the 'nipping frosts' of Virginia, but the initial trade in deerskins was the first real major export. Until 1712, the Carolinas were considered as a whole territory. In that year a division was made within the boundaries between the Savannah River, which bordered the Spanish-held territory of Florida to the south and Virginia to the north, and a separate governor was appointed to the northern area, which became North Carolina. The charter for the Carolinas was given to eight proprietors, most of whom were members of the King's inner circle. The originators of the idea of a new settlement were most likely Sir John Colleton and Sir William Berkeley. Colleton had spent the years during the Cromwellian regime in exile in Barbados, while Berkeley, formerly Governor of Virginia, stayed in Paris until the Restoration. At that point he again became Governor of Virginia. Both knew the potential as well as the problems of developing colonies. They also knew that colonial expansion was occurring, particularly in the Virginia area. The likes of Berkeley recognised that the English colonies were experiencing population growth to the extent that good land was becoming scarce. Virginia went from approximately 2300 in the 1630s, to 27,000 by 1670. After 1670, it grew to over 35,000. The most fertile lands along the tidal waterways were taken. Consequently, people began to move to the back country and further south in search of land. Colleton and Berkeley, along with five other investors were able to convince the King to charter a separate area from the Virginia grant in order for them to capitalise on what they saw as an opportunity for growth. In addition to migration from within, there were attempts to relocate people there from England and in 1670, the proprietors financed the first group of emigrants. Three hundred people set out but only 100 survived the journey. Eventually, a settlement was established at Port Royal on the coast. Later, a more amenable site was fixed at the junction of the Ashley and Cooper Rivers. This town became Charles Town, or as it later became, and is now called, Charleston.

Motives for settlement stemmed from imperial as well as colonial causes. In imperial terms, the settlement of the lower areas would provide a barrier to Spanish expansion from Florida. The Spanish Empire had extended from South America up into parts of North America. Florida was its foothold on the eastern coast of the northern continent. For most of the sixteenth century, Spain encountered little colonial competition in the New World. What competition there was came from France. French exploration concentrated largely in the upper regions of North America. However, the English began making a concerted effort to expand westward in the early seventeenth century. In the past, England had to face competition from Spain in Europe, and now their colonial claims were challenging those of the Spanish Empire. This was made clear in the second charter for the Carolinas granted by Charles II in 1665, which extended the southern boundary south to include the Spanish settlement at St Augustine. This in its turn prompted Spain to acknowledge England's claim to the area down to Charles Town.

## CONSTITUTIONS

The constitutional arrangements for the colony were laid out first in the Agreements and Concessions of 1665 and then in the Fundamental Constitutions of 1669. The first was prompted by the failure to attract sufficient colonists after a group from New England

*Map 4*   The lower south

abandoned the colony. It granted an Assembly and a generous land scheme promising the first settlers 150 acres for every family member. The Fundamental Constitutions were devised by one of the proprietors, Anthony Ashley Cooper, Earl of Shaftesbury, and his secretary/physician, John Locke. A significant feature of this constitution was its provision for religious liberty. The proprietors had been through the troubles of the English Civil Wars and experienced the religiously liberal regime under Cromwell, and therefore incorporated their own liberal beliefs into the colony's constitution. Locke's hand has been detected behind the Fundamental Constitution's arrangements for the distribution of land and power in the colony, though that of James Harrington has also been discerned. Certainly Harrington's thesis expounded in *Oceana* (1655), that power was based on landed property, and that too much land made men too powerful, is embodied in the document. The land was divided into two areas, with Albermarle to the north and Clarendon to the south, each further divided into counties. Landownership was to be based upon a hierarchical system with its own vocabulary. Thus, the proprietors were to be known as seigneurs, holding the most land at 12,000 acres each. The landgraves, holding a total of 48,000 acres, and 'cassiques' or 'caciques', holding 24,000 were to form the local aristocracy. Under these were the freemen, called leet-men, and tenant land owners. There was even a category for serfs!

The political system was one of an oligarchy or rule by the few. A Grand Council, controlled by the proprietors, was to propose bills which a representative Assembly of the aristocrats and people were merely to pass or reject. The Assembly was to meet every other November, and was to comprise the nobility, freemen and tenant farmers. The voting requirements were the ownership of at least 50 acres. Elections to the Assembly were to be by secret ballot. This great scheme, in the event, was a paper constitution which was never implemented. Instead, a governor appointed by the proprietors consulted a council and what came to be called the Commons House of Assembly. During the 1690s a separate Assembly began to meet in North Carolina, finding the distance to Charles Town too great to meet there. In 1712 the proprietors came to terms with this development by appointing a separate governor for North Carolina. North and South Carolina then developed as two separate colonies.

The land scheme in the Fundamental Constitutions also proved to be unworkable, not least because initially there were not enough settlements. The first settlers came from Barbados as well as from other colonies in North America. There were also some French Huguenots. However, the people migrating from within the colonies, particularly Virginia, were opposed to the political system with its rigid hierarchy. The large expanse of land was another detriment to the establishment of Shaftesbury's social hierarchy. The terrain of the northern area of the Carolinas within the Outer Banks was not conducive to the cultivation of a cash crop such as tobacco or rice. It concentrated on exporting lumber, pitch and other naval stores. There was little need at first for indentured servants or slaves.

Therefore, the settlements consisted mainly of self-sufficient white families and were not conducive to the building of a structured society in the way the more southern region developed. The proprietors took more interest in the southern region because of its accessibility to the sea. Here, a more prosperous community sprang up. In addition to the English immigrants who settled there, settlers from Barbados were offered financial inducements to settle the area. They were also induced to migrate to the mainland since the switch from tobacco to sugar cultivation on the island had disrupted the economy, leaving many of the poorer white settlers unemployed. However, it was not until the 1690s with the growing of rice in the southern region that its economy took off.

## RICE AND SLAVES

The Barbadians who migrated to the southern counties of Carolina brought with them their traditions and a drive for profit. They established large land holdings which needed a large labour force. They did not hesitate to use the blacks that they brought along, or the native population that they enslaved to do the work. They were also able, with the help of West Indians, to establish a trade in Indian slaves who would be shipped to the West Indies. An alliance with the Yamasee and Creek Indians enabled Carolina to capitalise on the slave market. This resulted in conflicts with the Indians thus destabilising the region. This, in turn, created resentment with other smaller landholders who did not have prime property, but land further back on the frontier. In 1711, the Tuscarora Indians, resenting the encroachment of whites on to their lands and people, attacked the coastal settlement of New Bern and killed its inhabitants. Retaliation by Carolinians and their Indian allies resulted in a devastating defeat for the Tuscaroras and their surrender. The Yamasees eventually fell out with the settlers over broken agreements and fell into conflict. That the settlers were able to defeat the Yamasees and drive them into Florida was due to the Cherokee allies and the arming of slaves. Although there would be further conflicts with the native was population, it was less a matter of white settler against native and was seen more in the context of a complicated and fluid change of alliances. Nevertheless, a slave-based society was one of the colony's earliest hallmarks.

The contribution of its black majority to South Carolina's economy and society was immense. It has been claimed that the cash crop of rice was cultivated by slaves who brought knowledge of African rice cultivation to the lower south. Certainly the white settlers, overwhelmingly from the British Isles, where the crop was unknown, were not familiar with the techniques of growing and harvesting it.

## CROWN COLONIES

The Carolinas remained proprietary colonies under the Stuarts. After the Hanoverian succession, however, they became Crown colonies; South Carolina in 1719 and North Carolina in 1729. Although the proprietors surrendered their political rights over the colonies to the Crown, the Earl of Granville refused to give up his territorial claims in North Carolina. This was to store up problems when the back country began to fill up with settlers who moved into the area of the Granville grant. During the 1750s, the population of the Carolinas expanded rapidly as people poured in from the north, many of them migrants from Ulster. In the words of the *South Carolina Gazette* for 11 March 1768: 'there is scarce any history either ancient or modern which affords an account of such a rapid and sudden increase in inhabitants in a back frontier country as that of North Carolina.' Around 1730, the piedmont area of the colony was sparsely populated. Then the great influx of settlers began, not from the east but from the north, as people moved down from Pennsylvania to fill it up. By 1750, the six westernmost counties had an estimated 22,000 inhabitants out of a total of 65,000 in North Carolina. On the eve of the War of American Independence, they numbered nearly 62,000 or 40 per cent of the colony's population.

## GEORGIA

Georgia, once a part of the Carolinas, had been founded as part of the crown's strategy to expand and create a buffer between the English colonies, particularly South Carolina, and the Spanish settlements in Florida. This was the primary reason for the creation of the colony. In 1732, King George II granted a charter to Colonel James Oglethorpe, Sir John Percival, Earl of Egmont, and 19 other trustees for a period of 21 years, after which it was to revert to the Crown. Oglethorpe, who went to the new colony, was also responsible for its defence. The threat from Spanish Florida took on reality in 1742 when 3000 Spanish troops and slaves, who had escaped from South Carolina, attacked Georgia. Though the attack was in response to Oglethorpes's previous incursion into Florida, the attacks and counter-attacks were part of the imperial contests over expansion.

Oglethorpe and Percival were also idealists. They believed that in an ideal society, the deserving poor or 'worthy poor' should be given the chance to have a better life. They saw Georgia as a place where one could start a new life. In the settlement of the colony, they had the opportunity to realize their vision of a better society. Insolvent debtors rotting in prison were released under the terms of the Trust and given a fresh chance in the colony. Poor families from all over Europe, as well as England, were also given transportation to the new colony. These emigrants included Germans, Swiss, Austrians, Italians and Scots. The requirements for immigrants were hard work and adherence to the Protestant faith. Upon arrival in the new colony, each settler received 50 acres, tools and enough supplies to last a year. Although not intended as immigrants, many Jewish members of European society migrated and settled in the Savannah region of Georgia. The organisation of the colony by the Trustees was based upon a utopian vision. Thus, in an attempt to stem greed, land was given away to the settlers and, likewise, the settlers were prohibited from selling their land. Large plantations of over 500 acres were also forbidden in the spirit of creating a quasi-equality among settlers.

There were limitations on this idealized society. Women could not own land and there was no elected Assembly. Moreover the celebrated decision of the Trustees to prohibit slavery in Georgia was based more on fears for its social stability than on any philanthropic motive. They recognised the danger of slave uprisings, especially if instigated by Spanish authorities in Florida. Their fears were realised in the Stono Rebellion of 1739 when blacks in neighbouring South Carolina, incited by offers of refuge in St Augustine, rose up and killed whites.

Initially, the colony did not prosper. The intentions of cultivating silk and grapes were not realised. Products such as rum, which were recognised as highly marketable commodities, were nevertheless prohibited. Rice and indigo became the colony's main export products. However, with the low numbers of settlers, most of whom had no previous experience of agriculture, there was not enough production, causing the colony's economy to suffer. Added to the settlers' dissatisfaction was their inability to participate in the political life of the colony. The disillusionment felt by the colonists caused many to leave Georgia and inhibited potential immigrants. In 1751 the Trustees revoked the ban on slavery. After the expiring of their charter in 1754, when Georgia reverted to the Crown, the colony began to prosper with the introduction of slaves, whose numbers rose from 500 in 1751 to 15,000 by 1775. Rice exports increased tenfold over the same period.

## SLAVERY IN THE LOWER SOUTH

The growth of slavery in the south was an inheritance from the West Indies and an answer to the labour shortage problem. By the eighteenth century, Carolinians discovered that growing rice would produce a very profitable return, but it was labour intensive and required manpower. The lack of indentured servants, partly due to improved standards of living back in England, and partly due to the inability of whites to adapt to the disease environment and fend off malaria, was offset by the use of imported slaves. Africans had the advantage of immunity to this disease because they had built up antibodies to it in the malaria-infested coast of West Africa. African slaves also appear to have brought with them their expertise in rice production.

Although blacks were considered in a lower class than white servants, while they still numbered in the minority they had considerable freedom. However, the racist element became entrenched more in the south than in the north. The primary reason was due to numbers. By the 1740s, the slave population grew exponentially so that whereas in the 1660s there were 49 whites for every one black, by the middle of the eighteenth century the ratio narrowed to less than three whites for every one black in North Carolina, while South Carolina's black population outnumbered the whites. The disproportionate numbers gave rise to fears of losing control of the slaves. Within the repressive system, slaves did have a certain amount of independence. This made practical and economic sense for the slaveholder. Although slaves worked harder and for a longer portion of their lives than did white servants, they were able to have time to tend their own plots and to sell their goods, sometimes to their own masters. The system relieved the master from expending more than he had in order to feed and clothe his slaves. Within their own economic system, slaves were able to improve their standard of living, albeit it remained worse than that of peasants in Europe. There was even the possibility that a slave could be set free by his master. Manumission, or the freeing of individual slaves, was not usual but not uncommon. Nevertheless, slaves were beginning to be seen dressing 'above their station', and their freedom of movement was noted in the towns where they gathered during the hours when not working, constituting increased fears over how to regulate them. The response by the South Carolinian government was to institute dress codes and curfews. To ensure these laws would be carried out, the colonial militia was given the responsibility over local slave patrols. The slaves reacted to this repression of their liberties with violence. Increasing number of arsons occurred and the number of runaways went up. Usually, the runaways went further south to Florida, where the Spanish government welcomed them not so much for the principle of freedom, but as a means to induce destabilisation in the English colonies. Tensions finally came to a head in 1739 when a group of slaves stole guns and ammunition from a store at the Stono River Bridge near Charleston. While making for Florida, they destroyed plantations and killed whites. Reprisals from the militia were brutal. A new and more repressive code was put into place in which slave owners were made more responsible of the discipline of their slaves on pain of fines. Manumission of slaves now required approval from the legislature.

By the eighteenth century, with the southern colonies becoming more prosperous and numerous, Spanish Florida became even more vulnerable. Because the Spaniards had always used the practice of assimilating the native population after conquering the area, they now invited Indians and black refugees to the territory in order to build up Florida's defence. This door of escape open to slaves had affected the stability of the southern colonies. Blacks who made it to Florida set up their own communities. Mose, established near St Augustine in 1738, was the product of years of black migration to the south. The Spanish government provided them with wage-paying jobs and enlisted them into militias as early as 1683. This was in response to Carolinian Indian allies who attacked and captured Florida mission Indians to sell as slaves. Border conflict ensued with blacks and Indians from Florida raiding Carolina and returning with captured slaves. Until the Spanish handed Florida over to the English as one of the stipulations in the 1763 Treaty of Paris, Florida was the Mecca for escaped slaves. With the English takeover, the Spanish government provided the blacks with land in Cuba. When the Spanish again acquired Florida in 1783, the colony became a haven for black slaves once more. Though relations with the newly formed United States was somewhat tense, the new government persuaded the Florida governor to rescind their policy on escaped slaves. Thus, the USA was able to neutralise the threat from its border and from within the southern states.

# 8 The West Indies

The mainland colonies are generally perceived as being the principal destinations of the settlers who went from Britain across the Atlantic in the seventeenth century. Thus, historians talk of 'the great migration' to Massachusetts in the 1630s, when 13,000 went there. But that pales into insignificance compared with the numbers who migrated to the Caribbean. It has been estimated that some 60 per cent of all whites who crossed the ocean went there, so that by 1660 the English islands contained 47,000 inhabitants, or 40 per cent of those in England's American plantations.

The most attractive destination was Barbados, whose climate was considered to be much healthier for settlers from the British Isles than that in other Caribbean islands. The white population increased to 23,000 by 1655. After that, however, it declined, while the numbers of slaves rose from 20,000 in 1655, to 46,500 by 1684. The reason for this demographic change was sugar. Barbados was originally given over principally to tobacco production, though as in other West Indian islands such plants as coffee, cotton, ginger and indigo were cultivated. They never concentrated entirely on one crop, albeit sugar eventually accounted for about 75 per cent of their exports, while in islands like Antigua and St Kitts it virtually monopolised them. The 1640s saw the switch to sugar first in Barbados. This had a dramatic impact on the island. Initially, there was a rapid increase in the population both from Europe and from Africa, making it one of the most densely populated of the colonies. Land therefore became scarce, forcing some settlers off it in the reign of Charles II. Many went to Jamaica or the Carolinas.

Although Jamaica was settled later than Barbados, it followed a similar demographic path. In 1655 the white population numbered 3000 compared with only 500 blacks. By 1696, the 10,000 whites were outnumbered by 30,000 blacks. This was despite the deaths of more than 2000 people in the Port Royal earthquake of 1692, and the

111

French invasion of 1694 when 2000 slaves were carried off. Diseases such as malaria and yellow fever carried off far more, for Jamaica was the most unhealthy of all the British islands in the Caribbean. By 1715 the white population had actually shrunk to 7000, while the slaves had increased to 55,000. The alterations in the ratios of whites to blacks were due, as in Barbados, to an increasing reliance on sugar production, together with its offshoots, molasses and rum.

The whites who went, and survived, were for the most part young adult males. This led, as in the early Chesapeake, to an imbalanced gender ratio, making family formation difficult. Unlike Virginia and Maryland, however, this was never adequately redressed, especially in Jamaica, where white society remained male dominated throughout the colonial period. This inevitably led to sexual relations between white men and black women, which was tolerated much more in the West Indies than in the southern mainland colonies. The Jamaican Assembly passed a law in 1733 unique in British America in recognising mulattoes as legally white when three generations separated them from their black forebears.

## SUGAR AND SLAVES

Investment in sugar production was costly, which in itself forced some whites out of the economy. Returns on successful plantations, however, were extremely profitable. Barbados' annual sugar crop was valued at £3,000,000 in the early 1650s. Some of the men who invested in the crop made fortunes. Thomas Modyford went to Barbados in 1645, when he acquired a plantation of 500 acres. When he died in 1679, he possessed plantations both in Barbados and Jamaica, with a labour force of over 600 servants and slaves. The Price family dominated the Jamaican planter aristocracy for three generations. In the third, Sir Charles Price owned 25,000 acres and 1300 slaves. At the end of the eighteenth century Simon Taylor, another 'sugar tycoon' in Jamaica, had an annual income of £47,000, while his estate was valued at £1,000,000, making him one of the richest subjects of the British Crown.

The method of producing sugar involved work so hard that a free labour force would not have undertaken it. Sowing and tending the cane was comparable with tobacco cultivation. But harvesting it, crushing the juice from the cane and boiling it in the heat of

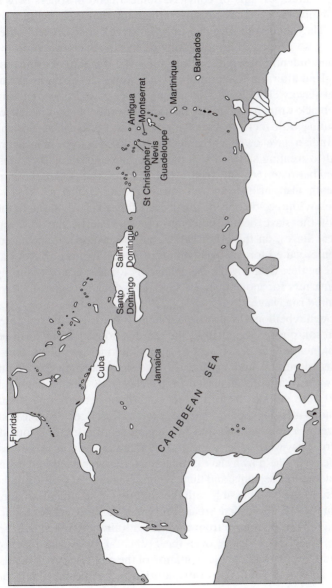

*Map 5*   The West Indies

a semi tropical climate was backbreaking. White labourers went out as indentured servants or convicts. Some 12,000 prisoners of war were shipped out to Barbados by Parliament after the English Civil Wars. They tended to succumb to yellow fever, dysentry and other diseases, so needed to be constantly replaced. As elsewhere in the colonies, indentured servitude dried up as the standard of living rose in England after the Restoration, so increasing recourse was had to chattel slavery. The death rate among slaves was also horrendous, while black women frequently miscarried, probably as a result of continuing with their backbreaking work into pregnancy. For the West Indian slave, owners became bywords for cruelty even in an era inured to treating slaves like cattle. The Slave Code of Barbados, enacted between 1661 and 1688, was draconian. It regarded slaves as 'an heathenish, brutish and an uncertain and dangerous kind of people'. Whites could only be fined, even if they killed a black. In the case of the slave being somebody else's property, the fine was heavier. Slaves, on the other hand, could be whipped or maimed, or even executed for relatively minor offences. In 1692 an Act was passed by the Assembly imposing hanging for absence or deserting their masters for more than 30 days. This does not seem to have prevented runaways.

Though rebellion was always punished by death, this did not deter a slave conspiracy, also in 1692, the ramifications of which terrified the colonial authorities. It was concerted among the skilled slaves, such as carpenters and smiths, who had been born on the island. They were clearly distinguished from field hands freshly imported. These were to kill their masters and then rendezvous at the governor's mansion. Some 4000 slaves were alleged to be implicated, who were to be organised into two regiments of horse and four of infantry. They were to seize the governor and the armoury, the keys to which were held by a slave. Apparently, they expected help from Irish indentured servants, and there seems to have been some Catholic element to the plot, possibly with the intention of securing Barbados for 'James III', the exiled Stuart Pretender to the English throne, and thereby to disengage from the war with France. When news of the English fleet's victory over the French at La Hogue reached Barbados it put off the implementation of the plot for several weeks. The plan was to gain control of the island's fortifications and the warships in the harbour. Once in control of the island, the white males were to be massacred and the females made to serve them as wives or whores, and servants. Many of the details might well have been the fevered imaginations of the terrified authorities who did not detect the conspiracy until it had been afoot three months, thanks to an oath of secrecy on the part of the plotters. The retribution was swift. A court martial examined those who were implicated, and tortured them by hanging them in chains until they either starved or confessed and revealed their accomplices. About 400 were rounded up and executed.

The Barbados Code was extended to Jamaica and similar laws were passed in the Leeward Islands. Such brutality helped to prevent the slave population increasing naturally. As a result there had to be constant importation of blacks, estimated at between 8 per cent and 10 per cent of the slave population per year, just to keep it constant. This was quite unlike the southern mainland colonies, where slave families not only reproduced themselves, but expanded their numbers naturally, even in the rice producing areas of South Carolina and Georgia. Unlike the mainland, too, slaves who ran away could generally escape from their masters, especially in the mountains of Jamaica, where they formed bands known as maroons. There was conflict between these and the white inhabitants in most years between 1700 and 1722, and again between 1729 and 1739, when the Jamaican authorities signed a treaty with them granting their independence in return for their help in policing runaways. This prevented large-scale resistance until Tacky's rebellion in 1760, when 400 slaves and 90 whites were killed. This was followed in 1765 by the St Mary's revolt and in 1776 by the Hanover revolt.

The slave populations of the islands were not merely sustained by imports from Africa, but continued to increase. By the middle of the eighteenth century, the black populations of Barbados and Jamaica respectively stood at 69,100 and 118,100. This labour force enabled sugar exports from the West Indies to increase from 22,017 tons in 1700, to 41,425 tons in 1748. Rum exports soared from 207 gallons in 1698, to two millions a year on the eve of the War of American Independence. By then, sugar production in Barbados had been outstripped by that of Jamaica, while the Leeward islands had also increased output. It was claimed that in Antigua, there was 'hardly one acre of ground, even to the tops of the mountains, fit for sugar canes and other necessary produce but what is taken in and cultivated'. St Kitts had become the richest colony in the British Empire through the cultivation of sugar.

The profitability of sugar did not pursue a uniform upward course in these years. On the contrary, competition from the French islands of Guadeloupe, Martinique and, above all, St Domingue, where sugar was produced between 15 per cent and 30 per cent cheaper than in the British West Indies, drove down prices. Indeed, British West Indian sugars became virtually confined to the home market in the opening decades of the eighteenth century. Hence, the concern of the West Indian lobby to get Parliament to protect its interests by passing the Molasses Act in 1733. The success of the campaign was tribute to the serious attention which the British government paid to the planters, whether they lived as absentee landlords in London or stayed on the islands. It also tied the sugar planters into the British economy, making them more dependent upon the mother country than were the continental colonists.

## THE PLANTER ARISTOCRACY

Owners of plantations who resided in the West Indies formed an elite of less than 10 per cent of the white population, which owned over half the land. The trend was for larger estates to expand at the expense of smaller holdings. By 1729 thirty planters owned nearly four-fifths of Barbados and three-fifths of its slaves. In St Kitts the number of sugar plantations shrank from 360 in 1724, to 110 in 1783. This process was assisted by the practice of primogeniture whereby, as in the mother country, the eldest son inherited the whole estate, unlike the continental colonies where property tended to be divided among siblings. Plantation owners dominated their small islands more completely than the ruling classes on the mainland.

The British West Indies were so small that parishes rather than counties became the basis of government and administration. Only Jamaica, the largest island, was carved out into three counties, and that did not occur until as late as 1758.

The parish was the basic unit for the island militias, in which every free white man between the ages of 16 and 60 had to enlist. The officers of the militia regiments were recruited from the planters, while their commanding officers were the royal governors. At first, these forces were needed for defence against attacks from other Europeans and from the Caribs who gave their name to the area and whose ferocity was notorious. In this respect, the model of 'garrison government' fits the West Indies more than the mainland. But increasingly, the parish militias acted as a police force to keep the slave population in awe of the whites. As early as 1647, Richard Ligon observed of the militias in Barbados that the slaves, 'seeing the mustering of our men and hearing their gun shot (than which nothing is more terrible to them) their spirits are subjugated to so low a condition, that they dare not look up to any bold attempt'. In the eighteenth century the Jamaican militia numbered 5000, while there were also 1000 regular troops stationed there.

The parishes also formed the constituencies which returned representatives to the Assemblies on the islands. Barbados acquired an Assembly in 1639, and during the following decades the other islands also obtained representation in them, They were largely controlled by the landed elite, who used them to pass local laws for their own advantage. Sir Charles Price contrived to ensure that the Jamaican Assembly met at Spanish Town. When a hostile governor moved it to Kingston in the 1750s, Price had him recalled and returned the Assembly to Spanish Town. Price used his clout in the Assembly to pass private acts in his own interest, including one that granted him a monopoly on tolls raised on the road between Spanish Town and the coast.

The West Indian planters have generally been portrayed as a hard-nosed, hard-drinking, argumentative, aggressive, cruel, irreligious and immoral elite. Certainly, the mainland colonists who petitioned against the Molasses Act of 1733 drew a moral distinction between themselves and the West Indians, claiming that they themselves were 'a laborious people who live with great frugality', whereas the planters 'live in wantoness and luxury'. They could indeed afford luxuries, being the nearest to the English aristocracy of any group of people in the American colonies. Their mansions, their furniture, their liveried servants, their coaches and equipages consciously aped the lifestyles of the richest subjects in England. Besides the landed gentry, there were professional men, clergy, doctors and lawyers. By 1710, thanks to a bequest from the Codrington family, Barbados even boasted its own college. The typically Georgian buildings of Codrington College were built between 1721 and 1738. Barbados was exceptional, however, in this respect. The other islands in the British West Indies, including even the largest, Jamaica, never developed an infrastructure to make them culturally self-contained. Even those 'creole' planters who were born there regarded Britain as their home, and felt themselves to be mere sojourners before leaving for the mother country. Many of the elite who dominated the Assemblies and the professions had received degrees and legal and medical qualifications in Britain. They sent their children to be educated at 'home', many of whom did not return to the West Indies. By the middle of the eighteenth century some 300 children a year were sent from Jamaica to Britain to be educated, one-third of whom stayed there.

Society in the West Indies thus differed markedly from the mainland, even in South Carolina and Georgia with which it had most in common. Ties with Britain, and especially with England, were much stronger in the islands than on the continent. This was to make their reaction to the demands of the British government after the accession of George III very different from the 13 colonies which declared their independence from him.

# PART III
# The Imperial Connection

# 9 The Glorious Revolution in England and America

## ENGLAND: THE 1680s

During the 1680s there was a drift towards absolute kingship in England under Charles II as well as under James II. Charles II was able to dispense with Parliament after the dissolution of 1681, never meeting another before his death in 1685. This was in defiance of the Triennial Act of 1664 which required Parliament to meet at least once every three years. He was able to get away with this because the commercial boom of the decade, largely due to the expansion in trans-Atlantic trade, increased customs revenues to the point where he at last realised the £1,200,000 income from taxation voted him by Parliament in 1660. James II's Parliament voted him the same revenue in 1685, and increased it to nearly £2,000,000 with the addition of short-term supplies to pay for the suppression of the rebellion of the Duke of Monmouth that summer. Thus when he dispensed with Parliament's services that November, he could afford to do so. James then attempted to pack Parliament between 1687 and 1688. Had he succeeded, he would have reduced the Lords and Commons to a rubber stamp. The regulators of corporations, whom he used for the purpose of packing Parliament, were paid officials directly responsible to him and they reported favourably on the prospects of a compliant Commons when he chose to summon a new Parliament.

Both Charles and James used the revenues voted to them for the purpose of raising a standing army. This was a modest force under Charles, amounting to no more than 8500 men. James, however, thanks to the generosity of the Commons' response to Monmouth's rebellion, was able to increase it to nearly 20,000 by the end of 1685. This was a sufficient force to intimidate any of his subjects who might be tempted to follow Monmouth's example. The army was used as a police force in garrison towns like Bristol, Hull and York. These centres were effectively under martial law during James's reign. In March 1688 a standing court martial was set up, which indemnified the army from common and statute law, making it an instrument of the royal will.

The judiciary was also brought under royal control. The judges of the common law courts – Common Pleas, exchequer and King's Bench – could be appointed either on good behaviour or at the pleasure of the Crown. In the first years of Charles II's reign, both forms were used; but increasingly in the later years and exclusively in James's reign, they were appointed at pleasure. Thus, they could be dismissed at will and during the 1680s both Kings used their right of dismissal to purge the bench in an effort to procure compliant judges. James even established a prerogative court, the Commission for Ecclesiastical Causes. This was regarded by many as a revival of the Court of High Commission, which had been abolished by Act of Parliament in 1641. It even used a seal similar to that employed by the earlier court. James delegated to the commission his authority as supreme governor of the Church of England, which it used to deprive the Bishop of London of his spiritual powers, and to discipline the Fellows of Magdalen College, Oxford, when they refused to elect the King's nominee as their president. These measures adversely affected men who in Charles II's reign had been among the most stalwart supporters of the King and of the hereditary principle. James strained and then snapped the link between the Crown and its natural allies.

When this became obvious even to him by 1687, he turned to try to forge an alliance with Whigs and Dissenters who had tried to prevent him succeeding his brother in the Exclusion crisis. In 1687 he issued a Declaration of Indulgence, an edict of toleration which gave Dissenters as well as Catholics immunity from prosecution for breaking the laws requiring conformity to the established Church. He also embarked on a campaign to pack Parliament with members who would put the Declaration on the statute book. The most prominent of the Dissenters who collaborated with the King was the Quaker leader William Penn, founder of Pennsylvania. He became a close confidante of James, helping draft the Declaration of Indulgence, intervening in the Magdalen College affair, and even getting involved in the campaign to pack Parliament. His 'collaboration' throws much light on the motives of many Dissenters who played a role in these revolutionary years. What they sought was toleration. The question was, where were they to find it? If they looked to the Cavalier Parliament elected in 1661, which lasted until 1679, they were doomed to disappointment. So, far from offering relief from the penal laws against dissent, the bigoted Anglicans on the back-benches, determined to get their own back on those who had perse-cuted them in the Civil Wars and Interregnum, added to the statutes penalising non-attendance at the established Church. The only hope of relief in those years came from the King, who twice offered Declar-ations of Indulgence, only to be obliged to withdraw them after protests from Parliament. The Exclusion Parliaments by contrast had seen sympathy for the plight of Dissenters, and there were even bills to relieve them brought forward in 1680, only to be aborted by the prorogation of the session. Since then, however, the Whig party, which had dominated the Commons during the Exclusion crisis, had been virtually annihilated, its leadership cut off by treason trials and its support eliminated by the urge of the Parliamentary boroughs. Once more a Parliament with an intransigent Anglican majority had been returned, which again refused to cooperate with a King anxious to introduce toleration. As on previous occasions under Charles II, it made more sense for Dissenters to hope for help from the Crown than from Parliament. This is what makes the term 'collaborators', with its echoes of Europe under the Nazi occupation, so pejorative. Penn was not a Quisling. James II's Declaration of Indulgence brought immediate relief to fellow Quakers who were suffering the severest persecution they ever experienced during the 'tory reaction' of Charles II's closing years. Penn even justified the packing of Parliament on the grounds that it was the only way to bring about a Toleration Act as comprehensive as the King's Edict in the circum-stances of the time. And he recognised the force of the Marquis of Halifax's argument in *The Character of a Trimmer* that toleration based on the mere word of the King was very precarious, since twice the royal word had been recalled under Charles II. Only an Act of Parliament could give a permanent guarantee of freedom from persecution. At the same time, only a Parliament of members who shared the King's views would enact his Declaration of Indulgence.

Unfortunately, when James panicked on learning of the imminent embarkation of William's task force in September 1688 and threw his policies into reverse, those Dissenters who had cooperated with him were left high and dry. He abandoned the attempt to pack Parliament, and restored charters to many Parliamentary boroughs, including London. He wound up the Commission for Ecclesiastical Causes and reinstated the Bishop of London and the Fellows of

Magdalen college. This 'U-turn', as it would be called today, was intended to placate his 'old friends' the Anglican Tories. It mainly succeeded in revealing his total unreliability. Thus, he won over very few of the clergy whom he had alienated with his Declarations of Indulgence, yet at the same time he completely lost all credibility with the Whigs and Dissenters. The result was a consensus against the regime. As one observer put it:

> I question if in all the histories of empire there is one instance of so bloodless a Revolution as that in England in 1688, wherein Whigs, Tories, princes, prelates, nobles, clergy, common people and standing army were unanimous. To have seen all England of one mind is to have lived at a very particular juncture.

It was not that the nation rose in unity to rally to William III's cause when he landed in England on 5 November. Very few people actively participated in the revolutionary events. The majority in any Revolution play a passive role. What is crucial is whether or not they support the regime or its opponents. In 1685 at the time of Monmouth's rebellion, before James had had time to alienate his subjects, most of them favoured his crushing of the rebels and his rival stood no chance. In 1688 they were so alienated that they withdrew their allegiance, creating a vacuum which gave William and those who assisted him the opportunity to overthrow him. James fled to France in December rather than risk battle with William, who in the King's absence issued writs for the election of a Parliament. When it met in January 1689, it debated how to fill the vacuum left by the King's flight. In the event it offered the Crown to William and his wife Mary, James's daughter, who accepted in February. Their unique joint monarchy, however, was not to be absolute but limited. The Declaration of Rights condemned James II's use of the Crown's remaining prerogative powers, and asserted Parliamentary limitations on the king's freedom of action. The Declaration, which was later put on the statute book as the Bill of Rights, marked the change from absolute to limited monarchy. This crucial change in the conception of kingship was confirmed in the changes made to the Coronation Oath in 1689. James had sworn to 'grant and keep' the laws 'granted by the kings of England'. William and Mary swore 'to govern the people of this kingdom of England ... according to the statutes in Parliament agreed on, and the laws and customs of the same'.

## AMERICA

### The Dominion of New England

The formation of the Dominion and Territory of New England was a major cause of the Glorious Revolution in America. In 1687 James II incorporated the colonies of Massachusetts, Connecticut, New Hampshire and Rhode Island into one jurisdiction. The following year, he extended it to New York and New Jersey. In effect it brought into being one vast Crown colony extending over the whole area from Maine to the Delaware River. There are signs that it was intended to cover an even greater region. Writs of *quo warranto* demanding justifications of their jurisdictions were issued against the colonies of Maryland and Pennsylvania, including the three lower counties on the Delaware, during the reign of James II. It seemed as though the King wanted to make most of the mainland settlements directly subject to the Crown. The Revolution which caused him to flee to France in 1688 brought the policy to an abrupt conclusion. Although William III, who succeeded James, was a military man with a similar attitude towards colonial government, and much as he would have liked to retain the Dominion, the effects of the Glorious Revolution in America were to render any attempt to revive it unfeasible.

The first step in the conversion of the New England settlements from chartered to Crown colonies was the attack on the charter of Massachusetts in 1684. The previous year, Edward Randolph had reported on his commission to investigate breaches of the navigation Acts by the Bay colony. His report was a damning indictment, accusing it of blatant disregard for them throughout Massachusetts, where smuggling was rife and officials turned a blind eye to it, thereby incurring great loss of revenue to the King. Randolph also alleged that the colony was defiant of royal authority, 'usurping to be a body politic'; in other words, setting itself up as a virtually independent commonwealth or republic. It was on the basis of his report that Massachusetts was forced to forfeit the charter granted by Charles I in 1629. The Puritans had used the charter he issued to the Massachusetts Bay Company as the colony's constitution. For instance, their Assembly was called the General Court, the name used in the charter for the governing body of the company. They were therefore not able to put up much of a defence against a writ of *quo warranto* which required them to explain by what authority they exercised their jurisdiction. The charter was consequently recalled and the colony placed under the jurisdiction of the Crown. Where before the freemen had elected the governor, now governors were to be nominated by the King. Plymouth, which up until then had been a separate colony, was placed under the jurisdiction of Massachusetts. Joseph Dudley, the first royal governor of the Bay colony, also presided over New Hampshire, which had already been taken over by the Crown. He was instructed to govern without summoning an Assembly, only convening a Council of his own choice. Previously governors of Massachusetts had been elected by the 'freemen', those so-called 'visible saints' who were full members of the Congregational churches. From now on the rule of the saints was over.

After James II came to the throne, he recalled the charters of Connecticut and Rhode Island and incorporated them into the Dominion and Territory of New England. In December 1686, Sir Edmund Andros became the governor of the Dominion. Andros ruled by decree. Thus, he raised taxes without any semblance of representation, provoking resistance from some colonists who, claiming the liberties of Englishmen, protested that taxation could only be legitimately raised with the approval of the suppressed Assemblies. Their ringleaders were arrested and thrown into jail. Andros rigorously enforced the navigation laws, which had been so blatantly disregarded in New England, by allowing only five ports where customs could be cleared, all breaches of the laws were to be tried in admiralty courts without juries. The selectmen, who were elected to represent the New England towns, were only allowed to meet once a year. For practical purposes they were superseded by men nominated by Andros himself. Since many were his cronies who did not even reside in New England, it was depicted as being 'squeezed by a crew of abject persons fetched from New York'. The entire governing body was replaced subsequent to the revocation of the colony's charter. Edward Randolph, who was appointed as secretary to the Dominion, used his position to create a host of new officials, many of them Anglicans who succeeded to the functions formerly carried out by Puritans.

James II genuinely believed in religious toleration. He had introduced freedom of worship into New York when he became its proprietor. He was determined that those colonists who were members of the Dutch Reformed Church should live peaceably with his English subjects. The visible saints of Massachusetts were notorious religious bigots, completely intolerant of all sects other than their own. They were particularly severe in their treatment of Quakers. The Massachusetts General Court passed laws banning them from proselytizing. Any Friend found trying to convert a Puritan was subject to harsh penalties, that for a third offence being death. James insisted upon complete toleration in New England. Although Connecticut had been more tolerant than Massachusetts, the Congregationalists there also resented this policy which effectively disestablished their Church. The only New England colony which greeted it with enthusiasm was Rhode Island, where religious toleration was practised. The King was determined to replace the rule of the saints with religious toleration, and instructed Andros to introduce it into the Dominion. Andros did so with great zeal. The Congregational Church, which was virtually the established Church in Massachusetts as it was in Connecticut, was in effect disestablished there too. Its ministers were no longer maintained by local rates. Anglican services were permitted in its churches. On one occasion, the Congregationalists who frequented Boston south church had to wait outside while a service was held according to the rites of the Church of England.

Although the jurisdiction over which Andros presided is usually referred to merely as the Dominion of New England, its full title was in fact the Dominion and Territory of New England. That the addition of the word 'territory' was not a mere synonym for dominion became clear when Andros began to levy annual quitrents on landowners. They were required to produce the title deeds to their lands and to have them confirmed. Where before they had held them as freeholds, they were now to be regarded as being held from the Crown. As one Congregational minister complained: 'We received only the right and power of Government from the King's charter, but the right of the Land and Soil we had received from God.' He clearly appreciated the distinction between dominion and territory.

Although this experiment in colonial government was undertaken for a variety of reasons, the most pressing motive was undoubtedly defence. Despite the fact that England and France enjoyed peaceful relations in Europe there was friction between them in North America, especially on the frontier between New France and New York. Thus, in 1687, the French attacked some Indians in the Mohawk River valley allied to the English. It was due to this attack that James decided to incorporate New York and New Jersey into the Dominion of New England. This extension of the Dominion in 1688 from Maine to the

Delaware Bay was designed to be 'terrible to the French', to quote the auditor of Crown revenues in the colonies at the time. The Dominion in this respect came closest to establishing the 'garrison government' which Professor Webb insists was the main objective of the English government's policy towards the American colonies in the seventeenth century. Charles II might have been interested in introducing such a regime in Virginia, but he lacked not only the funds but the determination to bring it about. His successor, who possessed both, did introduce a form of 'garrison government' in the Dominion of New England. Andros presided over the whole, but his deputy Dongan was replaced in New York by Francis Nicholson. Nicholson resumed the Crown's rights of government over New Jersey, which the proprietors had exercised since 1680, albeit on dubious authority. As elsewhere in the Dominion, the Assemblies were suspended. The Dominion of New England thus acquired many of the characteristics of absolutism which Charles II and James II had established in old England. There was a standing army, censorship of the press and arbitrary imprisonment.

In England absolutism was linked with Catholicism in the slogan 'Popery and arbitrary power'. Since the King was himself a Catholic, and came to rely more and more on Catholics to advise him, the association had some basis in reality in his kingdom. It was less obvious in New England and New York, however. Nevertheless, Andros and his deputy Nicholson were accused of being crypto-Catholics. Nicholson's predecessor Dongan was a Roman Catholic who had retained his chaplain, as well as two Catholic officers in the militia. It was alleged that he had accompanied James to Mass while in England, and had been 'on his knees before the alter in a Papist Chapel'. Since there was so little popery in the Dominion of New England, however, the opposition to those who presided over its government were driven to accuse them of being in league with the Catholic French to impose popery on the American colonies, just as James II was accused of seeking to impose it on England.

**Revolution in Maryland**

In their search for evidence of a plot to impose 'Popery and arbitrary power' on the colonies, critics of James II's regime in America found the most convincing 'proof' of it not in the Dominion of New England, but in Maryland. The proprietor of Maryland, Lord Baltimore, was a Catholic, and although he was in England during James's reign, in 1688 he appointed as deputy in his proprietary colony a fellow Catholic, William Joseph. Despite the fact that Protestants in Maryland outnumbered them by four to one, and dominated the elected Assembly, Catholics were in a majority on the Council. After Joseph arrived in Marylan, he delivered an address to the Assembly on the subject of the divine right of kings. The Protestant Assemblymen expressed their objections to this harangue. Tensions between the two grew as James II's reign progressed, leading to the emergence of 'an association in arms for the defence of the Protestant Religion' led by John Coode, a former Anglican minister who had abandoned the ministry in England before going to Maryland. His supporters were paranoid about the intentions of the proprietary government, especially when, in January 1689, the Council called in all public arms, ostensibly for repairs, though Protestants were convinced it was a move to disarm them. Protestant paranoia reached a crescendo when a rumour began to circulate that there was a conspiracy of Catholics to kill them with the assistance of Indians. When news reached Maryland that James had fled to France, Joseph and the Council prorogued the session of the Assembly from April to October. The proprietor's supporters were suspected by the Protestant Association of buying time, and even delaying to acknowledge publicly that William and Mary were King and Queen.

Reliable reports, as distinct from rumours, about the events of the Glorious Revolution in England took time to reach the American colonies. Official intelligence that William and Mary had accepted the offer of the Crown in mid-February 1689 took until late May to arrive in Boston, albeit unconfirmed reports had found their way across the Atlantic earlier. This time gap led to curious delays in proclaiming the accession of William and Mary. It was not until November, for instance, that a proclamation was issued in Philadelphia. Maryland's Catholic government was therefore not the most dilatory about announcing the change of regime, though the Protestant Association took matters into its own hands on 16 July 1689 when they marched on the capital St Mary's to take over the state house and then to lay siege to Lord Baltimore's country house, where his deputy governor Joseph had fled. With his surrender on 1 August, the proprietary government collapsed. The Associators then held elections for a convention which met towards the end of August. The

Protestant majority assumed the government of the colony, setting up a grand committee of safety. Coode then proclaimed himself commander-in chief of the militia and naval officer for the Potomac. His *coup* was recognised by the new regime in England, which confirmed his control of the colony until a governor appointed by the Crown, and not by the deposed proprietor, reached Maryland. Lionel Copley, the first royal governor, did not arrive there until 1692.

### New England

Sir Edmund Andros was on the Maine frontier confronting hostile Indians when he picked up a rumour that James II had fled to France. Upon this he retreated to Boston, where the news was confirmed on 25 March. This indicates that his opponents did not anticipate events in England, but were pretty certain that the King had been ousted when they seized Andros on 18 April. The threw him and Randolph in jail and set up a Council of Safety and the conservation of the peace presided over by Simon Bradstreet, a former governor then in his eighties.

The mass uprising in Massachusetts demonstrated that the Dominion of New England had alienated the majority in the Bay colony. The recall of the charter in 1684 had already lost the support of any Puritans even before the Dominion antagonised most of the other colonists. Encouraged by the King's approach to Dissenters like William Penn in England, Increase Mather went there in early 1688 to petition for the restitution of the charter. In June, Mather had an audience with the King at which he complained about Andros's intolerant treatment of the Puritans in New England. James encouraged him to present their case in a petition, and upon being presented with one in July, he promised to take it into his consideration. When James panicked in September on learning that William of Orange was about to invade England, and started to restore borough charters, Mather anticipated the restoration of that for Massachusetts, too. However, although he had a final audience with the King in October, James had more urgent matters to consider than the reinstatement of a colonial charter. Furthermore, when William III came to the throne, he was not prepared to grant Mather's request either. The charter granted to Massachusetts in

1629 was never restored. Instead, a new charter was issued in 1691 making it a Crown colony. Although the General Court was again to be elected by the freemen, these were no longer restricted to full members of the Congregational Church.

The freemen at large, while they had been opposed to the Dominion of New England, had no more liking for the rule of the saints than they had for that of Andros. They had not participated in the town meetings or the General Court, which were confined to church members. Their suppression therefore did not directly affect them. However, they welcomed the new charter, which allowed them to vote in elections for selectmen and Assemblymen in the General Court, and indirectly for the Council, since it elected the Councillors.

The collapse of the Dominion of New England led to the revival of its constituent colonies, apart from Plymouth which remained an integral part of Massachusetts. There were elections for the Assembly in Connecticut in May 1689, held in accordance with its old charter. The former Rhode Island charter was used by men calling themselves an 'assembly of freemen' to nominate officials when they met on 1 May. And New Hampshire became a separate Crown colony again in 1692.

### New York

When news arrived in New York that the King had fled to France, Lieutenant Governor Francis Nicholson and the Protestants on the Council dismissed Catholic officials and convened a General Convention composed of Justices of the Peace and militia officers. Expecting war to break out with France, which would precipitate an invasion from Canada, they proceeded to fortify New York City. The deputy governor appointed a colonel in the militia as commander of the fort and ordered revenues to be collected to provide for the City's defence. Nicholson's authority to implement these measures aroused objections on the grounds that the King's abdication had dissolved governments appointed by him. The deputy governor's principal critic was Jacob Leisler, who seized control of the fort. His action led Nicholson to set sail for England, leaving a 'committee of safety' in control of the City.

On 10 December a letter arrived from William III directed 'to our trusty and well-beloved Francis Nicholson Esq; our Lieutenant

Governor and Commander in chief of our province of New York ... in his absence to such as for the time being take care for the preservation of the peace and administering the laws in our said province'. Leisler assumed that he was the appropriate addressee and began to style himself Lieutenant Governor. He appointed a council and began to call the committee of safety the General Assembly. This body asserted the right to raise taxes, levying a 3 per cent rate on property. At first, its effective authority was restricted to New York City and adjacent parts of Long Island. Leisler's assumed governorship was not recognised in the upper Hudson valley, where a Convention at Albany led by Robert Livingstone filled the vacuum of power left by Nicholson's departure. The sack of Schenectady by a raiding party of French and Indians in February 1690, however, led Livingstone to leave Albany to seek support from New England. In his absence, Leisler's supporters took over the town which accepted his leadership.

Meanwhile, Nicholson had arrived in England and explained the situation in New York to the King. So far from recognising Leisler as governor, William appointed Henry Sloughter to the post in January 1690. It took several months to organise his transportation to the colony, and when he eventually sailed he ran into a storm which swept him off course and shipwrecked him on Bermuda. Major Richard Ingoldsby, who had set out with Sloughter, made it to New York in January and claimed the colony for the new governor. Leisler, however, refused to recognise his appointment until he arrived with his commission. Ingoldsby attempted to seize the fort from Leisler, and on 17 March an armed clash occurred between men under their rival commands. Two days later Sloughter at last arrived, and Leisler surrendered the fort to him after being presented with his commission as governor. The rebel was promptly arrested and tried for treason. After being found guilty, he was executed on 17 May 1691. The Glorious Revolution in New York was over.

But the debate on its significance began immediately and has continued ever since. The answer has been sought in the complex ethnic, religious and social divisions in New York.

The colony had originally been settled by the Dutch West India Company as New Netherland. It had been conquered by the English and called New York in 1664, recaptured by the Dutch and renamed New Netherland in 1673, and finally acquired by England in 1674.

There are signs of this Anglo–Dutch struggle in Leisler's rebellion. Although he was German by origin, he had married a wealthy Dutch widow. When he took over the fort, he called it New Amsterdam before settling on Fort William, the name it had received during the Dutch reconquest in 1673. Yet to see his uprising against the leadership of the Dominion of New England simply in terms of Dutch Leislerians against English supporters of James II is to exaggerate ethnic considerations at the expense of some important religious and social dimensions. The so-called 'Dutch' of New Netherland were by no means all from the United Provinces. The inhabitants of the colony before the English conquest included Swedes, Finns, Germans, Scots and Irish as well as Dutch, Moreover, those from the Dutch Republic tended to come not from the core maritime provinces of Holland and Zeeland, but from those on the periphery bordering Germany. There was much intermarriage between the various ethnic groups. Jacob Milborne, an Englishman, married Leisler's daughter. He was to be executed along with his father-in-law for his part in the rebellion. The really dominant Dutch elements in the colony – who lived in the upper Hudson valley, where Dutch was spoken well into the next century – as we have seen, resisted Leisler's authority. Although he was a deacon of the Dutch Reformed Church, most of its clergy had upheld the Dominion and opposed his rebellion. There were doctrinal disputes between the 'Arminian' and 'Calvinist' elements in the Church going back to the Synod of Dordrecht in 1618. Strict Calvinists, who insisted that grace alone could save, accused the Arminians of reviving the Catholic notion of salvation by works. Many of the Dutch clergy in the colony were accused of Arminianism by Leisler, a zealous Calvinist. But there was also a social dimension to their disagreements. The Reformed Church was backed by some of the wealthiest Dutch colonists, while Leisler was accused by them of being supported by dramsellers, bakers, bricklayers and carpenters.

What essentially distinguished Leislerians from their opponents were distinct political differences. The government of New Netherland was autocratic. The governors did not summon Assemblies, while the towns were governed by self-perpetuating oligarchies and not by elected councils. The Dutch colonists were quite content with this situation. After all, the United Provinces, though they formed a republic, did not constitute a democracy. Political participation in the Dutch Republic and in its overseas settlements was much more restricted than it was in

England and most of its American colonies. When English colonists moved across Long Island Sound from New England to New Netherland, they showed a much greater drive for self-government, petitioning the governors to allow them to elect town councils.

After the conquest, the Duke of York, himself an autocrat by temperament, sought to perpetuate the Dutch method of government. Again, his Dutch subjects largely acquiesced in this objective. It was the English who put pressure on him to convene a New York Assembly. After the establishment of Pennsylvania, their demands increased, particularly from English merchants who felt that the Quaker colony threatened their livelihoods. They had reason for their fears. The rapid rise of Philadelphia had an immediate adverse effect on New York's economy. In 1676 assessments of property values in the City estimated them at £100,000. By 1685, they were calculated to be worth only £75,000. The competition from Pennsylvanian farm produce caused wheat prices to fall in New York from four to three shillings a bushel between 1680 and 1688. English merchants subscribed to the view that economic growth was promoted by a participatory system of government and was impeded by absolutism. They therefore demanded a constitution as liberal as that in the rival colony, with an Assembly. James, as Duke of York and worried about his own revenues during the economic depression, conceded their demands. When an Assembly eventually met in 1683, it passed a Charter of Liberties and privileges based on Pennsylvania's.

As King, James revoked this concession early in 1687 and the following year absorbed New York into the Dominion of New England. In 1689 those who wanted the Assembly to be restored rallied to Governor Nicholson, who began to purge the administration of Catholics. This was a move in the right direction as far as the English opponents of the Dominion were considered. As *A Letter from A Gentleman of the City of New York* put it: 'there was no need of any Revolution here; there were not ten Jacobites in the whole.' To such men, the events of 1689 simply restored the situation which had existed before the Dominion.

To Leisler and his supporters, however, it restored the situation which had existed during the Dutch reconquest of 1673, when the fort had also changed its name from James to William. The few English supporters of his rebellion had also collaborated with the restored Dutch regime during the 15 months before the English reconquest of the colony. They do not appear to have been concerned to recall either the Assembly or the Charter of Liberties. Leisler notoriously ruled arbitrarily through a committee of safety which became a General Assembly in name only.

The political cleavage in New York created by the rebellion lasted for a decade and more. Anti-Leislerians dominated the colony until 1698. The replacement of Governor Benjamin Fletcher by the Earl of Bellomont in that year, however, transformed the situation. Bellomont openly sympathised with the Leislerians, and presided over the exhumation of Leisler and Milborne and their burial with due ceremony. By then the factions in New York were being compared with English political parties, anti-Leislerians being identified with the tories and Leislerians with whigs. The validity of these parallels was only superficial. But they demonstrate the interaction of English and colonial politics.


AN IMPERIAL REVOLUTION?

This interaction was demonstrated in the Glorious Revolution in America. James II's subjects on both sides of the Atlantic responded to the propaganda that there was a Catholic conspiracy to suppress liberty. Anti-Catholic hysteria swept through the colonies in his reign. It even affected the islands in the West Indies. In Barbados the governor suspected that a Jesuit missionary from Martinique was a French spy who had the King's support. The Duke of Albermarle, Governor of Jamaica, aroused suspicions when he sent Dr Thomas Churchill, a Catholic priest, to England as the colony's agent. It seemed a fitting fate for Albermarle that he died after excessive drinking celebrating the birth of the Prince of Wales in 1688. There was no equivalent in the West Indies of the uprisings in New England, New York and Maryland, but Sir Nathaniel Johnson resigned the governorship of the Leeward islands to Christopher Codrington because he could not accept the Glorious Revolution. He was the only colonial governor to voluntarily quit his post out of loyalty to James II.

Though the Glorious Revolution was welcomed by colonists in America and the West Indies, its fruits were not extended to them. On the contrary, the rights of subjects recognised by the Crown in England were not granted to the colonies. For example, where during the reign of William III the permanence of Parliament was guaranteed, and the independence of the judiciary recognised by the appointment of judges on good behaviour and not at pleasure, as far as America was concerned these were not for export. There was no assurance that Assemblies should meet regularly in Crown colonies, while colonial judges continued to be appointed at the King's pleasure. This was to store up a great deal of trouble for the following century.

# 10 King William's War and Queen Anne's War

The principal reason which drove William of Orange to take the huge gamble of invading England, after the campaigning season had ended, was to get English resources to back his war with Louis XIV. When he succeeded beyond his wildest dreams, obtaining the jackpot of the Crown, he involved England as a major power in the war which had begun in Europe in 1688. Since it ended in 1697, Europeans called it the Nine Years' War. American historians, however, traditionally call it King William's War. The subsequent conflict, known in Europe as the War of the Spanish Succession, is likewise dubbed Queen Anne's War in America. It has been suggested that Americans give them these different names to lay the blame for hostilities squarely on the kings and queens of England, and not on the colonists themselves. Whether the implied criticism is appropriate or not, the labels are, since without the Glorious Revolution, which resulted in the reigns of William and Anne, the colonies would not have become involved in the essentially European conflicts.

## ANGLO–FRENCH RELATIONS

There was, however, friction between New France and English America which had produced conflict even in James II's reign when he enjoyed good relations with the French King. Indeed French territorial ambitions in North America had been a major concern in the formation of the Dominion and Territory of New England. Disputes over rival claims in Hudson's Bay actually escalated into violence in 1686. Commissioners were appointed by both sides to try to resolve the dispute in London. In November 1687 they reached an agreement which established 'that it shall not be lawful for any Governor or Commander in Chief of the colonies, islands, lands and territories belonging to either King's Dominions being in America to commit any act of hostility against or to invade the subjects of the other King'.

The commissioners also discussed disputes arising from French aggression against Indian allies of the English colonists in North America. In 1677 a so-called Covenant Chain had been negotiated at Albany between colonial representatives led by New York and the Iroquois nation. It was essentially a treaty of mutual defence against the French. In 1687 the Governor of Quebec, the Marquis de Denonville, launched a massive attack upon some of the Indians who were party to the treaty, destroying their villages, corn and livestock. The Governor of New York reinforced Albany to deter further French attacks, but this did not placate the Iroquois. The French complained to the English about their arming of the Indians. When the commissioners addressed the situation, they urged the King to 'give them all necessary aid and assistance to oppose the French in case of another invasion'.

There was therefore potential for conflict between England and France in North America in the reign of James II even though he was anxious to avoid hostilities with the French King in Europe. James was not the subordinate ally of Louis XIV which his enemies and subsequent historians have accused him of being. His anxiety to avoid European war was due to his awareness that he lacked sufficient resources to fight one without calling Parliament to vote supplies, which he was determined to avoid.


THE FINANCIAL REVOLUTION

When William of Orange replaced James on the throne, and committed England to war with France, he found that he was completely dependent upon Parliamentary revenues to finance his war against Louis XIV. During his reign this cost an average of £5,000,000 a year, while during that of his successor it cost £7,000,000. By contrast, the taxes voted to his predecessors were calculated to realise only £1,200,000 annually. To raise the unprecedented sums required to fight the wars against the French King meant annual meetings of Parliament to vote them. It also necessitated anticipating them by borrowing. The main tax was on land, the wartime rate being 20 per cent on landed incomes from rents. This was calculated to yield £2,000,000. As soon as the land tax bill received the royal assent, the Treasury arranged to raise a loan of £1,800,000 on its security. To facilitate borrowing a machinery of public credit was set up in the City of London, the lynchpin of which was the Bank of England founded in 1694. The creation of this mechanism has been seen as a financial revolution which brought into being a fiscal-military state.

## KING WILLIAM'S WAR

These developments enabled England to become a great power. It was able to sustain a struggle against France as the leader of an alliance which included the Austrian Empire and the Dutch Republic. William achieved success against James II's bid to regain his throne by way of Ireland when he defeated him at the Battle of the Boyne in 1690. Elsewhere, the war initially did not go well for England. The Irish victory was accompanied by defeat at sea off Beachy Head. It was not until 1692, when the navy obtained the victory at La Hogue over a French fleet, that the danger of an invasion of England could be ruled out. On the Continent the war took the form of a series of sieges rather than of pitched battles. This led to stalemate broken only by occasional successes such as the allied siege of Namur in 1695. By 1697 both sides were sufficiently exhausted to conclude the Treaty of Ryswick, bringing at least a temporary peace.

While the main cockpit was in Europe, William III was well aware of the threat to the American colonies on the mainland from the French to the north in Canada, and to the West Indian islands from Guadeloupe and Martinique. As far as these North American continental colonies were concerned he regretted the dissolution of the Dominion of New England, since like James II he realised its defensive potential. He did what he could to minimise the damage, attempting to get the colonies which had made up the Dominion to cooperate. Benjamin Fletcher, governor of New York, attempted to raise quotas of men from them in 1692 When this failed, he assumed the command of the militia of Connecticut as well as of New York. In 1692 his jurisdiction was extended to Pennsylvania when its proprietor, William Penn, was deprived of the colony because of his association with the deposed James II. Pennsylvania thus became a Crown colony. Fletcher attempted to draw it into the strategic plans for the defence of the colonies against French threats, but ran foul of the pacifism of the ruling Quaker oligarchy. Penn eventually got his colony back in 1694 when he assured William that he was not a Jacobite and offered to provide naval stores for the war effort. He also appointed his Anglican nephew, William Markham, as his deputy to offset the Quaker oligarchs. William's concern for colonial defence led him in 1695 to appoint Fletcher's successor, the Earl of Bellomont, not only as governor of New York, but also of Massachusetts and New Hampshire. The King also kept up the Covenant Chain with the Iroquois.

England's Indian allies in fact struck the first blow against the French in North America, attacking Lachine near Montreal in July 1689. The Comte de Frontenac, Governor of New France, retaliated by launching a three-pronged attack on Albany, and the English settlements on the Kennebec and Merrimack rivers. The attack on Albany was abortive, but when the French fell back on Schenectady they left 60 dead. The attacks on New England terrified those living on the frontier. They provoked New Englanders led by Sir William Phips, to sack Port Royal, the main French port in Acadia, in May 1690. The same year, he planned a more ambitious expedition against Quebec. While Phips went to the capital of New France by sea, up the St Lawrence, forces from New York advanced north to reach the river by way of Lake Champlain. The land attack was driven back. Phips took three weeks to get up the St Lawrence to Quebec, where he bombarded the town and engaged his troops in skirmishes with its defenders. They failed, however, in their main objective, and withdrew to Boston. The Caribbean theatre saw the French seizure of St Kitts from the English in 1689, only for it to be retaken the following year by Christopher Codrington, the commander of the Leeward Islands. His attempt to take Guadeloupe in 1691, however, was unsuccessful. There were hopes of a second onslaught against New France in 1693, when a fleet which had been sent out to the West Indies under the command of Sir Francis Wheeler, sailed north to New England after failing to take Martinique. Military preparations, however, were not sufficient to risk a raid down the St Lawrence, and the fleet attacked St Pierre in Newfoundland instead.

While the remaining years of the war saw stalemate in the West Indies, on the continent the French made significant advances. They took Fort William Henry, which Phips had constructed at Pemaquid in Maine, from the English colonial garrison in 1696. And in 1697 they seized Port York in Hudson's Bay, which they held until the Treaty of Utrecht in 1713. More importantly, they inflicted such blows on England's Indian allies that the Iroquois negotiated a treaty with the French in 1701, whereby they were to be neutral in Queen Anne's War.

## QUEEN ANNE'S WAR

The war is known in Europe as the War of the Spanish Succession because of the problems that arose when the last Habsburg King of Spain, the childless Carlos II, died in 1701. These problems had long been anticipated since Carlos was physically and mentally incapacitated, the victim of his family's inbreeding over many generations. The ruler of a vast Empire, which included not only Spain itself, but the Spanish Netherlands – modern Belgium – much of Italy and all of Sicily, and the colonies in the West Indies and South America, could not masticate his food properly on account of his deformed jawbone. There were two claimants to his extensive dominions: the Austrian branch of the Habsburgs, represented by the Archduke Charles; and the Bourbon dynasty of France, led by Louis XIV, whose grandson, Philip of Anjou, upheld its claim. The prospect of the whole inheritance going intact to either candidate had given European statesmen nightmares for some years, since it would inevitably upset the balance of power and make the favoured state a superpower. Attempts had been made to divide the Spanish Empire between the rival bidders in the late 1690s, but these had all been rendered abortive when Carlos II's will was published, in which he bequeathed the whole of it to Philip of Anjou. Louis XIV, not surprisingly, accepted this on behalf of his grandson, reputedly exclaiming 'now there are no more Pyrenees'. William III, just as predictably, refused to acknowledge the Duke of Anjou as Philip V of Spain and instead recognised the Habsburg candidate as Charles III. William presided over the formation of the Grand Alliance, the principal signatories of which were himself, the Austrian emperor and the Dutch. He died before hostilities commenced in 1702, his place at the head of the allies being taken by John Churchill, shortly to be made Duke of Marlborough by Queen Anne.

   Marlborough was to become one of England's greatest generals, inflicting defeats on the French and their allies at the Battles of Blenheim (1704), Ramillies (1706), Oudenarde (1708) and Malplaquet (1709). The first was a particularly impressive feat since it was on the banks of the Danube hundreds of miles from the allied bases in the Netherlands. Marlborough took an army up the Rhine across the Main and up the Neckar to reach Blenheim in time to intercept an attack on Austria by the French and their ally the Duke of Bavaria. At Ramillies he managed to free the Dutch-speaking areas of the Spanish Netherlands from French rule. These victories were in stark contrast to the stalemate which had characterised much of King William's War. Where he had set England on the road to great power status, Marlborough made sure it arrived there.

His victorious battles contributed to the success of the negotiations between the English and the Scots which concluded in the incorporating Union of 1707. Indeed, had they not been successful he had contingency plans to invade Scotland to impose a settlement on them. For the Union was intended to prevent the northern kingdom playing an independent role in European affairs by not accepting the succession to the Scottish throne of the House of Hanover. By merging the Parliaments of the two countries into one at Westminster, the Union avoided that prospect. It brought into being the United Kingdom of Great Britain and changed the status of the colonies from being part of an English Empire to incorporation in the British Empire.

As far as the American colonies were concerned, the chief difference between Queen Anne's War and the previous conflict was that the Spanish possessions in the New World, which had been aligned with the English in the 1690s, were now claimed by the rival Bourbon and Habsburg candidates to the throne of Spain. Most of Spanish America in the event recognised Louis XIV's grandson Philip V as the rightful ruler. This made the southern theatre of war in many ways more important than the main area of Anglo–French friction established in the previous war, along the borders of New France, New England and New York. Though the northern theatre was strategically important enough to the French for them to establish a fort at Detroit in the Great Lakes in 1701, the new significance of the southern theatre was recognised with their settlement at the mouth of the Mississippi of a new colony, named Louisiana after the King of France. Pierre Le Moyne d'Iberville established a base at Biloxi in 1699, and moved it to Mobile in 1702. His strategy was to use Louisiana as a staging post for raids against English colonies on the American mainland and in the West Indies. D'Iberville was to launch an attack on Nevis from Louisiana in 1706, while the French attacked Charleston. Governor James Moore of South Carolina anticipated this threat from France's new found strength in the Caribbean and Florida by launching a pre-emptive strike against St Augustine in 1702. He easily took the town, but found the citadel, the Castillo de San Marcos, impregnable. A seven weeks' siege was raised when a Spanish fleet from Cuba came to the garrison's assistance. Moore and his men retreated to Charleston over land. He had no better luck in a raid on Pensacola the following year. The English government also appreciated the significance of the French threat in the West Indies when they dispatched a fleet there under Admiral John Benbow. It captured St Kitts in 1702, but failed to take the Spanish treasure fleet in an engagement off Santa Marta. Benbow was killed in the action, and two of his officers were court-martialled and shot for failing to obey his orders. Sir Charles Wager was more successful when he attacked the flotilla in 1708 for, although the main treasure ship sank when its powder magazine exploded, Wager returned home with considerable spoils from the others. In the southern theatre the war went reasonably well for the English, who even mounted an expedition to Mobile in 1709.

In the north, New England at first bore the brunt of the fighting, since the neutrality of the Iroquois gave New York virtual immunity from French attack. Thus, the main incidents occurred in Deerfield in the Connecticut River valley and Haverhill, 30 miles north of Boston. Deerfield was sacked by French troops and their Indian allies in 1704, when 40 colonists were killed and over 100 were taken to Canada. Haverhill was similarly sacked in 1708. Two attempts by New Englanders to take Port Royal on Nova Scotia in 1707 failed miserably. It became clear that without help from Britain, the northern colonies were not able to turn a defensive into an aggressive war. Samuel Vetch realised this when he laid before the Board of Trade a scheme to take Quebec based on Phips's strategy in the previous war. A two-pronged attack by land from New York and by sea up the St Lawrence, this time with massive help from the British Army and the Royal Navy, was approved in 1709. Francis Nicholson, Deputy Governor of New York during the Dominion of New England, and subsequently Governor of Virginia and Maryland, a man of unique colonial and imperial experience, offered his services. He undertook to lead the forces sent overland to Quebec from Albany. To drum up interest in England for the scheme, he also arranged for four Indian sachems to be sent there. When they arrived in 1710, they proved to be extremely popular and generated a great deal of publicity for the cause. Unfortunately, it did not arouse the government's interest sufficiently for it to give priority to the American theatre. A fleet intended to spearhead the invasion of the St Lawrence instead was despatched to Portugal. This happened twice, in 1709 and 1710, demonstrating that the British ministers saw the main conflict as a European concern, In 1710 they sent six warships to Boston which Nicholson and Vetch employed in an attack on Nova Scotia. They took Port Royal, renaming it Annapolis after the Queen.

The change of government in Britain in 1710, when the Whigs lost power to the Tories, led to a change of priorities. The new Tory ministers were determined to run down British commitment to the land war in Europe, which they claimed was ruinously expensive and not in the country's best interests. England was a maritime power, they insisted, and should have made its main contribution to the Grand Alliance at sea rather than on land. This Tory 'blue water' policy, as it was known, gave the proposed attack on Quebec a new lease of life. Henry St John, the incoming secretary of state, threw his weight behind it. His instructions to Robert Hunter, Governor of New York, claimed that the French 'encircle all our plantations on the continent of North America which (if not prevented) they may in time dispossess us thereof and annex the great Empire of North America to the crown of France'. A fleet under the command of Sir Hovenden Walker, with 5000 men led by Brigadier General John Hill, was sent across the Atlantic, landing in Boston in June 1711. Despite difficulties recruiting more men from the colonies, and friction between the British and the Bostonians, the joint attack went ahead. At the end of July, Walker set out for the St Lawrence while Nicholson advanced from Albany. On 21 August the fleet entered the St Lawrence seaway. Walker was unnerved to find it shrouded in fog, and when some of his ships foundered on the north bank with the loss of 850 men, he called off the expedition and sailed for England. Nicholson did not get news of this decision for nearly a month, during which he was advancing up the Champlain valley. When he learned of it he was furious, throwing off his wig and stamping on it. By October he was back in Albany. The Iroquois, who had been persuaded to break their treaty of neutrality with the French to join the expedition, renewed it in 1712.

By then, the original five nations of the Confederacy had become six with the addition of the Tuscaroras, who migrated to the Great

Lakes from North Carolina after defeat in war with European settlers in the southern colony. There had been friction between the Indians and the colonists for some time, but it broke out into open warfare in 1711 when the Tuscaroras objected to a planned Swiss settlement in what was to become New Bern. They put up a fierce resistance to their enemies, employing defensive tactics copied from them, with elaborate forts capable of resisting artillery attacks. North Carolina appealed for help to its neighbours. Virginia supplied provisions but no manpower. South Carolina sent forces under the command first of John Barnwell, then of the veteran John Moore. These eventually suppressed the Tuscaroras. Those that did not join the Iroquois or go to Virginia were granted a reservation in North Carolina in 1713.

The end of the European war in 1713 at the Treaty of Utrecht brought about peace between the British and the French in North America. Philip V was recognised as King of Spain and of the Spanish possessions in the New World, on condition that the Spanish and French crowns should never be worn by the same monarch. The Habsburg claimant refused to recognise him and fought on for another year, but came to terms with reality and accepted the Spanish territories in Italy and the Netherlands in compensation. Britain obtained Gibraltar and Minorca in the Mediterranean. In America the French conveyed their claims to Newfoundland and St Kitts to the British, and also Arcadia, an area whose boundaries were ill-defined but which included Nova Scotia. This became the thirteenth British colony on the North American continent.

# 11 'Salutary Neglect'? British Colonial Policy under the First Two Georges

Edmund Burke used the expression 'salutary neglect' to describe British policy towards its American colonies before the passing of the Stamp Act in 1765. Americans, too, initially reacted to the Act not by campaigning for independence, but by agitating for a return to the situation before it was enacted, when they felt that they had been virtually left alone.

However, when we look back for that alleged golden age, it is not easy to pinpoint. Certainly, as we have seen, the colonies could not be neglected in the wars against France between 1689 and 1713. Thereafter, there was some justification of Burke's expression until war with France broke out again in 1744.

The dynamic approach to colonial affairs initiated by the creation of the Board of Trade in 1696 had largely petered out by the 1720s. The Board's authority had been overridden by other bodies involved in colonial administration. The Admiralty's role had been increased by the necessity to police the Navigation Acts after 1696. During the War of the Spanish Succession the Duke of Marlborough had assumed its function of appointing governors. After the Treaty of Utrecht, appointments did not revert to the Board but were taken over by the Secretaries of State. In 1715 commissioners learned of the appointment of George Vaughan as Governor of New Hampshire from the official government newspaper, *The London Gazette*. They protested that he would be unlikely to protect the King's forestry interests there because of his own financial interest in sawmills. As they observed 'to set a carpenter to preserve woods is like setting a wolf to keep sheep.' The Board recognised its decreasing influence in a major policy document of 1721 which sought to reverse it. Among many bold proposals for a concerted colonial policy, the report advocated that its president should have Cabinet rank, and that competing agencies should be eliminated from interfering in the administration of the colonies. These sweeping recommendations were effectively shelved for a generation. For the Secretary of State for the South appointed in 1724, the Duke of Newcastle, virtually took over the Board's responsibilities, especially for colonial patronage.


## THE DUKE OF NEWCASTLE

Thomas Pelham-Holles, Duke of Newcastle, has not had a good press from historians. Contemporaries rather wrote him off as an amiable buffoon, excessively neurotic and paranoid. Horace Walpole, one of his chief detractors, portrayed him as an eccentric whose phobias made him a laughing stock. Thus, his chronic fear of contracting illness from unaired beds led him to insist that a servant should lie between the sheets to warm them up before he himself retired. These stories extended to his colonial concerns. The novelist Tobias Smollett ridiculed him in *Humphrey Clinker*, wherein he describes a levee of the Duke, who mistakes a supplicant for a colonial governor, and advises him to: 'take care of our good friends of the Five Nations – the Toryrories, the Maccolmacks, the Out of the Ways, the Crickets and the Kickshaws'. He was also alleged to have been unaware that Cape Breton was an island when planning its defence against French attack.

American historians have also found the Duke wanting. They see him presiding over, not so much a system of salutary neglect, as one of scandalous negligence. Thus, James Henretta concluded that 'as Southern Secretary for a quarter of a century, Newcastle failed to make a single positive contribution to the functioning of the colonial system. Not one administrative measure, not a solitary piece of legislation, was connected with his name. His was an era devoid of achievement and vision, a period of culpable mismanagement and negligence which led directly to many of the intractable problems of the next generation.' Newcastle's use of colonial patronage was disastrous. The number of posts in the colonies at the disposal of the secretary was very small; a mere 41 in 1724, rising to about 60 by 1730, largely as a result of the Carolinas becoming Crown colonies. Newcastle used these not to build up support among colonists, but to reward sycophants and careerists in Britain. At one time, no fewer than ten of the places were held by inhabitants of Sussex, an English county which was his power base in Parliamentary elections. Thus, the secretary of New Jersey appointed in 1733 was his electoral agent in the county. An investigation by Stanley Katz into Newcastle's gubernatorial appointments in New York reached a similar conclusion. Those appointed, with hardly an exception, were 'inexperienced, ill-informed, poorly motivated and generally unsuited to hold public office'.

British historians, however, have tended to take a different view of Newcastle ever since he was rehabilitated by Sir Lewis Namier. Namier, one of the twentieth-century's leading authorities on British politics in the Age of the American Revolution, based his view of Newcastle on the Duke's massive archive, which forms the biggest single collection of any minister's papers for the whole eighteenth century. These document a diligence and a range of interests over nearly half a century in public life. They paint a very different picture of Newcastle as a politician than that depicted by his opponents. The Duke emerges from a study of them as a dedicated public servant whose sheer survival at the top of the greasy pole of Hanoverian politics demonstrates that he was not the buffoon of legend. On the contrary, he was a heavyweight figure in the political life of the period. This reassessment of his role in British politics has been extended to his colonial patronage. Newcastle was responsible for the appointment of 22 governors, of whom only four could be ascribed to pressure put upon him to reward undeserving careerists. All agree that the appointment of William Cosby, Governor of New York from 1727 to 1736, who was characterised by 'cupidity and stupidity', was a mistake. Otherwise, 'fitness for the post played a far more important part in the calculations of those concerned than has hitherto been recognised'.

## COLONIAL GOVERNORS AND THE RISE
## OF THE ASSEMBLIES

Some governors complained that the Duke neglected not so much the colonies as themselves. On receiving a letter from Newcastle in 1746 to inform him of his dismissal from the governorship of Barbados, the dismissed governor replied acidly that it was 'the very first from your Grace during an administration of more than four years'. Many also felt that they were not being supported in the struggles they engaged in with colonial Assemblies. Governor Clinton of New York sent Newcastle 'an account of his conduct and justification' in 1747. In it he claimed that 'the opposition he has met with could proceed from nothing but from a design to overturn his Majesty's government by wresting power out of the hands of his officers, and placing it in a popular faction'. Governor Glen of South Carolina observed in 1748 that

> almost all the places of either profit or trust are disposed of by the General Assembly. The Treasurer, the person that receives and pays away all the public money raised for his Majesty is named by them and cannot be displaced but by them... they appoint the commissary, the Indian commissioner, the comptroller of the duties imposed by law upon goods imported... much of the executive part of Government and of the Administration is by various laws lodged in different sets of commissioners. Thus we have commissioners of the market, of the workhouse, of the pilots, of the fortifications, and so on without number... No wonder if a Governor be not clothed with authority when he is stripped naked of power.

The rise of the Assemblies, and the decline of the powers of the governors, which has been seen as a crucial development in the ultimate struggle between the colonies and the mother country, providing a vital pre-requisite for American independence, took place during the period of neglect under the Duke of Newcastle. In 1754 Horace Walpole, the auditor general of plantation revenues since 1717, confessed to the Secretary of State 'as to other monies raised annually by the assemblies for public services I have no cognisance of them, they having long since taken the receipt, examination and audit of them out of the hands of the Crown into their own management, although my office was originally established with a view to have from time to time an account of all the monies raised and expended there'.

## 1713–1744

Even in the years 1713–44, however, there were signs of British concern with the colonies which scarcely demonstrates neglect. The taking over of the proprietary colonies of North and South Carolina by the Crown in 1729, the establishment of the first naval base in colonial America at Antigua, also in 1729, the launching of Georgia in 1732, the passing of the Hat Act in 1732 and the Molasses Act in 1733, and the outbreak of the War of Jenkins' Ear with Spain in 1739, were all provoked by interventionism rather than by indifference.

Parliament intervened in imperial affairs with a series of Acts to regulate trade and piracy. Of 29 such Acts passed between 1714 and 1739, nearly half were put on the statute book in the years 1727–33, which marked an oasis of intensive activity in the comparative desert of neglect. The Hat Act prohibited the export of the popular beaver hats from the colonies, insisting that pelts should be sent to Britain to be used by British hatters. Had it been effectively enforced, it would have had the effect of crippling their manufacture in America. The Molasses Act was a tribute to the pressure which British West Indian interests could exert in London. The owners of plantations in the sugar islands carried more clout in the corridors of power for much of the eighteenth century than did the colonists on the mainland. This was partly due to the fact that many of them were absentee landlords, resident in Britain. They employed stewards to tend their West Indian estates and slaves to cultivate the sugar, and lobbied members of Parliament to safeguard their interests. These were threatened by the production of cheaper sugars on the French islands of Guadeloupe and Martinique. Although trading with the French sugar islands had been banned, this ban had proved ineffective in preventing colonial American merchants, especially from New England, from illegally importing French produced sugar for use in the distillation of rum. Hence the pressure for the Molasses Act. Its aim was to force colonial merchants on the mainland to purchase sugar from British islands rather than from French producers in Guadeloupe and Martinique. In 1731 'the gents of the northern colonies', representing all the seaboard settlements from Nova Scotia to South Carolina, in vain petitioned Parliament to protest against the proposed duties on sugar from sources other than the British West Indies. The Act was passed. Colonial merchants were allowed to trade directly with French producers, but had to pay prohibitively higher duties than on British sugar.

## ANGLO–SPANISH RELATIONS

The main threat in the Caribbean came not from French, but from Spanish possessions. Even after the Treaty of Utrecht there was friction with Spain, which broke out into hostilities in Europe from 1718–20, and again from 1727 to 1728. During the first war, the Royal Navy destroyed a Spanish fleet off Cape Passaro, while an abortive expedition backed by Spain attempted to restore the Stuart Pretender to the British throne. The war spread to America in 1720 when Spain launched an invasion of the Bahamas, which the British repelled. In 1727 the Spanish government challenged Britain's possession of Gibraltar and laid siege to the Rock. Britain retaliated by blockading Spanish ports until peace was agreed in 1728. The intervals of peace in Europe meant little in America, however, where Spanish coastguards constantly intercepted British shipping suspected of illegally trading. Legal trade was defined by the terms of the Treaty of Utrecht, whereby the South Sea Company was permitted to supply slaves to Spanish colonies, and to send one ship a year to Central America. This concession led to many more ships than one sailing annually to the area, to run the gauntlet of coastguards who became increasingly aggressive in their interceptions. It was to prevent this harassment that Britain built up a naval base in Antigua in 1729, while Admiral Hosier made an abortive attack upon Porto Bello, a major Spanish coastguard station on the isthmus of Panama.

Relations with Spain across the Atlantic were thus already strained when in 1732 George II granted a charter for the creation of a colony immediately below South Carolina, on territory which the Spaniards claimed was theirs. The new colony, named Georgia after the King, came about out of concern for the plight of debtors released from prison by an Act of 1729. Philanthropists, led by Thomas Bray, a leading member of the Society for the Propagation of the Gospel, who had been involved in the creation of parishes in Maryland, took up their cause. When Bray died in 1730 James Edward Oglethorpe continued his efforts, and petitioned for the charter, which vested the colony in trustees charged with settling it with 'worthy poor'. Oglethorpe himself took the first group of 114 settlers to the Savannah River in 1733. Spain immediately protested that the colony should be abandoned as it occupied the north of Spanish Florida. By 1736 friction was so intense that Oglethorpe, himself a veteran soldier, planned to lead an expedition to Florida. Tension was eased when the Spaniards acquiesced in the establishment of the colony, changing their objections to questioning its southern border. The British government gave Oglethorpe permission to raise a regiment in England to defend it. The men raised were sent across the Atlantic with three warships, doubling the naval capacity off the coasts of the southern colonies. In 1738 the British Parliament voted £500,000 to pay 10,000 newly recruited sailors.

Although these hostile moves against Spain were popular in Britain, the prime minister, Sir Robert Walpole, was anxious to avoid war, and signed the Convention of the Pardo with Spain in January 1739. The negotiations, however, were undermined by the continuing depredations of the coastguards in the Caribbean, who captured 12 merchant ships between 1737 and 1739. Anger at their seizure was inflamed by the story of one merchant, Jenkins, who claimed to have had an ear sliced off by a Spanish coastguard as long ago as 1731, and to have kept it pickled ever since. From this alleged incident, the ensuing conflict was known as the War of Jenkins' Ear. It began successfully for Britain when Admiral Vernon took Porto Bello in 1739. News of his success led to an outbreak of chauvinistic hysteria in England, where Vernon was feted as a hero. The celebrations were short-lived. Vernon lacked the resources to keep Porto Bello, while an attempt to take Cartagena in 1741 proved a costly failure. As Walpole had caustically predicted in 1739 when forced to declare war by his hawkish Cabinet colleagues: 'they are ringing their bells; they will soon be wringing their hands'.

The war inevitably involved hostilities between Georgia and Florida. Oglethorpe tried to besiege St Augustine in 1741 but was repulsed. The following year, he was able to repel a Spanish attack on his own capital at Frederica. In 1743 the American theatre became a sideshow to the European when George II became embroiled in the War of the Austrian Succession. Since he was the last British monarch to lead his forces into battle, at Dettingen in June 1743, the ensuing conflict truly deserves the name of 'King George's War'.

## KING GEORGE'S WAR

War had begun in Europe when Frederick the Great of Prussia invaded the duchy of Silesia in 1740. The duchy was one of the hereditary territories claimed by the Austrian branch of the Habsburg family, which had been inherited by Maria Theresa. The accession of a woman to the crown of Austria was disputed by other powers, including France, which declared war on her in 1742. The British were allies of the Austrian Habsburgs and tried to prevent their Italian possessions being attacked by Bourbon Spain, but were unsuccessful. They also sent troops to the Austrian Netherlands. Although George II personally engaged the French at Dettingen, it was as an ally of Maria Theresa. War was not formally declared between France and Britain until 1744. For Britain, 1745 proved the crisis year of the war. In Flanders, the young Duke of Cumberland was no match for the wily Marshal Saxe, suffering defeat at the Battle of Fontenoy in May. Although the Austrian Netherlands now lay open to the French, Cumberland was recalled to counter a Jacobite invasion aimed at toppling his father from the throne. Before that rebellion was crushed at Culloden in April 1746, Brussels was in French hands, while Antwerp fell to them shortly afterwards. Cumberland duly returned to Flanders, but was again outsmarted by his old antagonist, Saxe, who defeated him at Roucoux in October. The following year the French beat the allies again at Laufeldt.

Britain's setbacks in Europe had been offset, however, by developments across the Atlantic. There the New Englanders, stung by French attacks from Louisbourg on the fisheries of Nova Scotia in 1744, determined to launch a counter-attack. Massachusetts organised a force led by William Pepperell, who took it to Cape Breton in the Spring of 1745, under the protection of British ships commanded by Peter Warren. While Warren blockaded the harbour of Louisbourg, the New England militia landed and attacked the fort, which surrendered in June. The fall of what was reputed to be an impregnable fortress to New England forces, with financial help from the middle colonies, was extolled as a great American victory. Governor Shirley of Massachusetts was made a colonel, while Pepperell was knighted. The colonists were furious when Louisbourg was returned to the French in 1748 at the peace of Aix la Chapelle.

## 1748–1754

While the period between Queen Anne's War and King George's War might be regarded as an era of 'salutary neglect', the years between the latter and the outbreak of the French and Indian War, or Seven Years' War as it was known in Europe, certainly cannot be. On the contrary, the British ministers were aware of the threat posed to the colonies by the French in North America, and kept up spending on their defence. Between 1740 and 1748 the government had spent an average of £148,000 a year on its American empire. During the interval between the wars it actually rose to £268,000. This significant change of British policy towards the colonies came about with the accession of the Earl of Halifax to the Presidency of the Board of Trade in 1748. He injected a dynamism into the workings of the Board which it had not experienced since the 1720s, making it once more the major agency when dealing with colonial affairs. He persuaded the Duke of Newcastle that the French looked upon the peace as a breathing space and would present a real threat to the British in North America. Newcastle was so impressed by his energy and ability that he persuaded the King to admit the President of the Board of Trade to Cabinet discussions. Halifax's impact can be seen in the renaming of a former French fort in Nova Scotia after him in 1749. Some 4000 men were garrisoned on Halifax at an annual cost of £95,000. It became the principal base for the Royal Navy operating in North American waters. Its strategic importance was so great that Halifax became concerned about the loyalty of its French-speaking inhabitants. To counter their perceived threat he engaged in what would today be called 'ethnic cleansing'. In the mid-1750s he forced over half of the 13,000 French out of Nova Scotia and dispersed them throughout the colonies. Many of them found refuge in Canada or the new French colony of Louisiana. Their place was taken by English-speaking colonists, mainly from New England. Harsh though this policy undoubtedly was, the government justified it on the grounds that the original colonists of Nova Scotia presented a security threat to the British at a time when war had actually broken out with the French in North America.

# 12    The French and Indian War

Where the conflict in Europe between 1756 and 1763 is called the Seven Years' War, in America it is known as the French and Indian War. Chronologically, it makes sense to distinguish it from the European conflict, since it began in North America in 1754. Its imperial dimension has led some historians to call it 'the Great War for Empire'.

## ANGLO–FRENCH RELATIONS IN NORTH AMERICA

It was clear that the Treaty of Aix la Chapelle of 1748 was merely a breathing space until Britain and France recovered their strength for a renewal of conflict. Although the inhabitants of New France were vastly outnumbered by those of the British colonies in North America, there was a genuine fear that the French were preparing to sweep their rivals into the sea. They were supplied with military and naval *matériel* from France, which they used to equip a series of forts from Quebec and Montreal across to the Ohio River valley and down the Mississippi to Louisiana. They massively fortified Louisbourg on Cape Breton when they got it back at the peace, rebuilt Fort St Jean near Lake Champlain, constructed Fort Rouille on the site of the later city of Toronto, and established four forts linking Lake Erie to the confluence of the Allegheny and Monongahela Rivers with the Ohio. On the location of the present Pittsburgh, they built Fort Duquesne.

The whole of the Ohio region was disputed between France and Britain; contemporary French and British maps show it as belonging to each. In 1744 representatives of the colonies of Pennsylvania and Virginia, both of them claiming that the region was within their boundaries, along with others from Maryland negotiated the Treaty of Lancaster with the Iroquois, who largely occupied the Ohio valley.

As far as the colonists were concerned the Indians ceded the right to settle there. The Ohio Company had then been formed in 1747 to exploit this terrain, and in 1749 had been granted 200,000 acres by the British Crown in the vicinity of Fort Duquesne. The French could not ignore this threat to their imperial claims, and sent an expedition to enforce them, which planted lead plates at intervals proclaiming 'the renewal of the possession that we have taken of the said River Ohio'.

## THE ALBANY CONGRESS, 1754

Faced with the challenge from the French, the British government took the unprecedented step of convening a congress of representatives from the mainland colonies at Albany in 1754. The immediate issue before them was the threat of the Mohawks to withdraw from the Covenant Chain, a serious problem given the deteriorating relations with New France. For the Mohawks had been the most friendly of the Iroquois confederacy, the only one of the six nations to fight for them in King George's War. Although the Congress is remembered for its remarkable Plan of Union, in fact its proceedings were marked more by disunity. The plan was a scheme of Benjamin Franklin's to organise the colonies into a union for mutual defence. All those on the mainland, except Nova Scotia and Georgia, were to be represented in a council which would coordinate defence and relations with the Indians. The King was to appoint a presiding officer. Although the Congress adopted it, the colonies represented in it could not even agree on measures to be taken immediately. Thus, a proposal put forward by New York to pay for forts along its northern border was effectively vetoed by the New England colonies. The Plan for Union failed to be ratified by a single colony, while the British government gave no support to it.

## HOSTILITIES BEGIN

Before the Congress met, in April 1754 the French took a British fort on the site where they were to build Duquesne. The first shots had been fired in the war for North America. Within a month the Virginia militia, commanded by George Washington, marched into the region, known as the Great Meadows. There, on 28 May, they inflicted a defeat followed by a massacre of French forces by Indians allied to the Virginians. They then hastily constructed a fort to defend themselves against French reprisals, which they called Necessity. Washington used Fort Necessity as a base from which to advance towards Duquesne, but was driven back by French forces and their Indian allies. On 3 July he was forced to surrender.

This confirmed the British government's view that American forces were not up to the task of fending off French encroachments. 'All North America will be lost', the Duke of Newcastle gloomily predicted, unless French aggression was checked by regular forces. Two battalions, commanded by Major General Edward Braddock, were sent across the Atlantic in 1755 to avenge the defeat of the Virginia militiamen. On arrival in America they set out to Fort Cumberland in Maryland, slowly but without much difficulty. From there the passage to Fort Duquesne was impeded by thick forests, through which Braddock's men had to cut a broad swathe to allow their wagons and supplies through. Progress was slowed down to a crawl. It took from 30 May to 9 July to trek from Fort Cumberland to the Monongahela river, within eight miles of Fort Duquesne. There, they ran into an ambush of French troops and their Indian allies. The surprise led to confusion and panic, especially when the hostile Indians let out war whoops which terrified the British. This fatal reaction to unnerving yells had been a feature of the rout at Prestonpans in the '45 Rebellion, when Highlanders in the Jacobite army emitted similar cries. At least the defeated redcoats had been able to flee the Scottish battlefield. In the dense woodland of the Monongahela there was no convenient exit, and in the ensuing confusion 977 of the 1459 British troops were killed, including Braddock himself. It was not only a total defeat, but a humiliating disaster for the prestige of the regulars, who had previously looked down on the colonial militiamen as their inferiors. The arbitrary and arrogant demeanour of the British had generated resentment among the colonists. It has been argued that this, coupled with the disgraceful evidence that they were not invincible, gave rise to sentiments which ultimately fostered feelings of American independence.

Yet, though negative attitudes towards each other characterised relations between the British and colonial Americans, they were largely confined to the opening stages of the conflict, which went badly for Great Britain in North America. When the tide of war turned, culminating in the great victories of the 'glorious year' of

1759, these were transformed into positive euphoria that both were mutually engaged in a glorious enterprise, a 'great war for empire'.

## INITIAL SETBACKS

The immediate consequences of Braddock's defeat, however, were anything but glorious for the British and their American colonies. His defeated army retreated all the way to Philadelphia, exposing the western frontier settlements of Pennsylvania to the mercies of the Indians. Previously, the province had managed to sustain the friendly relations with native North Americans established by its founder, William Penn. Although these had been strained by such developments as the notorious 'walking purchase' of 1737, open hostilities had been avoided. Now the territory west of the Susquehanna experienced savage warfare in which settlements were sacked and their inhabitants scalped and raped. Many fled east before the Indian advance. They appealed to the Assembly for help, but the dominant Quaker majority would do little beyond voting money for the frontiersmen to purchase weapons to defend themselves. It was to take a coup of non-pacifist Assemblymen in 1756 to oust the pacifists from power before Pennsylvania made official efforts to defend itself.

Meanwhile, the French had taken almost everything before them. In the days before Braddock's defeat, the British had made confident plans to break the stranglehold of forts which New France had erected on their frontiers. While Braddock took Fort Duquesne, William Shirley was to advance from Albany to take Niagara, where Braddock was to join him. Another force was to seize Crown Point on the southern end of Lake George, and yet another was instructed to attack two French forts on the borders of Nova Scotia. In the event the only one of these ambitious designs to be realised was the last, when two French forts that threatened the British colony, Beausejour and Gaspereau, were taken from them in June 1755. Beausejour was renamed Cumberland after the Duke, who was the Commander in Chief in Britain. Otherwise the campaigns in the northeast failed to achieve their objectives. Shirley only got as far as Oswego, miles from Niagara. The attack on Crown Point was initially successful, but the fortification of Ticonderoga by the French persuaded Colonel William Johnson, who led the expedition, to retreat to the bottom end of Lake George, where he built Fort William Henry.

## WAR IN EUROPE

All these military actions between the British and the French had taken place in North America while Britain and France were at peace in Europe. Despite this, two new commanders were sent out in 1756 to continue the conflict across the Atlantic, the Marquis de Montcalm to New France and the Earl of Loudoun to New York. By the time Loudoun arrived in July with two battalions of regular troops, however, war had been declared between the two European powers. The official declaration of war between Britain and France occurred against the backdrop of the so-called 'Diplomatic Revolution', which had transformed Europe's political landscape. In an effort to protect George II's electorate of Hanover, Britain constructed a defensive alliance with Prussia; her erstwhile ally Austria now courted France to aid her schemes to recover Silesia from Frederick II. Actual hostilities broke out in May 1756 when the French seized Minorca from the British. This opening disaster in the Mediterranean Sea was followed by a defeat at Oswego on Lake Ontario. Montcalm had made the capture of the forts there a military priority, and invested it with 3000 men in August. After a brief siege the defenders surrendered. Montcalm offered the prisoners safe conduct to Montreal, but could not prevent Indians in his ranks from killing many of his prisoners.

The disasters of Minorca and Oswego led to the collapse of the government of the Duke of Newcastle, who had presided over them. Among his sternest critics was William Pitt, who had acquired a formidable reputation as an opposition spokesman in the House of Commons. Newcastle had been inclined to buy him off, but the King, who detested Pitt, would not hear of it. Now he had to promote him to the post of Secretary of State, while his ally the Duke of Devonshire became first lord of the Treasury. The Pitt-Devonshire ministry proved short-lived, since it patently lacked the backing of George II, while Newcastle had a considerable contingent of Members of Parliament in the Commons to harass the new ministry. In April 1757, it was forced to resign. Three months of haggling followed before the obvious solution, the formation of a ministry jointly headed by

Pitt and Newcastle, was adopted. The Pitt-Newcastle ministry was to infuse a determination to win the war which ultimately led to the 'wonderful year' of 1759.

Before that, however, there were further humiliations to bear. In 1757 the Duke of Cumberland was defeated by a French army at Hastenbeck in July, while in North America Fort William Henry, at the southern end of Lake George, was captured by a Franco-Indian force in August. As at Oswego, Montcalm's assurances of safe conduct for his prisoners were completely ignored by his Indian allies, who proceeded to massacre them, an incident which forms the central episode in James Fenimore Cooper's *The Last of the Mohicans*. A British soldier stationed in Boston thought they would all have been 'murdered had they not saved themselves by flight, though under the protection of the French – in short the French hold us so cheap there is nothing they dare not do'. In 1758 the British again lost a major engagement with the French in North America. This took place in July at Ticonderoga at the head of Lake George. General James Abercromby, who had replaced Loudoun as commander, led 15,000 men there to attack the French Fort Carillon, where Montcalm had about 3500 men to defend it. But they inflicted such heavy casualties on the attackers, leaving 2000 dead or wounded, that Abercomby felt obliged to order a retreat.

## RECOVERY IN NORTH AMERICA

While this shameful defeat was a major blow to the prestige of British arms, elsewhere in North America the tide had turned in Britain's favour. On 26 July 1758, Louisbourg on Cape Breton island was taken. This was the culmination of a joint military and naval enterprise, the soldiers being commanded by General Jeffery Amherst and the sailors by Admiral Edward Boscawen. A month later John Bradstreet, with 3000 men picked from Abercromby's defeated army, made a daring raid on Fort Frontenac on the eastern end of Lake Ontario. The strategically situated fort fell easily into Bradstreet's hands. Knowing he could not defend it against forces sent from Montreal to retake it, after stripping it of all valuable stores he demolished it, and thus deprived the French of a vital link in their chain of forts. The year ended with the fall of Fort Duquesne to Brigadier General John Forbes. Forbes made his way there slowly and systematically, cutting a road west from Carlisle, Pennsylvania, to the Forks of the Ohio. When he got there on 24 November, he found the fort demolished and the site abandoned. Deprived of enough Indian allies to resist the approaching army, the commander had decided to abandon the fort. Forbes arranged for another to be built at the Forks, which was to be called Fort Pitt, later to become Pittsburgh.

## 1759: 'THIS WONDERFUL YEAR'

William Pitt, the prime minister who was acknowledged in the newly named fort, planned the invasion of Canada for the campaign of 1759. To effect it, he replaced Abercromby as commander in North America with Jeffery Amherst. Amherst was instructed to invade through Crown Point and Lake Champlain. Pitt also appointed James Wolfe to a separate command, instructing him to launch an attack on the French from Cape Breton up the St Lawrence River. While they were preparing these operations, a presage of the 'wonderful year' ahead was presented with the capture of the French sugar island of Guadeloupe by an expeditionary force under Major General Peregrine Hopson. Hopson initially landed his forces on Martinique, but hastily withdrew them when he appreciated the formidable natural defences they had to overcome. He then successfully invaded Guadeloupe in February, but succumbed to fever along with many of his men. Major General John Barrington, who replaced him as commander, captured the whole island by the end of April. In July, Fort Niagara was taken by the British, aided for the first time in the eighteenth century by Indians from all six of the Iroquois nations. This cut off the forts constructed to the west from Lake Ontario, leading to their abandonment. The western frontier of New France had thus effectively been moved away from the Ohio valley to the head of the St Lawrence River. Its southern frontier was pushed up to Lake Champlain with the capture of Fort Carillon, which the British called Ticonderoga, by Amherst in July and of Crown Point in August. Then, in September its eastern frontier collapsed with the taking of Quebec. On 13 September General Wolfe, who earned eternal fame by dying in the moment of victory, engaged Montcalm, who was also killed that day, in a pitched field battle, a rare event in North America before that. The discipline of Wolfe's forces prevailed over the mixture of French veterans, inexperienced militiamen and Indians who faced them. On 18 September, the ensuing siege of Quebec ended with the capitulation of the garrison. The taking of Quebec had been as much a naval as a military feat. Wolfe's men were escorted up the St Lawrence by a fleet of 49 ships. The 'annus mirabilis' of 1759 was celebrated in a sea shanty which contained the lines 'come cheer up my lads 'tis to glory we steer, to add something more to this wonderful year'. It ended on 20 November, appropriately with a great victory by the British navy over the French at Quiberon Bay.

The victories in America led Pitt to sound out whether or not the French were ready to discuss terms of peace. But though they had also been worsted in Africa, where they had lost Fort Louis on the Senegal River, and in India, they were still dominant enough in Europe to reject his overtures. For while Prince Ferdinand of Brunswick-Wolfenbuttel had led the Hanoverian army to victory at Minden in August, Frederick II had been defeated at Kunersdorf and had to surrender Dresden and most of Saxony to the Austrians. The war would continue for at least another year.

## THE FRENCH DEFEAT IN NORTH AMERICA

Pitt therefore gave priority to the total defeat of the French in Canada, instructing Amherst to take Montreal. The General undertook to do so with a three-pronged attack. He would lead a force from Oswego east down the St Lawrence. Another army would march north from Crown Point. And a third would advance on Montreal from Quebec. These men were not only British redcoats, but were also recruited from the colonies. As in previous years, most of the colonies raised a quota of men. Before 1758 their quotas had been assessed by the British commanding officer, and the Assemblies had been required not only to recruit them, but to raise taxes to supply a common treasury for their pay. They had been reluctant to accede to such demands, viewing them as arbitrary and a breach of their liberties. This had caused friction between the Assemblies and Generals Braddock and Loudoun. But Pitt had then given instructions that the Assemblies were to fix and pay their own quotas, most of the expenses to be reimbursed by Parliament. As a result they had raised and paid for more than had previously been required of them. This change in the way the colonies co-operated with the British Army created a feeling of their being involved as partners rather than as subordinates and this, together with the change from defeats to victories, had brought about euphoria for the empire among Americans. Thus, in 1760 the colonies from New Jersey northwards raised nearly 14,500 men to fight alongside the 20,000 regulars in the common cause.

The French attempted a pre-emptive strike by sending all the men they could muster, some 7000, from Montreal to try to retake Quebec. The British under Brigadier General James Murray advanced to meet them at Sainte-Foy on 28 April, but were forced back into the city. Fortunately, the arrival of ships of the Royal Navy on 12 May forced the French to retreat. Otherwise, as a British officer acknowledged, the French 'would again have had a supremacy in America'. While the ships made their way upriver to Montreal, the other two prongs of the assault on the city were also under way. The force that moved north from Crown Point took the French fort at Ile-aux-Noix, the last barrier between it and its target, late in August. Amherst had also to take Fort Levis before he could advance from the west down the St Lawrence to arrive in the vicinity of Montreal early in September. Faced with inevitable defeat, the French governor Vaudreuil surrendered on 9 September. New France became a colony of Great Britain.

Although the acquisition of Montreal virtually placed most of North America in British hands, until the peace terms were thrashed out Amherst could not take its absorption into the empire for granted. In 1761 the French island of Martinique was acquired, and there was talk in the run up to the Treaty of Paris of exchanging Canada for this and Guadeloupe. It is yet another measure of the imperial priority assigned to the sugar producing islands of the West Indies that such an exchange should be seriously considered even after the annexation of Newfoundland in 1762. When Spain entered the war that year on the side of France, a British expedition was sent under the Earl of Albermarle to Cuba. The veteran troops, most of whom had served in North America, besieged and took Havana between 8 June and 13 August. The cost in lives, however, was horrific. A total of 5366 died at the siege of Havana, about 40 per cent of the total British force there. Of these 4708 died not from wounds, but from disease.

## THE PEACE OF PARIS, 1763

When peace was agreed in 1763 it was on the basis of restoring Guadeloupe and Martinique to France and Cuba to Spain. The British retained all their conquests from the French in North America, leaving only those west of the Mississippi to France. Spain gave Florida to Britain in exchange for Cuba, and the French granted Louisiana to Spain by way of compensation. Spain suffered the last humiliation of the war when a British fleet took Manila in the Philippines in October 1763. Although it was restored to Spain in 1764 it was not before booty estimated at £1,300,000 had been seized there. The capture of Manila has been described as 'the crowning accomplishment of Britain's most glorious war'.

# PART IV

# The Imperial Crisis

# 13 British America at the Accession of George III

The growth of a collective consciousness of being American was greatly advanced by involvement in the imperial wars of the mid-eighteenth century. Before the reign of George II, the colonists seem to have considered themselves as Virginians or New Yorkers rather than being Americans. As we have seen, the different regions of the eastern seaboard produced very different societies under the Stuarts. Cultural ties bound them more to the mother country than to each other. Under the Hanoverians, however, the trans-Atlantic bonds were complemented by intercolonial links. The wars led Britain to cajole them into intercolonial cooperation. But other developments brought about a sense of American identity by the time of the accession of George III.

## THE GREAT AWAKENING

Perhaps the most significant was the religious phenomenon known as 'the Great Awakening'. There had been revivals before the 1740s, but they had been largely confined to specific regions such as New England. Contemporaries noted that this was an intercolonial experience which swept the land from Georgia to Maine. It began in New England and the Middle Colonies in the early 1730s. In Northampton, Massachusetts, the Congregationalist minister, Jonathan Edwards, described how hundreds of sinners were brought to repentance by his sermons warning them of the wrath to come. Prominent among revivalists in the middle colonies were the Tennents. William Tennent senior had emigrated to Pennsylvania in 1718 and established Log College at Neshaminy in 1725 to train Presbyterian ministers. Among them were his three sons, who became pastors in New Jersey: William junior at Freehold; John at Hopewell; and Gilbert at New Brunswick. Gilbert Tennent preached a sermon at Perth Amboy in

1735 inveighing against sinners just as vehemently as Edwards, denouncing 'drunkards, swearers, whoremongers, adulterers, sabbath breakers, thieves' who 'storm Hell, and endeavour to take damnation by violence out of the hands of the Devil'. Jonathan Dickinson pastor at Elizabeth-Town, New Jersey, published *A Display of God's Special Grace in the conviction and conversion of sinners so remarkable of late begun and going on in these American parts* in 1742. 'He must be a stranger in Israel', the Preface claimed, 'who has not heard of the uncommon religious appearances in the several parts of this land among persons of all ages and characters.' What swept up the revivals in different regions of the colonies into an American experience was the evangelising mission of George Whitefield. He arrived in 1739 from England, where he had been a prominent member of the Methodists associated with John Wesley. They had quarrelled, however, over the issues of predestination and free will. Whitefield was a strict Calvinist, who believed that only the unmerited grace of God could effect salvation, and that was confined to the elect. Wesley, by contrast, was an Arminian who held that Christ died for all men, and that they could merit salvation through good works. While Wesley reaped a rich harvest in England, leaving only the gleanings for Whitefield, the latter found a much more congenial soil for his beliefs in the colonies. For the Great Awakening there stressed a return to strict Calvinism and denounced Arminianism. The 'New Lights' among the Congregationalists and the 'New Sides' among the Presbyterians insisted that they were preaching the pure doctrine of Calvin, which they claimed had been diluted by 'Old Light' and 'Old Side' preachers.

From his arrival on 31 October 1739 at the start of his first tour, until his departure on 10 December at the end of his third, Whitefield engaged in a barnstorming mission which took him through the 13 colonies from New Hampshire to Georgia. He preached 169 public sermons. Their message was that, unless men experienced the reception of God's grace like a new birth, they would not be saved but damned to the eternal tortures of hell fire. Everywhere he went he attracted huge crowds and prominent notice in the colonial press. 'This celebrated itinerant preacher, when he visited America, drew the attention of all classes of people', observed Isaiah Thomas, 'The blaze of his ministration was extended through the continent.' In some ways Whitefield can be considered as the first American.

By the time he returned to America in 1745, the Great Awakening had passed its peak. Its role in uniting Americans nevertheless continued to inspire Americans in their zeal to defeat the French, who as Catholics, or 'papists' as the Protestants called them, were depicted as 'the whore of Babylon' and 'anti-Christ' in revivalist rhetoric. The capture of Louisbourg was seen by Nathaniel Ames as a triumph of American arms over 'superstitious Papists bold and base'. The French and Indian War similarly was upheld as a Protestant Crusade. And some historians have even seen Britain replacing France as the devil incarnate once the French were expelled from North America. Thus, the depiction of the Quebec Act of 1774 as a sinister plot to extend popery at the expense of Protestantism has been represented as a product of the Great Awakening.

This is, however to take its unifying effects too far. As well as uniting Americans, the Awakening also divided them. As we have seen, it polarised Congregationalists into Old and New Lights and Presbyterians into Old and New Sides. Between these were moderates, known in New England as 'Regular Lights'. The nature of these divisions has been variously explained. Perry Miller, the great authority on New England Puritanism, saw tensions between traditional societies increasingly confined to the frontiers and more secular communities emerging along the seaboard behind the Awakening. As he put it: 'the Great Awakening was the point at which the wilderness took over the task of defining the Puritan errand.' Certainly, in Massachusetts it was much more a feature of the Connecticut River valley in the west of the colony than of the Bay. In Virginia, too, where the revival had less impact against the established Anglican Church, it made some inroads in the piedmont county of Hanover rather than in the tidewater. Perhaps a more convincing explanation of why it was less prominent in the south than in New England or the Middle colonies, however, is that the landed elite were afraid of the appeal the revival might have to the slaves in their midst. A study of the Baptists in Virginia during the central decades of the eighteenth century concluded that they made conversions among socially inferior groups, including servants and slaves. One magistrate actually accused Baptist preachers of 'carrying on a mutiny against the authority of the land'. An investigation of the Awakening in the towns of Boston, New York and Philadelphia also saw it as dividing their inhabitants along class lines. The revivalists appealed largely to the lower orders, tradesmen, craftsmen and the labouring poor, and were accused by their critics of being levellers.


## URBAN SOCIETY

Boston, New York and Philadelphia, along with Newport, Rhode Island and Charleston, South Carolina, all had several thousand inhabitants by 1760. Philadelphia, with a population of 18,000, was the largest city in North America. As elsewhere in the colonies, the rich were getting richer and the poor were getting poorer. From the evidence of inventories, it emerges that the distribution of wealth in Boston and Philadelphia changed for the worse between 1684 and 1699 and again between 1756 and 1765. In the first period the top 4 per cent owned 25.9 per cent of personal wealth in Boston and 21.7 per cent in Philadelphia, while by the second period they commanded 46.4 per cent and 55.8 per cent respectively. Meanwhile, the share of the poorest 30 per cent in both cities had declined from 3.3 per cent to 2.0 per cent in Boston and from 4.5 per cent to 1 per cent in Philadelphia. Average annual expenditure on poor relief in the major cities over the century also indicates a substantial increase in the numbers of paupers. From the 1700s to the 1750s, it rose from £173 to £1204 in Boston, and from £119 to £1803 in Philadelphia, while in New York it increased from £259 in the second decade of the century to £1667 by the seventh.

Even in their leisure activities, cities seem to have become more class conscious as the eighteenth century progressed. Thus, in Philadelphia taverns were frequented by all classes of men during the early 1700s, but by the accession of George III there were distinct establishments which catered exclusively for the elite, such as the City Tavern. The proliferation of taverns and coffee houses gave colonial towns amenities which had become commonplace in British urban life for a century. Another feature that they shared was the press. Most cities in Britain had their own newspapers, while some had two or even three, and London several more. Similarly, Boston, New York, Philadelphia, Williamsburg and Charleston published their own papers, Boston boasting no fewer than four. Possibly, a higher proportion of the population was able to read the outpourings of the press in New England than in old England. Prior to 1800, generally, people were more literate than their more southern neighbours, whose population makeup constituted large numbers of single indentured female servants. By 1760, New England's literacy rate was 70 per cent among men and 45 per cent amongst the female population. The south saw a lower rate of between 50 per cent and 60 per cent for men and 40 per cent among women. In Britain literacy varied greatly, both geographically and socially. By and large, urban areas were more literate than rural. While the upper classes were almost entirely literate, illiteracy was widespread among the lower orders. Initially, colonial newspapers reported mainly British and European news, but, increasingly, they carried reports of events, such as religious revivals, throughout the colonies, helping to forge the intercolonial bonds which supplemented those which bound the empire together. The creation of these public spaces on both sides of the Atlantic also gave them common ground. The Boston of 1760 had more in common with contemporary Bristol in England than with Winthrop's 'city upon a hill'. A visitor to Philadelphia in the 1740s overtly compared it with Newcastle upon Tyne, finding many similarities. The Reverend William Slatter observed in the middle of the eighteenth century that 'when contemplating the towns ... and the sensible inhabitants, living in the same manner, enjoying the same culture, pursuing the same business, and differing but little from Europeans, I could scarcely realise that I was in reality in a different quarter of the world.'

## RURAL AMERICA

Town dwellers, however, formed but a fraction, around 5 per cent of the total population of the colonies, which numbered over one and a half millions by 1760. And although the towns continued to grow, they did so less rapidly than the rural areas, so that of the estimated two and a half million colonists on the eve of the War of American Independence perhaps only 4 per cent lived in towns. Typically, white American colonists lived in small communities scattered throughout the countryside and engaged in rural pursuits such as farming and fishing.

In rural America, too, there are signs that society was becoming more like the mother country than it had been in the seventeenth century. In New England the mean age at marriage, which had been significantly lower, moved upwards towards the norm in Britain. Family sizes accordingly adjusted downwards to come into line too.

In the Chesapeake the gender imbalance, which had marked much of the previous century, evened out. During the early years of settlement in Virginia, the gender ratio was three males to one female. Even as late at 1700, the balance was still in favour of women by three to two. While New England did not experience as great an imbalance as its southern neighbour, nevertheless they were still the minority. It was not until 1720 that the ratio between the sexes became more even throughout the colonies.

## WOMEN

The gender imbalance had served to give women more scope for advancement in the colonies than in England during the seventeenth century, which has been seen as a golden age for colonial wives seeking to improve their status through marriage. This view has been effectively challenged, however, on the grounds that the relative scarcity of women merely led to them marrying younger than their sisters in the mother country. It did not lead to their being treated more equally in their economic activities or in their legal status. As in England, women were formally excluded from political life, being denied the vote. This did not prevent some from campaigning for male candidates at elections, as the wives of two prominent planters did in Georgia in 1768. Most women, however, played little part in politics.

Religion afforded opportunities for some women to participate in the public sphere. It has been estimated that after 1680, women constituted between 55 per cent and 70 per cent of most colonial congregations. This gave them collective clout when it came to such issues as discipline and hiring ministers. However, membership had its limits. The outcome of Anne Hutchinson's activities was a salient lesson in the perils of becoming too publically involved in the male-dominated Church of New England. The more liberal atmosphere of the Baptists and Quakers in the middle colonies and the south allowed women equal participation in terms of voting and speaking on issues such as improper preaching. Quaker women, in particular, had much more freedom in self-determination, at least in the religious sphere, than in other religious organisations. But although Quaker women carried clout in decisions over marriage and religious passports, they were circumscribed from joining in the wider political sphere that their male counterparts engaged in. In general, though, the essential decision-making bodies from the offices of ministers, wardens, elders, treasurers and the like were held by men. Even so, religion was one sphere where women could contribute and still fulfil expectations of female piety, humility and charity.

The experience of women was not uniform throughout the colonies, for there were significant geographic and ethnic differences in the degrees of equality among the sexes in colonial America. While the southern and northern colonies exhibited to a large degree common ethnic and religious characteristics, the multicultural makeup of the middle colonies affected the status of women in them. Before the English take over of the New York area, Dutch law allowed much more equality between the sexes. Women could invest, sell and contract debt over property. Their status did not necessarily change with marriage. They were not, as English law implied, materially dependent upon the husband and therefore less under his control.

Urbanisation contributed to women's expanding roles as well. This was more obvious in the northern colonies where the principal cities were located, in which business prospects for women opened up. Thus Boston, New York and Philadelphia provided public spheres of employment to a greater extent than in the rural areas, especially among the lower ranks in society. By 1760, however, the evening out of the gender ratio to that which existed in England meant that colonial women no longer had the advantage over their sisters in the mother country. For example, in Britain, woman's primary role was to be a dutiful wife and daughter, fruitful mother and efficient homemaker. The conditions in British North America only allowed for modification of these requisites and only operated within the patriarchal framework. The family was the centre of social and economic life, especially in the country. And at the head of the family was the husband, who demanded obedience. Wives, children, servants and slaves were subordinate to him. Only through remaining single, becoming widowed, or being legally separated could women exert some control over their lives. Even then, employment opportunities for single women were severely limited, being confined to school teaching, shop keeping, or selling skills on the labour market. These were mainly available in urban areas. Most women, however, married, and remarried if they became widows. As wives they were expected to bear and raise children. Any education they received was normally to train them to supervise the household if they were upper class, or to run it if they were middle or lower class. However, women's domestic roles were not just given to sewing and rearing offspring, they were a decisive factor in domestic decision making. They were often seen as partners to their spouses, who left them to manage their affairs while they were away from home. Throughout rural America, women worked alongside men on the farms. In the south, plantation life accorded an elevated status to upper-class women. There race reinforced gender stereotypes. The sanctity of white womanhood, which was to become an ideology in the next century, was not unknown in the colonial south.

In the southern colonies by the mid-eighteenth century, the status of African American women, both free and enslaved, had changed. A succession of laws made it increasingly obvious that they were constrained not only by gender, but by race as well. In 1672, free blacks were forbidden to purchase white labour. 1691 saw the intro- duction of laws which further segregated social interaction such as interracial marriages. A 1705 law disallowed blacks from testifying in court or holding any public office. While this last law did not affect the black female because she had already been restricted by her gender, it did set her apart in terms of race. Nevertheless, race was always a factor to some degree. The case of Mary Johnson, a free black, is an example of the racial undercurrent even before 1672. When the family farm on the Eastern Shore of Virginia was devastated by fire, Mary's husband petitioned the Northampton county court that she and their daughter be released from taxation. Although they were free, according to a 1643 Virginia law African women were labelled as 'tithables' which meant that they were liable to be taxed. Their white counterparts were not included under this law. Thus, a distinction based upon race emerged which helped to facilitate the legal institutionalisation of slavery.

While the slave community became more cohesive as the plantation system in the south grew, the role of the female was relegated to more menial work than that of the male slave. For instance, where women worked in the fields with the men, with the increased use of the plough, only male slaves were taught how to operate them in order to plough the fields. Women, on the other hand, were not taught any such skills, and remained using the hoe to clear away debris from the land in order to prepare it for ploughing. In gender terms, women were considered the weaker sex, intellectually and emotionally. With the institutionalisation of slavery and race, slave women were regarded not only as lawful possessions, but as lustful sex objects which many white slave owners openly used as concubines, giving rise to a whole separate class of mulattos. The slave codes ensured that the children of enslaved women took their mother's status, thereby safeguarding the white father's property rights in his offspring by them. Nevertheless, the self-contained plantation gave slaves the opportunity to have more stable relationships with partners and offspring.

The urban areas of the north afforded slaves more scope for independence. Unlike the southern colonies, which mainly used the old or very young female slaves in the house, slave women in northern cities were more inclined to be employed in domestic service. However, they lacked the reinforcement of fellow Africans that plantation life afforded. This is because slave holdings were too few and too small to encourage families. So while northern slaves were employed in relatively less gruelling work, their livelihoods were less secure.

## ANGLICISATION

From many points of view, by the 1760s colonial society was tending to become more like that of Britain than it had been a century before. In one important respect, however, given the geographic origins of those who migrated to America, it was becoming less like the mother country.

Although those that took the lead in the dispute with Britain stressed that their forefathers came from the British isles, or even from England, in fact they were more cosmopolitan than that. 'Europe, and not England, is the parent country of America', insisted Thomas Paine, 'not one-third of the inhabitants even of [Pennsylvania] are of English descent.' Paine had a point, though as usual he exaggerated by choosing Pennsylvania for his example, as that was the most polyglot of all the colonies. There had been Dutch and Swedes there before the English arrived. By the 1760s only 19.5 per cent of those of European extraction were English, while 33.5 per cent were German and the rest came from Ireland, Scotland or Wales. Elsewhere, those of English stock were more prominent. In this respect New England deserved its name since perhaps as much as 75 per cent of the white inhabitants were of English origin. In other regions of North America, however, they formed a minority.

Yet the Founding fathers stressed their rights as Englishmen and that these had been undermined by the British government. They felt that they shared an English culture, and there is evidence of the Anglicisation of America as the eighteenth century wore on. Consumer goods, denounced as 'baubles from Britain', flowed into all the colonies from over the Atlantic, the flow increasing to a flood as the colonists prospered and could afford an increasing range of imports. Not only such manufactures as clothing, cooking utensils, cutlery, furniture, tools and other necessities, but luxuries like books, engravings and paintings filled the rooms and decorated the walls of the wealthy landowners, and even of the business and professional classes. The houses of the southern planters, like the Byrds's Westover and the Washingtons's Mount Vernon in Virginia emulated the mansions of the country gentlemen in England. Their occupants read English literature, including conduct books like the Letters of Lord Chesterfield in order to acquire the veneer of aristocratic manners. But the merchants too had their substantial houses and also read the conduct books, adapting those written for a more genteel readership to bourgeois lifestyles. The upper and middle classes of the colonies became more and more English in their patterns of consumption and codes of behaviour after about 1720.

## THE WEST INDIES

The most English of all colonists, however, were the white populations of the Caribbean islands. The elites who dominated them copied the lifestyles of the aristocracy of the mother country. Their houses were mansions devoted to conspicuous consumption of luxuries for which they had become infamous. Luxurious living was somewhat curtailed in the second quarter of the eighteenth century when sugar prices slumped and profits were reduced. Some returned to England. Others adopted a less extravagant lifestyle, although their standard of living was still conspicuously greater than their counterparts in the mainland southern colonies.

Their Englishness extended to their religious observations. Although visitors were shocked by their indifference to spiritual concerns, accusing them of atheism, they paid outward conformity to the Church of England. The Anglican Church had a virtual monopoly in the West Indies throughout the colonial period and beyond. There were

Dissenters from it, such as Scottish Presbyterians and Quakers, but they did not succeed in establishing themselves as separate sects for worship as they did in the mainland colonies. There were no signs of the Great Awakening which affected the continental colonies. This was despite – or perhaps even because – there was more toleration in the West Indies, where Jewish communities established themselves in Barbados, Jamaica and Nevis.

Many of the white elite had received their own education in Britain and sent their children to be educated there. Nearly one-fifth of the members of the Assemblies of Antigua, Barbados, St Kitts and Jamaica attended Universities in Britain or the Inns of Court in London in the years 1763 to 1783. Between 1753 and 1776, 148 West Indians attended Eton College and 37 went to Harrow, compared with only 22 and two respectively from the 13 colonies which broke with Britain.

Below the elite there were too few whites to form a distinct middle class. Unlike the mother country or the mainland colonies, which witnessed the emergence of middle classes during the colonial period, the experience in the islands saw the reverse, as small landholdings were absorbed into the larger plantations. George Washington noted that the inhabitants of Barbados were 'either very rich or very poor', there being 'few who may be called middling people'. Yet Barbados had a greater proportion of small estates than in the other islands. The great divide in the Caribbean was not between classes, but between races. Whites were outnumbered by blacks nearly ten to one, which distinguished them even from South Carolina, the continental colony with which they had most in common.

## BLACK AMERICANS

By the accession of George III probably 20 per cent of the population on the mainland were blacks, most of them slaves. Their distribution throughout the colonies was very uneven. In New England less than 4 per cent of the population were of African origin. In the middle colonies the ratio rose to about 7 per cent. In the upper south it was around 40 per cent and in the lower south nearer 60 per cent. Indeed it was over 60 per cent in South Carolina, which made that colony the closest on the mainland to the sugar islands of the West Indies, which all had a majority of blacks.

By 1760, there was a distinct black hierarchy. Where most blacks in the seventeenth century were field hands, during the eighteenth century more and more were employed as domestic servants or in skilled trades. The domestics and tradesmen had generally been born in the colonies and spoke English. They tended to look down on the newly acquired slave labourers, especially those imported directly from Africa, whose unintelligible speech they dubbed 'Gullah'. Where the new arrivals sought to escape their enslavement by fleeing in groups, which was almost inevitably bound to end in capture, slaves employed by their masters in the household or in workshops were more inclined to run away individually. Those who did so might hope to find refuge among free blacks. There had been free blacks in the south in the seventeenth century, notably on the eastern shore of the Chesapeake Bay. Some had owned land and even their own slaves. But these had died out by the eighteenth century, when most free blacks were to be found in the towns employed in urban trades. Since urbanisation was more advanced in the north than in the south, this again distinguished the two regions. The differences between the north and the south caused by the 'peculiar institution' of slavery, which were to emerge very quickly after Independence, were firmly entrenched by the end of the colonial period.

## FRONTIER FRICTIONS

Yet the regional contrast which had most impact on the 1760s was not that between north and south, but the tension between the settled areas of the eastern seaboard and the unsettled conditions in the back country. In 1764 the Paxton Boys protested against the poor protection they received in the Susquehanna valley against Indian raids from the authorities in Philadelphia. They took the law into their own hands, lynched Indians who had been taken into Lancaster gaol for their own safety, and threatened to march on the colonial capital.

Even more serious were the regulator movements in the Carolinas. The regulators in South Carolina had much in common with the Paxton Boys. They complained that the authorities in Charleston had no regard for the security of settlers in the back country who were exposed to attacks from Indians. On the contrary, in the eyes of frontiersmen they were more inclined to appease the natives than to defend their fellow countrymen. In this respect the violence in Pennsylvania and South Carolina was similar to that experienced in Virginia in Bacon's rebellion when the settled communities of the tidewater were accused of ignoring the concerns of the settlers on the frontier. All three movements demanded that the colonial governments paid more attention to the plight of the back country.

## THE NORTH CAROLINA REGULATORS

The regulation in North Carolina was very different, protesting that the authorities were making too heavy demands on the new settlers in the piedmont in the form of taxes and fees. In the spring of 1767, Governor Tryon of North Carolina left the colony's capital at New Bern to travel 300 miles or so into the interior, visiting what was the frontier in order to survey a boundary line between the colonists and the Cherokee Indians. Reporting on his visit to the Secretary of State in England he observed: 'I found on those hilly or back settlements a race of people sightly, active and laborious, and loyal subjects to his Majesty.' The following April he received a letter from Edmund Fanning, judge of the superior court in Orange county, informing him that 'the people are now in every part of the county meeting conspiring and confederating by solemn oath and open violence to refuse the payment of taxes and to prevent the execution of law.' Tryon was astonished. 'Is it possible that the same men, who I received with so much pride and happiness last year', he asked, 'should now be loaded with the opprobious titles of insurgents and violators of the public peace?'

The answer was that the piedmont counties had indeed erupted into violence. About a hundred men armed with clubs and other weapons had gone to Hillsborough, the capital of Orange county, to recover a horse taken from one of them by the sheriff in lieu of taxes. Others had taken over the court-house in Salisbury in nearby Rowan county. There Fanning had been assaulted, run out of town and his house destroyed. These men, calling themselves regulators, belonged to an association which had been formed the previous January. In their articles of association, 'for regulating public grievances and abuses of power', they had undertaken to pay no fees or taxes beyond what was legally allowed. Fanning tried to restore order to the back country by arresting their ringleaders, Herman Husband

and William Butler. They were kept in custody awaiting trial from May to September. Meanwhile, the governor again visited the area, this time to raise a militia to protect the court-house from regulators who threatened to disrupt the proceedings. At the trial, Husband was acquitted, while Butler was fined £50 and sentenced to six months in prison. Tryon subsequently pardoned him and two others fined with him. The regulators got off lightly, while Fanning was found guilty of taking excessive fees.

This outcome of the immediate crisis postponed a violent resolution of it for two years. In 1769 it was channelled into the legitimate arena of the elections for the North Carolina Assembly. While there were cross-currents to the movement, it was predominantly a dispute between the settled areas of the east and the highly unstable back country. The tidewater was settled mainly by colonists from England, while the interior was filled up by Ulstermen and Germans. The east was characterised by large farms with slave labour, the back country by small family farms. The long settled areas were predominantly Anglican, while the piedmont counties were populated by Presbyterians, Lutherans, Baptists, Moravians and Quakers. These religious divisions underlay the ideological friction between the Assembly and the regulators. But above all, the old counties were well represented in the Assembly while the new counties were poorly represented. Five of the eastern counties returned five Assemblymen apiece. The newer ones had two. As counties were carved out of the interior, the eastern counties were subdivided to keep them preponderant. To this insult of under representation was added the injury that taxes extorted from the west seemed to be lining corrupt pockets in the east. This grievance was symbolised in 1766 when the Assembly voted funds for the erection of a governor's mansion which was inevitably nicknamed 'Tryon's palace'. It was the perception that the over-represented counties of the east were using their majority on the Assembly to fleece the back country with taxes and fees that was the fundamental cause of the regulator movement in North Carolina. Regulator candidates did well in the piedmont counties.

Unfortunately for them, the prospect of making headway through the Assembly was thwarted by the clash between it and the governor over the issues raised by the Townshend duties. The session was abruptly ended when Tryon disapproved of the resolution passed by the Assembly against the British government. In the next elections held in March 1770, the regulators lost ground.

Frustrated in their hopes of achieving their ends at the polls, they turned again to direct action. Throughout 1770 it was almost impossible to raise taxes or sue for debts in the affected counties, while in September there occurred the most violent demonstration to date, again involving the court-house in Hillsborough. When the next session of the Assembly opened in December, the governor asked it 'to provide for the raising of a sufficient body of men to march into the settlements of those insurgents in order to aid and protect the magistrates and civil officers'. Hearing that regulators were on the march from the back country to the capital, the Assembly voted £500 for the raising of armed forces to suppress the insurgents. They also passed a Riot Act which included a draconian clause whereby anyone indicted for riot who did not surrender within 60 days to stand trial was declared to be guilty, and could be lawfully killed and their lands forfeit to the King 'for the use of government'. The Privy Council in London was aghast when they received the Act containing this clause, declaring it to be 'irreconcilable with the principles of the constitution, full of danger in its operation and unfit for any part of the British Empire'. Such savage measures stiffened regulator resistance. They declared Fanning an outlaw to be killed on sight and threatened to kill all lawyers. Tryon then went to Orange county at the head of over 1000 men, where he encountered a force of regulators which he claimed numbered 2000, at Alamance Creek, a few miles west of Hillsborough. There, on 16 May 1771, the Battle of the Alamance was fought, in which the regulators were routed. The episode of the North Carolina regulation had been brought to a bloody end.

On the site of the battlefield today there stands a monument claiming it as the first armed conflict in the War of American Independence. It perpetuates a romantic view which saw the regulators as heroes fighting for their rights against the tyranny of British officials represented by Governor Tryon. This is historical nonsense. In reality, the reverse was true. When the war came, the regulators were either neutral or even loyal to the King. The officers in the armed forces raised to crush them were future revolutionary leaders of North Carolina.

Several strands made up the regulator movement. One was class conflict, pitching poor frontier farmers against lawyers, officials and merchants who they saw as fleecing them. Another was religious, opposing the largely Anglican establishment of the east to Ulster

Presbyterians, Quakers and other Protestant sects in the back country. What wove them together was an ideology which accused the government of employing corruption and military force to undermine liberty.

This political philosophy was borrowed from the arguments developed by critics of the Whig ministries constructed by the Hanoverians in Britain, and especially the administration of Sir Robert Walpole, who was prime minister from 1720–42, the longest serving premier in British history. His opponents accused him of perpetuating his rule by using public money to bribe members of both Houses of Parliament in order to create a corrupt majority. They also criticised him for maintaining a standing army in time of peace to use as an internal police force. Such methods had destroyed liberty in ancient Rome, with which parallels were constantly drawn in opposition propaganda. Outstanding among Walpole's critics were John Trenchard and Thomas Gordon, who developed this ideology in a series of articles they titled *Cato's Letters*. Bound together in four volumes in 1724, these went through many editions in the eighteenth century, being published not only in England but also in the colonies. They provided the main texts of the ideological origins of the American Revolution, informing critics of the imperial regime throughout North America. When, following the accession of George III, a ministry came to power pledged to raise taxes in the colonies to pay the salaries of imperial officials, and the wages of soldiers kept on foot to police America, the worst scenario portrayed in this opposition ideology seemed to be realised.

# 14 Adjustment to Empire, 1763–1770

The euphoria that attended the successes in the French and Indian War seems in retrospect to have evaporated remarkably quickly. Shortly after the signing of the Peace of Paris in 1763 friction arose between the colonies and the mother country which some see as the start of a sequence of events which culminated in the Declaration of Independence.

## INEVITABLE INDEPENDENCE?

Hindsight has led historians to look for the origins of the quarrel between the Americans and the British in the years before the accession of George III. Nor is it entirely with the benefit of hindsight that a case can be made for seeing the seeds of rebellion in the previous reign. Peter Kalm, a Swedish visitor to the colonies in the 1740s, claimed to 'have been told by Englishmen, and not only by such as were born in America but also by those who came from Europe, that the English colonies in North America in the space of thirty or fifty years would be able to form a state by themselves entirely independent of Old England'. Others predicted that if the French threat were to be removed, then the colonists would no longer need Britain for protection. Such predictions appear to document that independence was, as one observer put it, 'in the womb of time'.

Yet other observers protested that the idea was not widely held before the 1770s. 'No part of his Majesty's dominions contained a greater proportion of faithful subjects than the thirteen colonies', protested Joseph Galloway, referring to the Seven Years' War against France, 'The idea of disloyalty at this time scarcely existed in America.' As late as 1774, Benjamin Franklin maintained that he had represented 'the people of America as fond of Britain, concerned for its interests and its glory, and without the least desire of a separation from it'. Although Thomas Paine asserted that he never met anybody on either side of the Atlantic who had not been of the opinion 'that a separation between the two countries would take place', he qualified it by adding 'one time or another'. His qualification is a corrective to the theory that the two sides in the War of American Independence were on a collision course long before it broke out. While the notion that the colonies would break away from the mother country one day might have become a commonplace, the rupture was always placed some way off in the future. George Grenville's political opponents blamed him for bringing on 'a crisis twenty or possibly fifty years sooner than was necessary'.

## THE GRENVILLE PROGRAMME

George Grenville was prime minister of Great Britain from April 1763 to July 1765. He had emerged from the political upheaval which attended the accession of George III, when the new King had determined to nominate his own ministers and replace those whom his grandfather had relied on. Pitt had resigned in 1761 in protest when George interfered with his running of the war, and had thereafter criticised the moves towards peace as a disgraceful selling short of the great victories he had presided over. The Duke of Newcastle had been dismissed in 1762. George turned to his tutor, the Earl of Bute, to replace them at the head of the ministry. Bute, however, a timid man, could not face the barrage of opposition he received over his conduct of the peace negotiations. Some of the criticism amounted to crude xenophobia, since he was vilified for being a Scot. When he resigned rather than continue to be subjected to abuse, George promoted Grenville, who was made of sterner stuff.

Grenville has been credited with a 'programme' for dealing with the colonies. One of his ministerial colleagues was Lord Halifax, who had been president of the Board of Trade. Grenville was presumably aware of his plans to reassert the authority of the Crown over the colonists. These had been shelved for the duration of the war, and could now be implemented. Whether his measures deserve the name of 'programme' is, however, debatable. They can be seen not as the implementation of long-delayed policies so much as reactions to post-war conditions. One of the most important decisions, to retain 7500 troops in North America, was taken before Grenville became prime minister. These were mostly stationed in the newly acquired colonies in Canada and Ohio.

The Royal Proclamation of October 1763 was another response to the acquisition of vast territories from the French. It is chiefly remembered for its limitation of westward expansion to the crest of the Appalachian mountains. Since settlers had already poured over them and down into the Ohio River valley this was bound to produce resentment in the colonies. It was intended to appease the Indians who were in turn resentful and apprehensive of encroachment on their territory. Their apprehensions found expression in the so-called 'Pontiac Uprising', in which Indians fought against British expansion in the Detroit area during the years 1763–65. The Proclamation also made provision for the creation of four new colonies from the territories taken from France; one in Quebec, two in Florida and the fourth, Grenada, in the West Indies. 'That our loving subjects should be informed of our paternal care for the security of the liberties and properties of those who are, and shall become inhabitants thereof', the king proclaimed, 'we have given express power and direction to our governors of our said colonies, respectively, that so soon as the state and circumstances of the said will admit thereof, they shall . . . summon and call general assemblies. . . .'

Parliament did not appear to demonstrate the same concern for the liberty and property of the colonists when it passed the Sugar Act of 1764. The preamble stated that 'it was just and necessary that a revenue be raised [in the colonies] for defraying the expenses of defending, protecting and securing the same.' The Act thereby directly linked the cost of maintaining troops in North America to taxing the colonies so that they bore part of the burden. Though it increased the tax on sugar imported into North America from five shillings per hundredweight to one pound seven shillings, it actually halved the duties levied on foreign molasses by the Molasses Act of 1733, from sixpence a gallon to threepence. But where previously there had been massive evasion, now the intention to collect them was made clear with the establishment of a vice-admiralty court at Halifax to try violators. At the new rate the duty was expected to raise £78,000, compared with the total cost of maintaining forces in North America, which was estimated at £384,000 a year, most of which would still fall on the British taxpayer. Grenville clearly thought this was an eminently fair demand, and Parliament agreed for there was no opposition to the measure in either House.

There were, however, protests in America. Some West Indians objected to the reduced duties on molasses, which meant that prices became even less competitive with that produced by the French. They also found the administrative and judicial measures adopted to enforce the Act irksome. But on the whole, they benefited from the legislation, particularly from the prohibition of the importation of foreign rum into North America, which gave them a legal monopoly of the most lucrative trade. Objections to the Act came principally from those colonies in the north which needed molasses for the distilling of rum. Complaints were made in Massachusetts, Rhode Island and New York against the burden of the duties. Although some also voiced objections to Britain's right to tax them on principle, these were relatively muted since Parliament had passed legislation imposing duties on colonial goods for well over a century, though the object had been to regulate trade rather than to raise revenue. Moreover, since customs duties were external or indirect taxes, they did not fall directly on individuals.

## THE STAMP ACT

This was not the case with the stamp duty which Grenville proposed to place on a wide range of colonial documents, including conveyances, contracts, newspapers, pamphlets, playing cards and wills. Few would escape this tax, which hit hardest journalists and lawyers, the most articulate and vociferous professional men in the colonies. Any evasion of it would be tried in vice-admiralty courts to be set up in Boston, Philadelphia and Charleston in addition to that at Halifax. Together with the molasses duty, it was expected to contribute one-third of the cost of the army in North America, for which all revenues raised by the two measures were earmarked. When in March 1764 Grenville announced his intention to impose the stamp duty the following year, he indicated that he was prepared to consider alternative proposals from the colonies. As Thomas Penn wrote from London to James Hamilton in Philadelphia on 9 March 1764: 'it is proposed also to lay a stamp duty on the colonies and islands, as is done here, in order to defray all expences of troops necessary for their defence; we have endeavoured to get this last postponed, as it is an internal tax, and wait till some sort of consent to it be given by the several Assemblies, to prevent a tax of that nature from being laid without the consent of the colonies.' None were forthcoming, though there were plenty of criticisms of the scheme. These simply stiffened the prime minister's determination to pass the Stamp Act, which was effected between February and March 1765. Again there were hardly any objections to it in Parliament, though a few Members did raise some, including Isaac Barré, who called the colonists 'Sons of Liberty'. Even he did not question Parliament's right to tax the colonies.

Many colonists questioned it, however, the lead being taken by the Lower House of the Virginia Assembly. Patrick Henry persuaded it to pass four resolutions which upheld the notion that there should be no taxation without representation. He failed to persuade the Assemblymen to pass a further three denying that the British Parliament had any jurisdiction in Virginia. All seven of his 'Virginia Resolves', as they were known, were nevertheless published in the newspapers as though they had been passed. This inspired other colonies to follow the lead given by Henry and nine sent delegates to a Stamp Act Congress in New York. On 19 October the Congress adopted 14 resolutions. The third asserted: 'that it is inseparably essential to the freedom of a people, and the undoubted right of Englishmen, that no taxes should be imposed on them, but with their own consent, given personally, or by their representatives'. The fifth proclaimed: 'that no taxes ever have been, or can be constitutionally imposed on them, but by their respective legislatures'.

The fourth resolution of the Stamp Act Congress maintained: 'that the people of these colonies are not, and from their local circumstances, cannot be represented in the House of Commons of Great Britain'. This was a response to Grenville's claim in the Commons that, though the colonists were not actually represented there, they were virtually. Virtual representation nowadays seems to be a dubious doctrine. But in the days before democracy it made some sense. Fewer than a quarter of adult males had the right to vote in Britain, as Grenville pointed out. Notions of representation were not based on numbers but on interests. Thus, the House of Commons was said to represent the landed interest, the monied interest, the trading interest and so on. Those members who sat for London and other large ports such as Bristol and Liverpool were held to represent the interests not only of their constituents, but of other places engaged in overseas trade, such as Whitehaven, which did not send representatives to Parliament. Those Americans who complained that they were not virtually represented could scarcely do so on democratic grounds. For though the right to vote for the Lower Houses of Assembly in the colonies was more extensive than it was for the House of Commons, it was nevertheless restricted to property owners. The concept was not challenged in principle, but only in practice. For all practical purposes, those members of Parliament who represented the interests of merchants involved in the colonial trade could only virtually represent those resident in Britain. American merchants did not enjoy a harmony of interests with them, but on the contrary were often in competition with them. Therefore the concept of virtual representation was not a fiction; it was merely inapplicable to the circumstances of the colonists.

Other demonstrations of dissatisfaction with the Stamp Act were less refined. In August a Boston mob attacked Andrew Oliver, who was suspected of being the designated distributor of stamps in Massachusetts. They hanged him in effigy and destroyed his house, forcing him to flee for his life and resign the post. Two weeks later it was the turn of the lieutenant governor of the colony, Thomas Hutchinson, to have his house gutted. There were even riots on the West Indian islands of St Kitts and Nevis, although Barbados and Jamaica on the whole accepted the duty, despite it being higher in the West Indies than on the mainland. These violent episodes led other distributors throughout the colonies to resign rather than face the same treatment. While these activities effectively nullified the Act, what its opponents sought was its repeal. To exert pressure on the British government in order to effect this, therefore, merchants in New York began to boycott British goods. Their non-importation agreement was followed by others in Boston and Philadelphia.

## THE REPEAL OF THE STAMP ACT

By the time these initiatives got under way, the government in Britain had changed. In July 1765, George III dismissed Grenville not on account of his handling of the colonial crisis, but for personal reasons. He replaced him as prime minister with the Marquis of Rockingham, who had taken over from the Duke of Newcastle as leader of the 'Old Corps' Whigs whom the King had removed after his accession. Rockingham, like Newcastle, had not been responsible for the Act and could therefore propose its repeal without appearing to be inconsistent. Yet it would have to be repealed by the same House of Commons that passed it, for there had been no general election since 1761. Ministries in the eighteenth century were formed by the king and not usually as the result of a changing Parliamentary majority brought about at the polls. One of the features of the rapid changes of ministry after the accession of George III was that between 1761 and 1768, when the next election was held, they had to deal with the same Members of Parliament. To persuade them to perform what would now be called a U-turn required considerable managerial skill. Rockingham accomplished it by simultaneously passing a Declaratory Act which asserted that Parliament had the right to legislate for the colonies 'in all cases whatsoever'. This was Parliament's riposte to the resolutions of the Stamp Act Congress. It enabled members to yield in practice to the crisis caused by the Act without yielding in principle. Nevertheless, the proposal ran into opposition. Grenville opposed it, protesting that the repeal of his Act would reward violence in the colonies. William Pitt, while accepting that Parliament could legislate for the colonies, denied that it could tax them, a distinction lost on most members.

## THE TOWNSHEND DUTIES

In July 1766 George III made another change of ministry, replacing Rockingham with Pitt, whom he had elevated to the peerage as Earl of Chatham. Chatham's manic depressive tendencies, however, became acute during his premiership, and he was often unable to do more than preside over measures which were in reality initiated by other ministers. This was particularly the case in his administration's dealings with the American colonies. The repeal of the Stamp Act meant that the contribution to the armed forces in North America it was expected to yield never materialised. Nor did that of the Sugar Act, for though it remained on the statute book it raised a mere £5200 in 1764 and £4090 in 1765. The shortfall led the Chatham ministry to seek to increase colonial contributions to the burden of maintaining a military presence in America by enforcing billeting and increasing taxes. Both provoked hostile responses in America.

The Quartering Act of 1765 had provided for soldiers to be billeted in licensed premises if there were not sufficient accommodation in barracks, and in uninhabited buildings should there not be enough beds in inns, taverns and alehouses. It also laid down that they should be provided with 'fire, candles, vinegar, and salt, bedding utensils for dressing their victuals, and small beer or cider, not exceeding five pints, or half a pint of rum mixed with a quart of water, to each man, *without paying anything for the same'*. Those who supplied the provisions were to be reimbursed not by the army, but by the colonial Assemblies. This provisioning clause proved to be a source of grievance as colonists claimed that it was a backdoor tax, one that was particularly unfair since the army was not stationed in every colony, its presence being principally felt in New York. In May 1766 the Assembly there refused to supply the provisions specified in the Act. General Gage, the commanding officer, complained to the government. The Cabinet instructed the governor to require the Assembly to conform to the law. The assembly defiantly refused to vote any money for provisions. In Chatham's absence the Cabinet, on a suggestion of the Chancellor of the Exchequer, Charles Townshend, agreed to bring in legislation to suspend the New York Assembly until it had complied with the Quartering Act. The Assembly gave in before an Act was passed.

Townshend was also responsible for the American Import Duties Act of 1767 aimed at 'further defraying the expenses of defending, protecting and securing' the colonies. 'Champagne Charlie', as he was known for a brilliant Parliamentary speech delivered under its influence, was well versed in colonial affairs. He had served as a commissioner of the Board of Trade under Lord Halifax, and had later become president himself. His experience led him to agree with the view of his political mentor, Chatham, that the colonies were right to resist direct taxation, but had reluctantly accepted the validity of indirect or external taxes. He amended the Sugar Act, reducing the duty to a penny a gallon, but extending it to British as well as to foreign molasses. It thus became avowedly a revenue raising measure rather than one protecting the interests of the West India planters. He also introduced a revenue bill placing customs duties on such items as tea, glass, lead, paper and painters' colours, predicting that it would raise £40,000. This money was to be used to pay the salaries of governors and other royal officials in the colonies, making them financially independent of the Assemblies. Another Act established an American Board of Customs in Boston. Having completed a system of colonial administration suggested by Halifax and only partially implemented by Grenville, Townshend unexpectedly died at the age of 42. By then, too, Chatham was a spent force, and his premiership was assumed by the Duke of Grafton. He and his Cabinet colleagues were left to face the consequences.

They did not have to wait long. In December, John Dickinson published the first of 12 *Letters from an American Farmer*. These were reprinted in newspapers throughout the colonies. Dickinson admitted that Parliament could regulate colonial trade, but denied that it could tax the colonies. The debate had gone beyond distinctions between internal and external taxes to the issue of sovereignty. The prevailing British view was that it lay with the king in Parliament. The counter-claim of the Crown had been eliminated in the Glorious Revolution. Although theories of popular sovereignty survived 1688, and were even to be revived in the reign of George III, they did not command enough support to challenge the dominant view. This was that the king in Parliament was the sovereign power which could not be lawfully resisted. They had supreme authority over all British subjects, whether they were resident in Britain or in her American colonies.

Colonists opposed to taxation without representation objected to this assertion. They claimed that the colonies owed their origin to the authority of the Crown in the seventeenth century and were still subject to it and not to Parliament. The Stuarts had granted colonial charters, giving colonists the right to have representative Assemblies and to pass laws which were not contrary to English law. This proviso indicated that the laws of England did not automatically apply to the colonies. While the independent power of the king might have been merged with that of Parliament in the Revolution Settlement as far as England, and after 1707 Scotland, was concerned, this transfer had not included the colonies too, which continued to be under the Crown. Dickinson advised the colonists to petition the King to redress the grievances they had against Parliament. A similar attitude was adopted by the Massachusetts legislature which not only petitioned the King, but sent a circular letter to other colonial Assemblies, desiring them to harmonise their responses to the duties. The letter, drawn up by Samuel Adams, proclaimed that they were 'infringements upon their natural and constitutional rights'. The appeal to the laws of nature as well as to the liberties of Englishmen was to become a cornerstone of American arguments against the actions of the British government.

The British government's response to this defiant letter was the responsibility of the Earl of Hillsborough, who had just been appointed to the newly created post of Secretary of State for the Colonies. In April 1768 he wrote to the governors of all the colonies to urge their Assemblies to take no notice of 'this flagitious attempt to disturb the public'. If they did countenance it, they should be immediately dissolved. Anticipating trouble in Massachusetts, Hillsborough also ordered General Gage to send a regiment to Boston 'to give every legal assistance to the civil magistrate in the preservation of public peace'. Before they arrived there in October, the town meeting passed a series of resolutions objecting not only to arbitrary taxation, but also to standing armies in time of peace. The meeting then appointed James Otis, Thomas Cushing, Sam Adams and John Hancock to 'a committee in convention' to meet with delegates from other towns in Faneuil Hall on 22 September. When Parliament discussed this and other developments in Massachusetts the following February, it condemned the convention as a design 'to set up a new and unconstitutional authority independent of the Crown of Great Britain'.

The two Houses also denounced all denials of its own sovereignty over the colonies as 'illegal, unconstitutional and derogatory of the rights of the Crown and Parliament of Great Britain'. Assemblies in the colonies responded by repudiating the sovereignty of Parliament, but respecting that of the king. They claimed in effect that there were two constitutions within the dominions of the British monarchs. One applied to the United Kingdom of Great Britain, and embodied the sovereignty of the king in Parliament. The other pertained to the remaining dependencies and concerned the Crown alone. A major exception to this appears to have been Ireland. For although there was a separate Irish Parliament, a British Statute of 1720, the Declaratory Act, asserted the right of the Parliament of Great Britain to legislate for Ireland 'in all cases whatsoever'. This was a precedent for the Declaratory Act of 1766, which declared Parliamentary authority to legislate for the American colonies. Yet, as defenders of Irish and colonial independence of British legislation pointed out, this claim of theoretical sovereignty over Ireland was never used in practice to raise revenues there. The attempt to do so in America was a violation of what has been dubbed 'the imperial constitution'. The Americans had a point when they appealed to George III against the claims of Parliament. British politicians were apprehensive of this approach since the doctrine of Parliamentary sovereignty had been developed to counter the claims of the Crown. They were afraid that the influence of the Crown was still a threat to the liberties of Parliament. Were the King to succumb to American overtures, they feared that it would result in a significant increase in his influence. Fortunately for them, George III sided with Parliament.

The colonists followed up their theoretical claims with the non-importation strategy which had been effective in their campaign for the repeal of the Stamp Act. Against the Townshend duties, however, it was rather less so. Although merchants in Boston and New York did their best to impose it, those in Philadelphia were less enthusiastic than they had been previously. It has been suggested that the Stamp Act boycott was more determined because a post-war recession in the colonies left merchants with warehouses packed with goods which they could not sell. An embargo therefore made economic as well as political sense. By 1768 the colonial economy had picked up, not least through the continued presence of troops. Demand therefore exceeded supply, rendering non-importation unattractive economically. Whatever the reason, the agreements were ended when the British government repealed all the Townshend duties except that on tea.

## THE REPEAL OF THE TOWNSHEND DUTIES

The repeal came about as a result of yet another change of government. Lord North replaced Grafton as prime minister in 1770. The instability which had marked the rapid changes of ministries during the 1760s now came to an end. North's ministry was to last until 1782, when the news of the defeat of British troops at Yorktown led to its collapse and set in train a process which led to the peace of Versailles in 1783, whereby the British government recognised the independence of the United States of America.

Until he fell from power North sought to impose the doctrine of the sovereignty of the king in Parliament on the colonies. Thus, though he was advised to drop the tax on tea as well as the other Townshend duties, he refused, keeping it as a token of Britain's right to tax the colonies as expressed in the Declaratory Act. It would be erroneous, however, to portray the period of Lord North's ministry as a continuation of the confrontations of the 1760s. In many ways his premiership marked a new departure. It was not just that George III had at last found what he had been seeking in vain for a decade – a minister congenial both to himself and the House of Commons.

The late 1760s differed from the early 1770s in other respects. The period between 1763 and 1770 had been one of adjustment to the new empire which Britain had acquired in the Seven Years' War. It ended with an event which symbolically marked the conclusion of that era, the so-called Boston massacre.

## THE BOSTON MASSACRE

The 'massacre' occurred on 5 March when a crowd confronted troops guarding the customs house in King Street. There had been a similar incident on 2 March, when insults and then blows had been exchanged. On this occasion, however, the soldiers retaliated to the cry 'fire, damn you, fire' by actually firing shots. Three men died immediately, while another eight were wounded, two of them mortally. The 'massacre' could have escalated into a series of bloody confrontations if the authorities had not withdrawn troops off the streets of Boston into Castle William in the harbour and brought Captain Preston, the officer commanding those at the customs house, and the men under his command, to trial. The jury acquitted Preston of the charge of having ordered the men to fire. While two soldiers were found guilty of manslaughter, they were not hanged but merely branded on the thumb. The lenity of the judgements and the fact that Preston and his men were defended by John Adams and Josiah Quincy, both later prominent in the colonial cause, indicates that this incident marked, not the firing of the first shots in the American Revolution, but the last ones in the French and Indian War.

# 15  The Imperial Crisis: 'Tis time to part

## THE 'PERIOD OF QUIET'

So far from events escalating to an inevitable war, the years 1770–73 witnessed what has become known as a 'period of quiet'. In Britain there was almost a complete silence. Parliament, which had devoted many debates to the colonial issues raised since the Sugar Act, rarely discussed the colonies. The British press, which had given considerable coverage to the crises over the Stamp Act and the Townshend duties, reported hardly any event in North America during these years. In the colonies, too, there was a relaxation of tension. There were, to be sure, disputes between Assemblies and governors in some. In Maryland the governor proclaimed a scale of fees for officers in defiance of the Assembly. In Georgia the Assembly's choice of a speaker was rejected in 1771. In North Carolina the Assembly set up a new superior law court in defiance of instructions to the governor from the Secretary of State for the colonies. But such incidents were commonplace in colonial politics. Only with hindsight can they be seen as precursors to revolution. The so-called Wilkes fund controversy in South Carolina was more serious. For some time the Lower House of the Assembly in that colony had asserted the right to vote money for purposes of its own from the public purse without seeking the assent of the governor or council. When in 1769 they voted £1500 to the English radical John Wilkes, the British government instructed the governor to stop its payment. The Assembly protested at this infringement of its alleged rights, and the dispute continued until it was overtaken by the war for independence.

Yet even the Wilkes fund affair might have been contained within the normal parameters of imperial politics if events elsewhere, mostly in New England, had not kept up the tensions of the 1760s The *Gaspee* incident in Rhode Island and the debates between

Governor Thomas Hutchinson and the general court in Massachusetts sustained the antagonisms raised by the clash over taxation.

In June 1772 the *Gaspee*, a customs schooner stationed in Rhode Island, ran aground on a sandbank. It had previously been the focus of attention by ship owners who accused its captain of arbitrary action in seizing their vessels. Some took advantage of its being crippled to board it, put the captain and crew ashore, and then burn it to the waterline. The captain was then put on trial for his seizures of ships and found guilty in the colony's courts. To add insult to injury, he was also court-martialled by the Royal Navy for losing his ship. A royal commission was set up in 1773 to investigate the circumstances of its loss, but failed to find convincing evidence to bring anybody to trial.

In Massachusetts the Boston town meeting set up at Sam Adams's instigation a committee of correspondence in November 1772. The committee was 'to state the rights of the colonists and of this province in particular as men, as Christians and as subjects; to communicate and publish the same to the several towns in this province and to the world ...'. The committee produced a pamphlet, again largely the work of Adams, with the title *The State of the Rights of the Colonists*. This provoked Governor Hutchinson to convene the general court in January 1773 and to harangue its members with a denunciation of the pamphlet. A debate ensued between the governor and the court in which he claimed: 'I know of no line that can be drawn between the supreme authority of Parliament and the total independence of the colonies.' Led by Sam Adams and John Hancock the Assemblymen agreed, claiming that the colony was dependent upon the Crown alone. To Hutchinson's chagrin, the issue had been exposed in stark clarity. Even the British government felt that the governor had erred in putting it so crudely. The Earl of Dartmouth, newly appointed Secretary of State for the colonies, confided to Benjamin Franklin that the ministry wished he had not been so frank. Hutchinson made clear where he stood in letters he wrote to Thomas Whately in England, which fell into Franklin's hands. Franklin sent them to Massachusetts where they were published, one of them with the unfortunate phrase 'there must be an abridgment of what are called English liberties'. The governor was consequently impeached by the General Court. The clash between Hutchinson and the colonists led by Sam Adams persuaded the British government that Massachusetts was at the heart of the colonial resistance to its authority.

This impression seemed to be confirmed when the main attack upon its next imperial scheme came from Boston in the notorious tea party of 1775.

## THE BOSTON TEA PARTY

On 16 December colonists dressed as Indians dumped 342 chests containing 90,000 pounds of tea into Boston harbour. This was a reaction to the implementation of North's Tea Act passed earlier in the year. The Act was designed to assist the nearly bankrupt East India Company repair its financial situation by permitting it to ship tea directly to designated merchants in Boston, New York, Philadelphia and Charleston. Lord North again declined to remove the duty on tea, which would have lowered the price substantially in the colonies. As it was, the company could offer it for sale at prices which would undercut the merchants who had not been earmarked by it to distribute the tea, who included legitimate traders as well as smugglers. These organised protests against the Tea Act serve as another demonstration of the British government's determination to tax the colonists without their consent. In Philadelphia a series of resolutions were passed in October, one declaring 'that it is the duty of every American to oppose this attempt'. In New York the 'sons of liberty' formed an association in December denouncing the measure as one which would 'enslave' Americans. 'If they succeed in the sale of that tea', they asserted, 'then we may bid adieu to American liberty.' Massive demonstrations were also mounted against the company's ships when they arrived in the four ports. In Philadelphia their captains and the Delaware pilots were warned in handbills signed by 'the committee for tarring and feathering' that they faced that excruciating, and potentially lethal, ordeal if they landed the tea. Those bound for New York and Philadelphia turned back. Those which arrived at Charleston were allowed to unload their cargo, but not to sell it. In Boston, Governor Hutchinson was determined to have them not only discharge the tea, but also to pay duty on it, while the town meeting, presided over by Sam Adams, was equally determind to prevent them. The impasse was finally resolved in the Boston Tea Party.

When news of the 'party' arrived in Britain, it provoked outrage. Even the 'friends of America' could not condone the deliberate destruction of the East India Company's property, worth an estimated

£9000. 'I suppose we have never had since we are a people so few friends in Britain', Franklin wrote from London, 'the violent destruction of the tea seems to have united all parties here against our province'. The province the British government singled out for punishment was Massachusetts. Hutchinson was replaced as governor of the Bay colony by General Gage. He was instructed that 'the sovereignty of the king in Parliament over the colonies requires a full and absolute submission' and until that was achieved the capital of Massachusetts should be removed from Boston to Salem. Gage was also to try to discover the ringleaders of those who dumped the tea and to bring them to justice. 'People talk more seriously than ever about America', Gage wrote to Hutchinson, 'that the crisis is come when the provinces must be either British colonies, or independent and separate states.'

## THE COERCIVE ACTS

Lord North determined to punish Massachusetts for the destruction of the tea with a series of statutes known as the Coercive Acts. As he put it in a speech to the House of Commons: 'for the course of five, six, or seven years the town of Boston has invariably been the ringleader of all the disorders, the discontents and disturbances'. The Boston Port Act closed down the harbour there until compensation had been paid to the East India Company. The Massachusetts Government Act altered the charter issued to the Bay colony in 1691. That had provided for the council to be selected by the Lower House of Assembly. It had long been considered regrettable that this vestige of the semi-autonomy enjoyed by the Puritans in the seventeenth century, when they had also chosen the governor, had survived when Massachusetts became a Crown colony after the Glorious Revolution. There had been discussions about transferring the choice from the Lower House to the King before the Tea Party. Now that transfer was made in the Act. Town meetings were also restricted to annual sessions. The Administration of Justice Act gave the governor the right to have capital cases tried in another colony, or even in Britain if he felt that a fair trial could not be had in Massachusetts. The Quartering Act allowed the governor to requisition 'uninhabited houses, outhouses, barns or other buildings' as barracks for troops.

North had full backing for these Acts from the King and the British Parliament. 'The dye is now cast, the colonies must either submit or triumph', George III wrote to him in September, 'by coolness and an unremitted pursuit of the measures that have been adopted, I trust they will come to submit.' He called a general election shortly after they were put on the statute book – six months before one was strictly necessary under the Septennial Act of 1716 – in order to get the electorate's endorsement for his policy. This was not, of course, a test of public opinion. Most constituencies were small and their electorates subservient to the local elite, many of whom supported the government. There were, however, constituencies such as counties and cities where the electors could express an independent choice. These were divided on the government's policy towards the colonies. Counties in which the gentry and the Anglican clergy were dominant by and large supported coercion. Cities, by contrast, especially those in which there was a significant number of Dissenters from the Church of England, tended to advocate conciliation. This was manifest even in those which did not have their own members of Parliament, since they could sign petitions and addresses urging either course, and tended to be sympathetic to the American cause. Appeals were made to the voters in the larger constituencies by both sides. The Dissenter Joseph Priestley published *An Address to Protestant Dissenters* justifying the opposition of the colonies to Parliamentary taxation. Samuel Johnson's *Taxation No Tyranny* supported the government. Johnson's views were probably more typical of the independent electors at large. The Rockingham Whigs, the mainstay of the ministry's opponents and seen as 'friends of America' lost seats, though Burke was returned for Bristol as were radicals from London and Westminster. They lost the popular constituency of Southwark, where William Lee, an American, stood. The result of the election was an increase in North's majority, giving him the support of the House of Commons throughout the rest of the 1770s.

The reaction of the American colonies was very different. If North thought that he could confine his critics to Massachusetts, he was sadly mistaken. As Joseph Lee wrote from Philadelphia to warn him: 'if the Boston Port Bill and the other proceedings against that province have been founded on a supposition that the other colonies would leave them to struggle alone, I do assure you there never was a greater mistake.' By altering the colony's government, North raised apprehensions in others. 'The words Rhode Island, Connecticut, New York etc.', observed a Pennsylvanian, 'are written with lime juice and only want the heat of the fire to appear.' In this respect the prime minister had acted rather like a schoolmaster who punishes the whole school when a few pupils break his windows. It was not necessary to remove the chartered rights of men in the Connecticut River valley for actions perpetrated by Bostonians over 100 miles away. It bore all the marks of taking advantage of the tea party to change the charter along lines proposed before it took place. Lord North thereby overreacted and was therefore primarily responsible for the consequences. He was also unfortunate, as the colonists added the Quebec Act to the four 'intolerable Acts'. It was merely a coincidence that a statute designed for the government of Canada was given the royal assent in the same session as the legislation passed in reaction to the Boston Tea Party. The government of the new territories acquired in 1763 had not developed along the lines laid down in the Royal Proclamation of that year. Not enough Protestants had migrated to them for Assemblies to be chosen. At the same time, the vast majority of Catholics could not be left in the status of second-class citizens. The Act therefore arranged for rule through councils nominated by the governors, and recognised the Roman Catholic Church as an established church, whose clergy could receive tithes. It also upheld French civil law, which rarely allowed for trial by jury. The failure to provide elected Assemblies, the establishment of Catholicism and restrictions on juries alarmed the American colonists, coinciding as they did with the coercive measures against Massachusetts. The fact that the Quebec Act also annexed the vast area north of the Ohio River to Canada seemed to be another blow at their freedom.

'There is not an American from New England to South Carolina who would so far shame his country as to accept this baneful diet [tea] at the expense of his liberty', claimed a letter from Philadelphia published in the London *Morning Chronicle* of 1 February 1774, before the Coercive Acts were passed. 'Fleets and armies will never subdue the noble spirit of freedom which fills our breasts.' When news of the Boston Port Act reached the port in May, the committee of correspondence sent a circular latter calling upon other colonies to suspend trade with Britain. They responded not with a boycott of British goods, but with proposals for the convening of a general congress at Philadelphia in September.

## THE FIRST CONTINENTAL CONGRESS

When the first Continental Congress met in Carpenter's Hall 55 delegates from all the colonies which eventually declared their independence turned up, with the single exception of Georgia. They soon divided into two parties, one of conservatives who wished to reach an accommodation with Britain and another of radicals who were determined to defy British claims of Parliamentary sovereignty. The radicals seized the initiative and got the Congress to adopt the so-called Suffolk Resolves. These were a series of defiant resolutions passed in Suffolk county, Massachusetts, and rushed to Philadelphia by Paul Revere. They denied that any obedience was due to Acts of Parliament or to royal officials. Conservatives led by Joseph Galloway tried to offset the effects of the adoption of the Suffolk Resolves by proposing a Union which would establish a president-general appointed by the King and a grand council chosen by the colonial Assemblies. These would have jurisdiction alongside Parliament over imperial affairs. They would form 'an inferior and distinct branch of the British legislature, united and incorporated with it for the aforesaid general purposes'. Galloway's proposal was shelved by the Congress for future discussion. When it was discussed again, it was rejected, and all reference to it in the proceedings of the Congress was expunged. On 1 October a virtual bill of rights was adopted which the Congress claimed their inhabitants enjoyed 'by the immutable laws of nature, the principles of the English constitution, and the several charters'. These included the right to life, liberty and property, all the rights of Englishmen, and to assemble and petition the king. They declared that the maintenance of a standing army in any colony without the consent of its Assembly in time of peace was illegal, though they were prepared to acknowledge Parliament's right to regulate colonial trade. The Congress did agree to a complete ban on trade wth Great Britain, on imports with effect from 1 December 1774, and on exports after 10 September 1775 unless colonial grievances had been redressed before then. Before they adjourned they set up an association to implement this embargo, with committees in every county, city and town which served as constituencies for the Assemblies to monitor its implementation. Any violators of its provisions were to be named 'in the gazette, to the end that all such foes to the rights of British America may be publicly known and universally condemned as the enemies of American liberty'. The Association was to last until a whole range of laws imposing taxes, enforcing them in admiralty courts and for trying offences outside the colony where they were committed, as well as the Coercive Acts, were repealed. Having sent a petition to the King and an address 'to the people of Great Britain', the Congress adjourned its meeting to May 1775.

The committees of inspection to supervise the realisation of the aims of the Association were set up throughout the colonies. They inspected ships and warehouses to see that the embargo was enforced, and vetted individuals accused of breaches of it, such as drinking tea. Enforcement of the Congress's resolutions on the non-consumption of British commodities could involve a great deal of intimidation, obliging people to sign up to the association, with the threat of violence if they refused. The committees also tried to implement the resolutions of the Congress aimed at frugality, so that Americans could survive without importing British goods. These included efforts to increase the numbers of sheep and thereby the availability of wool, and the discouragement of 'every species of extravagance and dissipation, especially all horse racing, and all kinds of gaming, cock fighting, exhibitions of shows, plays, and other expensive diversions and entertainments'. Committees of inspection regarded themselves as responsible not to the Assemblies but to Congress. They functioned in New York, even though the Assembly was the only one of the 12 colonies who attended the Congress that did not endorse its resolutions. As local government collapsed when war broke out, they became Committees of Safety, replacing the agencies appointed by the imperial authorities.

## LEXINGTON AND CONCORD

Faced with widespread civil disobedience colonial governors refused to convene the Assemblies. In their place sprang up provincial Congresses. One was even convened in Georgia to adopt the Association, even though no delegates from that colony had gone to Philadelphia. Another met in Virginia in March 1775 and prepared for hostilities, prompting Patrick Henry to make the apocryphal speech: 'is life so dear, or peace so sweet, as to be purchased at the price of chains and slavery? Forbid it, Almighty God! I know not what course others may take; but as for me give me liberty or give me death.' In Massachusetts the provincial congress met at Concord. Learning that Gage was expecting reinforcements, the delegates undertook to raise an army of 13,000 men. Gage was informed that they had stored weapons at Concord, and in April 1775 sent a body of men under Colonel Francis Smith there to seize them. Paul Revere rode from Boston to raise the alarm, but only got as far as Lexington where he was captured. Another patriot, Samuel Prescott, carried the message from Lexington to Concord. Warned about the approaching troops, patriots, known as minutemen from their boasted ability to be ready for action in a minute, prepared to intercept them. On 19 April those at Lexington faced Smith's men. Heavily outnumbered, the minutemen started to obey the order to disperse, but did not surrender their weapons. Their failure to lay down their arms caused the British to open fire on them, killing eight and wounding ten. The first shots had been fired in what was to become the War of American Independence. Smith advanced then to Concord, where his men engaged with the provincial forces and sustained casualties. The decision was taken to retreat to Boston. All along the 17-mile road the British were sniped at by minutemen. By the time they got there, 73 of their number had been killed. They were pursued by the colonists who laid siege to the town.

## THE SECOND CONTINENTAL CONGRESS

As Boston was besieged, delegates made their way to the second Continental Congress, which opened in Philadelphia on 10 May. Clearly some decision had to be made about the military situation in Massachusetts, not least since the first Congress had pledged help to the colony if it were attacked. On 26 May the resolution was taken to put the colonies in a state of defence. In June, George Washington was appointed commander of 'the American continental army' and despatched to Boston. Before he got there, the Americans had engaged the British in what is known as the Battle of Bunker Hill, though much of the fighting took place on nearby Breed's Hill. Although the British forced the Americans off these hills on 17 June, it was at a heavy cost. Gage ruefully wrote to Lord Dartmouth that 'the rebels are not the despicable rabble too many have supposed them to be.'

When George Washington arrived in Cambridge early in July, he published *A declaration by the representatives now met in General Congress in Philadelphia setting forth the causes and necessity of taking up arms*. Written by Thomas Jefferson and John Dickinson, this was in one respect a dry run for the Declaration of Independence. When the latter was published a year later, it was due to 'a decent respect to the opinions of mankind [which] requires that they should declare the causes which impel them to a separation'. This earlier declaration was due to 'obligations of respect to the rest of the world, to make known the justice of our cause'. They assured their 'friends and fellow subjects in any part of the empire' that they were not yet ready 'to dissolve that union which has so long and so happily subsisted between us, and which we sincerely hope to see restored'. They then rehearsed the history of their relationship with the mother country since their forefathers left it, which had been of mutual benefit until the end of the French and Indian War which Pitt had directed 'so wisely and successfully'. But after the war George III changed his ministers. 'From that fatal moment the affairs of the British empire began to fall into confusion, and gradually sliding from the summit of glorious prosperity ... are at length distracted by the convulsions that now shake it to its deepest foundations.' So the root cause of the imperial crisis lay in the King's choice of ministers. The measures they had adopted had reduced the Americans 'to the alternative of choosing an unconditional submission to the tyranny of irritated ministers, or resistance by force. The latter is our choice.'

Their friends and fellow subjects would wish to know why the Congress had rejected overtures of conciliation which Lord North had made earlier in the year. He had held out an offer to any individual colony not to tax it so long as it made its own contribution to the common defence and the civil government and administration of justice in the colony, the sums raised to be disposable by Parliament. The only exception would be duties to regulate commerce, the proceeds of which were to be 'carried to the account' of the colony. The Declaration was silent on this grudging concession, which had probably only been made to appease opposition in Britain. At the end of July, however, Congress did draw up an explanation of its rejection of North's offer on the grounds of it being 'unreasonable and insidious'. The proposed deal would only last as long as colonies continued to make gifts of money for the common stock. It would give Parliament the right to spend it on the internal administration of the colonies, which was their affair alone. The British did not give up their right to tax the colonies. Anyway, the issue had moved far beyond questioning that right. The Coercive Acts had arrogated powers to Parliament over the colonies, such as altering their charters, which if allowed by the colonists would leave them with no security for their lives or property.

This explanation was drawn up by a committee composed of John Adams, Benjamin Franklin, Thomas Jefferson and Richard Henry Lee, all radicals. Conservatives took alarm at what seemed like a threat to declare independence if the British government did not back down completely. One of their leaders, John Dickinson, persuaded Congress to petition the King. This too put the responsibility for the crisis squarely on the shoulders of the ministers. It then appealed for the restoration of the former harmony between the mother country and the colonies. The conservative cause received a blow with George III's reaction to their petition. He refused to accept it. Instead, he issued a Proclamation acknowledging that there was rebellion in North America and denouncing its abettors in Britain. Any subject who gave succour to the enemy should be brought 'to condign punishment'. The King convened Parliament in October and told the two Houses that the 'rebellious war' in America was 'manifestly carried on for the purpose of establishing an independent empire'. He had consequently increased the armed forces and made arrangements to hire foreign mercenaries to deal with the rebels. Parliament proceeded to pass an Act prohibiting trade with all 13 colonies and declaring their shipping forfeit to the Crown. This extended earlier restrictions on commerce with all but New York, Delaware, North Carolina and Georgia. A member who opposed the measure described it as 'a Bill for carrying more effectively into execution the resolves of Congress'.

Certainly, these reactions in Britain played into the hands of the radicals in Congress. The King, on whom the conservatives had relied, had betrayed their trust. Appeals had been made to him against Parliament and his 'evil counselors', but to no avail. Thomas Paine articulated what many Americans were thinking when he made an attack on monarchy in general and George III in particular in *Common Sense*, which appeared in January 1776. The King was not a benevolent constitutional monarch, but a 'hardened, sullen-tempered Pharaoh', the 'royal brute of Great Britain'. In order to achieve independence, the American people had symbolically to execute their king. This proposition, previously unthinkable to most, became common sense in the course of 1776. What also struck Paine and his readers as common sense was that men were now fighting and dying. For what? As far as the radicals were concerned it was not just to return to 1763, which is what the conservatives proposed. Independence was the only cause worth the sacrifice of lives.

## THE WAR OF AMERICAN INDEPENDENCE

War had indeed spread far and wide throughout North America by the Spring of 1776. Washington's siege of Boston forced the British to abandon the town on 17 March, transporting their troops to Halifax, Nova Scotia. Elsewhere, the Americans were less successful. Washington had sent a force of 1100 men, led by Benedict Arnold, to take Quebec. It seemed an easy target, since Ethan Allen had led a successful attack on Ticonderoga in May 1775, which had been followed up by the seizure of Montreal in November. But the assault on Quebec was repelled in January, and though Arnold stayed on in Canada until the summer, he was forced to withdraw to New York in June. The British bombarded towns from Falmouth in Maine in October 1775, to Norfolk in Virginia in January 1776 and Charleston in June. At the end of June, General William Howe landed in New York City with 32,000 men and 30 ships. This was to be the British base for the rest of the war.

These reverses did not convince conservatives that it was common sense to challenge the greatest power in the world at the time. On the contrary, one of their more persuasive arguments in favour of seeking accommodation with Britain was that the colonies would be crushed in the event of all-out war. Even the radicals accepted that they could not win on their own. But they urged that foreign help would not be forthcoming unless the colonies declared their independence, as European rulers would not assist rebels against a legitimate government. Congress too accepted that outside assistance was needed, and in March appointed Silas Deane to go to France to seek the help of the French. He sailed from America in April on a mission that was to lead to French intervention in the war on behalf of the colonies after they had declared themselves the United States of America.

INDEPENDENCE

By the spring of 1776, British government had effectively broken down in many of the colonies. The functions of Assemblies and courts under royal jurisdiction had ceased. If anarchy were not to ensue, some institutions would have to take their place. In June 1775, Congress had authorised the Massachusetts provincial Congress to resume the powers granted by the charter of 1691, which had been abrogated by the Massachusetts Government Act. When the New Hampshire Assembly asked Congress in October for guidance in setting up a new form of government, they were advised to settle on one which would be most conducive to the happiness of the people. Such requests from colonies led Congress to resolve in May 1776 'that it be recommended to the respective assemblies and conventions of the united colonies where no government sufficient to the exigencies of their affairs have been hitherto established to adopt such government as shall, in the opinion of the representatives of the people, best conduce to the happiness and safety of their constituents in particular and America in general'.

These new representative institutions faced up to the issue of independence in the early months of 1776. On 12 April the convention in North Carolina instructed its delegates to support any resolution that Congress might make to separate from Great Britain. It was followed by Rhode Island in May. But it was the Virginian Assembly which bit the bullet and authorised its delegates to introduce a resolution for separation. On 7 June, Richard Henry Lee proposed that 'these United Colonies are, and of right ought to be, free and independent States, that they are absolved from all allegiance to the British Crown, and that all political connection between them and the state of Great Britain is, and ought to be, totally dissolved.' There was still reluctance to go along with it in the middle colonies, however, so the debate was postponed until 1 July. By then all the middle colonies except New York had been persuaded to vote for independence. John Dickinson of Pennsylvania, although he spoke against it on 1 July, abstained when the vote was taken on the following day. Lee's resolution was passed. On 4 July the Declaration of Independence penned by Thomas Jefferson was signed.

# Conclusion

The Declaration of Independence accused King George III of 'having in direct object the establishment of an absolute tyranny over these States'. It went on to list a series of charges against him to substantiate this claim 'to a candid world'. If they are read candidly, however, few seem to demonstrate that he was in fact a tyrant. The first accused him of vetoing legislation passed by colonial Assemblies. Yet the Crown retained the theoretical right to veto bills passed by both Houses of Parliament as well as by legislatures in the colonies. The fact that none had been vetoed in Britain since 1708 was a constitutional convention, not a relinquishing of the power. George was also charged with dissolving Assemblies, yet the prerogative of dissolution of all legislative bodies, including Parliament, whenever it suited the King, was still possessed by the Crown, and exercised on both sides of the Atlantic. The fact that most Parliaments were allowed to run the full course prescribed in the Septennial Act was another convention, one which was occasionally flouted. Thus, Lord North had got the King to dissolve Parliament in 1774, six months before it was required, in order to cash in at the polls on the popularity in Britain of his Coercive Acts. George was criticised for appointing judges 'dependent on his will alone, for the tenure of their offices'. The appointment of judges at pleasure had been taken from the Crown in England by the Act of Settlement of 1701, which had settled the succession in the House of Hanover. After the Hanoverians succeeded the Stuarts in 1714, they could only appoint judges on good behaviour, and they could only be dismissed by a two-thirds majority of both Houses of Parliament. Another charge was that the King had maintained a standing army in time of peace without the consent of the Assemblies. Again, the right to keep troops on foot in peacetime had been taken from the Crown in England by the Bill of Rights in 1689. The opening charges against George III in the Declaration of Independence in effect amount to a claim that the benefits of the Glorious Revolution, and subsequent constitutional restrictions on the monarchy in Great Britain, should have been extended to the colonies. As we saw in Chapter 9, these were not regarded as being for export to the American colonies. In many ways the colonists were fighting the battles Parliament had waged against the English Crown in the seventeenth century.

The Declaration of Independence had to admit that, in giving his assent to laws which they found oppressive, the King had not acted alone but had 'combined with others'. The 'others' were of course his ministers and both Houses of Parliament. The statutes objected to were mainly the so-called 'intolerable Acts', including the Quebec Act. This had been passed, it was claimed, 'for abolishing the free system of English Laws in a neighbouring Province, establishing therein an arbitrary Government, and enlarging its Boundaries, so as to render it at once an Example and fit Instrument for introducing the same absolute rule into these colonies'. Such an interpretation was pure paranoia, fuelled by hatred of French popery. The fact that Congress was seeking an alliance with the French to help to maintain the independence of the colonies brought its objections to the arrangements Britain had made for Canada close to hypocrisy. Had they included a charge in an early draft of the Declaration that George had encouraged the 'execrable commerce' of the slave trade, it would have been even closer. As Samuel Johnson observed in *Taxation no Tyranny*, 'how is it that we hear the loudest yelps for liberty among the drivers of negroes?' In the event, the charge was judiciously dropped.

The final charges related to events since hostilities had broken out. To blame George for taking steps to suppress rebellion was to disclaim any responsibility for the violence which had brought about the confrontation. To conclude on the basis of these accusations that he was 'a Prince, whose character is thus marked by every act which may define a Tyrant' was to stretch the definition of tyranny to breaking point.

Yet the outbreak of war made it essential both to break with Britain in the eyes of those who signed the Declaration of Independence, and to seek to justify it to a candid world. The genuine grievances which had brought them to this point were no longer negotiable. Although the King was not a tyrant, he could not see that the demands of the colonists were reasonable. Like his ministers, and indeed most contemporary politicians, he was so locked into the doctrine of the sovereignty of the king in Parliament that he saw no merits in the notion of the sovereignty of the people. Perhaps this was because there was so little popular participation in politics in Britain. The electorate played less and less of a role in the construction of a Parliamentary majority. Where in the years 1695–1715 there had been frequent general elections, one every two years on average, since the passing of the Septennial Act in 1716 they had been held roughly every six years. Moreover, the number of constituencies which actually went to the polls had fallen from over a third in the early eighteenth century to under a fifth by the 1760s. By contrast, elections to the colonial Assemblies became more frequent under the Hanoverians. In Pennsylvania annual elections were mandatory under the Frame of Government. New York obtained a Septennial Act in 1743, but elections there were held far more frequently than every seven years, ten occurring between 1743 and 1775. Elsewhere, they were at the discretion of the governors, but were still regular occurrences. They also tended to provoke more contests. Two-thirds of Virginia's districts went to the polls at most elections. The proportion of white adult males qualified to vote in Assembly elections was considerably higher than in Britain. At the beginning of the century perhaps as many as one in four could vote in England, though far fewer in Scotland. By the reign of George III, population growth had actually reduced the ratio of voters to non-voters. Eligibility varied from colony to colony, but was at worst confined to 50 per cent of white adult males and at best extended to 80 per cent. Although turnouts tended to be low on both sides of the Atlantic, nevertheless Americans had far more experience of participating in the political process than their British counterparts. This exacerbated the mutual misunderstandings over the issue of no taxation without representation. By 1775 these had caused a complete breakdown in the relationship between America and the mother country.

The way out of the impasse was not to return to the relationship with Britain which had existed prior to 1763. The only way forward was to declare independence from the mother country, to become a sovereign state, and to defend that status by fighting the British.

Immediately following the Declaration of Independence, the military outlook did not bode well for the new country. On 27 August the newly formed continental army under George Washington was defeated by the British, commanded by General Howe, at the Battle of Brooklyn Heights and retreated across the East River to Manhattan.

Although the British drive to take New York City was checked at Harlem Heights on 16 September, in November Washington was driven over the Hudson and then over the Delaware into Pennsylvania. Howe made his base in New York City and stationed troops on the New Jersey banks of the Delaware. With Philadelphia threatened, Congress moved to Baltimore. The gloomy prospects prompted Tom Paine to publish *The American Crisis*. 'These are the times that try men's souls', he wrote, 'the summer soldier and the sunshine patriot will, in this crisis, shrink from the service of their country; but he that stands it *now*, deserves the love and thanks of man and woman. Tyranny, like hell, is not easily conquered; yet we have this consolation with us, that the harder the conflict, the more glorious the triumph.' Paine's words rallied the ranks of the continental army at a time when their morale was at its lowest, even though elsewhere American forces had been more successful, inflicting defeats on the British in South Carolina and on Lake Champlain. Washington's men were inspired to follow him across the Delaware on Christmas Day, when Howe was celebrating in New York and his scattered forces in New Jersey were exposed to attack. The British garrison at Trenton was surprised and overpowered. Washington then moved on to take Princeton on 3 January 1777.

The campaign of 1777 culminated in Howe's capture of Philadelphia in September and Burgoyne's defeat at Saratoga in October. Contrary to traditional accounts, there was no concerted strategy for the two British generals to unite in the Hudson River valley. Howe took his army by sea from New York City down the Atlantic coast and up to the northern end of Chesapeake Bay, where they were disembarked to march towards Philadelphia. Washington intercepted them at Brandywine Creek on 11 September, but was defeated, leaving the way clear for Howe to take Philadelphia, forcing Congress to flee once more, this time to Lancaster, Pennsylvania. Washington attempted to dislodge the British from Germantown in October, but was again unsuccessful, and withdrew to Valley Forge to spend the severe winter there, while Howe passed it in comfort in Philadelphia. Meanwhile, Burgoyne had advanced from Canada down Lake Champlain and across to the Hudson River, where his army marched towards a heavily defended position which he twice attacked before surrendering on 7 October.

If, by capturing Philadelphia, the British hoped to inflict the same kind of defeat on the Americans as the taking of a European capital such as Paris or Berlin would have done on the French or the Prussians, they must have been deeply disappointed. In that respect America was different from Europe. At the same time, it is a myth to imagine that the Americans succeeded because the redcoats could not adjust to fighting in a wilderness, whereas their enemies could engage in guerilla warfare, using their militias as well as their regulars. The British had shown in the French and Indian War, as Washington fully appreciated, that they could adapt their tactics to North American conditions. Burgoyne was beaten in regular battle, not in irregular skirmishes.

The victory at Saratoga finally persuaded the French, who had given clandestine help, to offer the Americans a formal alliance in February 1778. They undertook not to make peace with Britain until it recognised the independence of America. Their own recognition of the United States made the war an international conflict. In order to cope with its extension, the British withdrew from their exposed position in Philadelphia to entrench themselves in New York City. Washington left his winter quarters at Valley Forge to chase them across New Jersey, catching up with their rearguard at Monmouth court-house on 28 June, where they inflicted damaging blows on the retreating troops. Having failed to cut off what they considered as the hard core of the rebellion in New England from the other rebellious colonies, the British now decided to consolidate the loyalism which they were convinced pervaded the south. The southern strategy, however, turned out to be based on a similar deception to that which held that the rebellion was largely rooted in Massachusetts. For, following initial successes, the British encountered more and more determined resistance.

In the winter of 1778–79 the British took Georgia, and held off an attempt by the Americans and their French allies to take Savannah. They then moved north, laying siege to Charleston, which surrendered to them in May 1780. General Cornwallis inflicted a defeat on an American army under Horatio Gates at Camden in August. The arrogant behaviour of the British, and especially of their loyalist allies, after these apparently easy successes, however, antagonised those who were neutral and stiffened the resistance of American patriots. The latter inflicted a severe defeat on loyalist forces at King's Mountain in October. Washington sent an army under Nathanael Greene into South Carolina to stiffen patriot resistance to the British and their loyalist allies. A detachment from Greene's army led by Daniel Morgan advanced towards the area of King's Mountain early in 1781. Cornwallis sent a force of loyalists led by Banastre Tarleton to intercept them at Cowpens in January. Tarleton, who had a reputation to uphold as a butcher, was determined to crush Morgan's forces, but instead found himself on the losing side. Morgan then retreated into North Carolina to link up with Greene, while Cornwallis chased after him. The two armies met at Guilford court-house in March 1781. Though the British held the field, they sustained many more casualties than the Americans, so many indeed as to make Cornwallis seek an exit strategy rather than risk another battle. While he marched his men northwards to Virginia, Greene went south to succour the patriots in South Carolina and Georgia. The battle to win the hearts and minds of the southerners had been won by the Americans, for the British held little beyond Charleston and Savannah until they were obliged to withdraw from those towns in 1782.

Meanwhile, Cornwallis had withdrawn to Yorktown, on a peninsula between the York and James Rivers on the western shore of Chesapeake Bay. He fortified it with the apparent intention of using it as a base from which to continue the conflict in the south after being reinforced from New York. Sir Henry Clinton, the Commander in Chief in New York City, did indeed dispatch ships to the Chesapeake, more with a view to evacuating Cornwallis's troops than to reinforcing them. Unfortunately for the British, a superior French fleet was blockading the entrance to the Bay, making it impossible to relieve Cornwallis. His troops were now trapped for there was no escape by sea, while an army of Americans and French commanded by Washington and the Comte de Rochambeau was approaching Yorktown. Cornwallis tried to retreat northwards across the York River, and sent Tarleton to secure a bridgehead for him. A squall, however, prevented a mass evacuation of Yorktown and on 17 October 1781 Cornwallis surrendered to Washington.

This, in fact, sealed the American victory. For, when news of the defeat reached England, it took the will to fight out of those who had previously supported North's ministry, and the prime minister resigned in March 1782. He was succeeded by the Marquis of Rockingham, forming his second administration after an interval of 16 years. Although Rockingham died later that year, to be succeeded as prime minister by the Earl of Shelburne, he set in train the negotiations at Paris which his successor was to complete in 1783, when Britain recognised the independence of the United States of America.

There was no logistic or economic reason why the British abandoned the struggle. Although Spain and other European powers came to side with America and France, Britain could still have launched another expedition, and still had the financial resources to sustain it. They did indeed continue to defend the West Indies from French attack, regaining naval supremacy over the French there at the Battle of the Saints between Guadeloupe and Dominica in April 1782.

The West Indies remained loyal to the British Crown, unlike the planters of the Chesapeake and lower south. Why they did not rebel has been the subject of some debate among historians. Partly, it was due to their strategic position in the empire. Unlike the continental colonies they were not attached to a land mass, British dominion over which extended considerably by 1763. Although the French surrendered the 'ceded islands' of Dominica, Grenada, St Vincent and Tobago in 1763, they still retained Guadeloupe, Martinique and St Domingue. It was the removal of the threat from France in 1763 which created the conditions on the continent for the American colonists to confront Britain. In the Caribbean the continuance of a French presence necessitated the stationing of the British Navy in Antigua. It also led to the seizure of St Lucia in 1778 to serve as an additional naval base in the Lesser Antilles. This did not prevent the French from retaking Dominica in 1778, St Vincent and Grenada in 1779 and St Kitts in 1781. The British also inherited from the French in Grenada and Dominica both maroon colonies of escaped slaves similar to those in Jamaica and the Caribs of St Vincent, who had a fearsome reputation and fought British troops in the Carib War of 1772–73. The white inhabitants of the islands faced a much greater threat from their black populations than any mainland colony, even in the south, as the slave uprising on Jamaica in 1776 dramatically proved. Given the constant need to suppress their slaves, there was very little possibility of any resistance to British rule from the Caribbean colonists. Indeed, where the presence of troops on the mainland became a major grievance, the inhabitants of the islands, with the exception of Barbados, welcomed their presence. About a quarter of all those on duty in America after 1763 – about 2500 men – were stationed in the West Indies, in barracks constructed for them by the Assemblies. These were essential, as a petition from Jamaica pleading for more in 1764 made clear, 'to preserve the peace and tranquility of the island from the secret machinations and open insurrection of their internal enemies'.

Many wealthy planters were absentees who lived in Britain. The huge profits to be made from sugar made this possible, whereas the cash crops in the southern mainland colonies did not enable anything like as many to retire to the mother country. By 1740, over one-third of those who owned plantations in Jamaica resided in Britain, a proportion which rose to two-thirds by 1800. Those who remained on the islands numbered only 50,000 in 1776 compared with two millions on the mainland. Although about as many emigrated from the British Isles to the West Indies as went to North America, the death rate was so horrendous in the Caribbean that they failed to reproduce themselves, much less increase as in the continental colonies. They were therefore in no position to rebel even if they had wanted to do so.

In fact, there is no sign of any major rebellion against Britain occurring in the West Indies. Economic prosperity perhaps accounts for the lack of interest in resisting the mother country. Following the depression of the second quarter of the century, there came a 'silver age' when buoyant demand for sugar in Britain caused prices to increase, and the islands' share of British trade to grow from 10 per cent to 20 per cent. Increased demand from the mother country was the result of a growing population coupled with more consumption per head, which expanded from 4 pounds in 1700, to 10 by 1748 and by 1800. During the 1760s, demand for West Indian products other than sugar, such as coffee, ginger and indigo, also began to rise. This helped to offset the ban on imports from the West Indies by the rebellious mainland colonies, although the economic threat this posed to their livelihoods alarmed the Caribbean colonists at the outset of the imperial conflict. There were petitions from Jamaica in 1774 and Grenada in 1775 calling upon the King to intervene to end the quarrel between Parliament and the colonies. Although the economy of the West Indies was severely depressed during the war, especially after the French joined with the Americans, there was no significant support in the islands for the Declaration of Independence.

Perhaps, above all, this was because the West Indians felt that they benefited politically from being part of the British empire, whereas the mainland colonists came to feel that they no longer did. The imperial government, which derived more revenue from the sugar islands than from the continental colonies, treated them as a special interest. The Molasses Act, reinforced as the Sugar Act in the 1760s, was one sign of this. Another was the Free Port Act of 1766 which established four Jamaican ports open to foreign ships, with a view to attracting Spanish traders, and two on Dominica to attract French. British protection was seen as essential to sustain the elite in power and prevent slave insurrections. A powerful West India lobby emerged to protect the interests of the islands with the 'home' government. In 1774 there were ten agents in London representing them. The islanders also recognised that, unlike the 13 colonies on the continent, they could not go it alone. As the Speaker of the Assembly in Barbados admitted in 1766, the island 'could not so much as exist without the constant protection and support of some superior state'.

Though the British were determined to keep their possessions in the Caribbean, as the Battle of the Saints demonstrated in 1782, by then they lacked the political will to continue the conflict with the 13 colonies which had declared their independence. For what were they fighting them for by 1781? To return them to the allegiance which they had owed to the British Crown before the war was clearly impossible. It would have been necessary to occupy North America with a large army indefinitely, just to retain in practice the King's theoretical claim to sovereignty. North himself had always hoped for a political solution to the problem, and had been prepared to resign if one were not found. Even the 'hawks' in his Cabinet, like Lord George Germain, did not seek a permanent military solution. Yet that seemed to be the only alternative to dropping all claims to sovereignty and recognising the United States as independent.

But the achievement of independence was not the American Revolution. The War of American Independence could be seen merely as a war of colonial liberation. Yet it was not just a question of whether or not the Americans should get home rule. As Carl Becker famously put it, it was also a question of who should rule at home.

The answer to the question varied almost from state to state. In this respect it was not an American revolution but the sum of several revolutions – in Virginia, in Massachusetts, in New York, in Pennsylvania and so on – through all the original 13.

Virginia perhaps witnessed the least disruption. There the last royal governor, Lord Dunmore, was virtually isolated in Williamsburg. When he left the governor's palace in 1775 he was accompanied by very few Virginians. Most of the colony's inhabitants, led by the great families which formed its ruling elite – the Byrds, Carters, Jeffersons, Randolphs and Washingtons – took the patriotic side. The planters did so largely because Dunmore made the cardinal error of promising slaves their liberty if they joined the British side. Faced with the appalling prospect of a slave revolt, which had haunted them all through the colonial period, the landed elite closed ranks. Those below them accepted their lead not because they adopted a deferential stance towards them, as used to be claimed. On the contrary, as a recent investigation of the Old Dominion on the eve of independence has shown, there was considerable tension between different social ranks. But the hegemony of the great land-owners was grudgingly accepted when they were forced to take the lead against the even-more hated British.

In Massachusetts social protest from below the level of the elite had marked the resistance to British measures from the days of the Stamp Act, when the 'Loyal Nine', comprised mainly of Boston artisans, had orchestrated the direct action against stamp distributors and Lieutenant Governor Hutchinson. In 1774 opposition to the Coercive Acts in rural Massachusetts was led by farmers who closed the courts. Yet the Massachusetts Government Act, by removing the choice of the council from the Assembly and placing it in the Crown, recognised that the leading men of the colony who had been elected as councillors were among the most alienated of the colonists in New England. They now sought election to the Assembly. There, they drafted the new state constitution, the principal draftsman being John Adams. They showed their confidence that they had the support of a great majority of the men in Massachusetts when they called elections to a convention to ratify it in which all adult males voted.

New York was more polarised. The elite was divided on the question of loyalty to Britain or support for independence. The number of loyalists is hard to gauge, though it has been estimated at between 15 per cent and 20 per cent of white adult males in the colonies as a whole. In New York it was probably higher, since the British army occupied New York City from 1776–83. Yet sufficient numbers of the elite took the revolutionary side for a compromise to be struck between them and those immediately below them who had opposed the British government ever since the Stamp Act, when they had formed the 'Sons of Liberty'. There was to be a governor and a senate, but these were to be elected by owners of freeholds worth £100. The

'Green Mountain men', who were simultaneously opposing both the British and the patricians of New York, and who were to succeed in carving out the new state of Vermont, protested against this constitution, preferring instead that adopted in Pennsylvania.

For Pennsylvania witnessed the most radical transformation. As the proprietary government of the Penn family collapsed, committees of merchants and craftsmen emerged to replace them. These bypassed the proprietary Assembly and elected a provincial convention to draft a new constitution in 1776. This was the most egalitarian of the new state constitutions, with no governor, no Upper House and an Assembly not of representatives, but of delegates who were accountable to the electorate. The adoption of this new constitution broke the deadlock in Congress over the issue of independence. More than any other shift in political power in the former colonies, it decided that there would be home rule.

After independence was achieved, however, it also kept the question of who was to rule at home at the top of the political agenda in the new republic. For the radicalism of the Pennsylvania constitution of 1776 alarmed conservative elements throughout the United States who, while they went along with the break with Britain, did not desire a social revolution as a consequence. It was partly to put a brake on such radicalism that the Constitutional Convention met in Philadelphia in 1787. But that is another story.

# Guide to Further Reading

The literature on Great Britain during the seventeenth and eighteenth centuries, and on the American colonies, is enormous and growing rapidly. This brief bibliography merely draws attention to a small number of crucial titles under the chapter headings. Although our knowledge of the histories of Britain and colonial America has been advanced considerably by articles in learned journals, such as *The English Historical Review*, *The Historical Journal*, *History*, *Past and Present* and *The William and Mary Quarterly*, only books are mentioned here, the date of publication being, wherever possible, that of the most recent paperback edition.

## Introduction

Daniel Boorstin, *The Americans: The Colonial Experience* (1988).
John Brewer, *The Sinews of Power: War, Money and the English State, 1688–1783* (1989).
Linda Colley, *Britons: Forging the Nation, 1707–1837* (1992).
David Cressy, *Coming Over: Migration and Communication between England and New England in the Seventeenth Century* (1995).
David Hackett Fischer, *Albion's Seed: Four British Folkways in America* (1991).
Alison Games, *Migration and the Origins of the English Atlantic World* (2001).

## The British Empire in America to 1750

Robert M. Bliss, *Revolution and Empire: English Politics and the American Colonies in the Seventeenth Century* (1990).
Nicholas Canny, editor, *The Oxford History of the British Empire, Volume 1: The Origins of Empire: British Overseas Enterprise to the Close of the Seventeenth Century* (1998).
Anthony Macfarlane, *The British in the Americas* (1995).
Peter Marshall, editor, *The Oxford History of the British Empire, Volume 2: The Eighteenth Century* (1998).
Stephen Saunders Webb, *The Governors General: The English Army and the Definition of Empire, 1569–1681* (1987).

219

## British Society in the Era of Western Migration

Bernard Bailyn, *Voyagers to the West* (1986).
Julian Hoppitt, *A Land of Liberty? England, 1689–1727* (2000).
Paul Langford, *A Polite and Commercial People: England, 1727–1783* (1989).
J. A. Sharpe, *Early Modern England: A Social History, 1550–1760* (2nd edition, 1997).
T. C. Smout, *A History of the Scottish People, 1560–1830* (1987).

## Anglo–Indian Relations

J. Axtell, *The European and the Indian: Essays in the Ethnohistory of Colonial North America* (1982).
M. Daunton and R. Halpern, editors, *Empire and Others: British Encounters with Indigenous Peoples, 1600–1850* (1999).
F. Jennings, *The Invasion of America: Indians, Colonialism and the Cant of Conquest* (1988).
James H. Merrell, *Into the American Woods: Negotiators on the Pennsylvania Frontier* (2000).
Alden T. Vaughan, *New England Frontier: Puritans and Indians, 1620–1675* (1995).
R. White, *The Middle Ground: Indians, Empires and Republics in the Great Lakes Region, 1650–1815* (1991).

## The Chesapeake

Charles E. Hatch, *The First Seventeen Years: Virginia, 1607–1624* (1991).
James Horn, *Adapting to a New World: English Society in the Seventeenth-Century Chesapeake* (1996).
Rhys Isaac, *The Transformation of Virginia, 1740–1790* (1999).
Allan Kulikoff, *Tobacco and Slaves: The Development of Southern Cultures in the Chesapeake, 1680–1800* (1988).
Edmund S. Morgan, *American Slavery: American Freedom: The Ordeal of Colonial Virginia* (1995).

## New England

Francis J. Bremer, *The Puritan Experiment: New England Society from Bradford to Edwards* (1995).
Richard L. Bushman, *From Puritan to Yankee: Character and Social Order in Connecticut 1690–1765* (1980).
Richard R. Johnson, *Adjustment to Empire: The New England Colonies, 1675–1715* (1981).

Carol F. Karlsen, *The Devil in the Shape of a Woman: Witchcraft in Colonial New England* (1998).
Edmund S. Morgan, *Visible Saints: The History of a Puritan Idea* (1965).


## The Middle Colonies

Richard Dunn and Mary Maples Dunn, editors, *The World of William Penn* (1986).
Mary K. Geiter, *William Penn* (2000).
Ned Landsman, *Scotland and its First American Colony, 1683–1765* (1985).
James T. Lemon, *The Best Poor Man's Country: A Geographical Survey of Southeastern Pennsylvania* (1972).
Gary B. Nash. *Quakers and Politics: Pennsylvania, 1681–1726* (1997).
Robert C. Ritchie, *The Duke's Province: A Study of New York Politics and Society, 1664–1691* (1977).


## The Lower South

Joyce Chaplin, *An Anxious Pursuit: Agricultural Innovation and Modernity in the Lower South, 1730–1815* (1996).
A. Roger Ekirch, *Poor Carolina: Politics and Society in Colonial North Carolina* (1981).
Robert M. Weir, *Colonial South Carolina: A History* (1997).
Betty Wood, *Slavery in Colonial Georgia, 1730–1775* (1984).


## The West Indies

Richard S. Dunn, *Sugar and Slaves: The Rise of the Planter Class in the English West Indies, 1624–1713* (1973).
Richard B. Sheridan, *Sugar and Slavery: An Economic History of the British West Indies, 1623–1775* (1974).


## The Glorious Revolution in England and America

David Lovejoy, *The Glorious Revolution in America* (1972).
W. A. Speck, *James II* (2002).


## King William's War and Queen Anne's War

Bruce Lenman, *Britain's Colonial Wars, 1688–1783* (2001).

## 'Salutary Neglect'? British Imperial Policy under the First Two Georges

James Henretta, *'Salutary Neglect': Colonial Administration under the Duke of Newcastle* (1972).

## The French and Indian War

F. Anderson, *Crucible of War: The Seven Years' War and the Fate of Empire in British North America, 1754–1766* (2000).
S. Brumwell, *Redcoats: The British Soldier and the War in the Americas, 1755–1763* (2002).

## British America at the Accession of George III

Carol Berkin, *First Generations: Women in Colonial America* (1997).
Patricia Bonomi, *Under the Cope of Heaven: Religion, Society and Politics in Colonial America* (1995).
Kathleen Brown, *Good Wives, Nasty Wenches and Anxious Patriarchs* (1996).
Jon Butler, *Awash in a Sea of Faith: Christianizing the American People* (1991).
Jack P. Greene and J. R. Pole, editors, *Colonial British America: Essays in the New History of the Early Modern Era* (1984).
Jack P. Greene, *Pursuits of Happiness: The Social Development of Early Modern British Politics and the Formation of American Culture* (1988).
Frank Lambert, *Inventing the 'Great Awakening'* (1999).
Philip D. Morgan, *Slave Counterpoint: Black Culture in the Eighteenth-Century Chesapeake and Lowcountry* (1998).
Gary B. Nash, *The Urban Crucible: Social Change, Political Consciousness, and the Origins of the American Revolution* (1986).

## Adjustment to Empire 1763–1770

John L. Bullion, *A Great and Necessary Measure: George Grenville and the Genesis of the Stamp Act, 1763–1765* (1982).
P. D. G. Thomas, *British Politics and the Stamp Act Crisis: The First Phase of the American Revolution, 1763–1767* (1975).
P. D. G. Thomas, *The Townshend Duties Crisis: The Second Phase of the American Revolution, 1767–1773* (1987).

**The Imperial Crisis: 'Tis time to part**

B. Bailyn, *Ideological Origins of the American Revolution* (1992).
S. Conway, *The British Isles and the War of American Independence* (2000).
Piers Macksey, *The War for America, 1775–1783* (1993).
P. D. G. Thomas, *Tea Party to Independence: The Third Phase of the American Revolution, 1773–1776* (1991).

**Conclusion**

Edward Countryman, *The American Revolution* (1985).
Andrew Jackson O'Shaughnessy, *An Empire Divided: The American Revolution and the British Caribbean* (2000).

# Index